J. C. Lightowe .
Feb. '67.

THE LANGUAGE OF CRITICISM

THE LANGUAGE
OF CRITICISM

JOHN CASEY

Fellow, Tutor and College Lecturer in English,
Gonville and Caius College, Cambridge

LONDON

METHUEN & CO LTD

First published in 1966 by
Methuen & Co Ltd
11 New Fetter Lane, London EC4
© 1966 by John Casey
Printed in Great Britain by
Butler & Tanner Ltd, Frome and London

TO

ROBIN

CONTENTS

PREFACE

Criticism is not, and does not seek to be, a science. It is, however, a rational procedure rather than the expression of a set of more or less arbitrary preferences. In this book I outline a view of the nature of critical argument which seems derivable from the work of some recent philosophers, and which allows to criticism a rationality proper to it. The discussion revolves round such topics as the justification of critical judgements, the place of 'emotion' in our response to works of art and literature, the possibility of the systematic study of patterns of literary symbolism, and the relations between critical and 'moral' judgement.

I examine the work of a number of well-known modern critics and aestheticians and in the course of this try to show that certain philosophical assumptions are compatible with the realities of aesthetic experience and that others are not. Underlying the argument is the thesis that English criticism since Wordsworth has been unable to rid itself of an unsatisfactory theory of the emotions, with the result that the 'irrational' element in both art and criticism has assumed a false preponderance.

The opening chapter I include with some hesitation. As a highly general account of the applicability of some of Wittgenstein's thought to aesthetics it will seem intolerably compressed to some and intolerably one-sided to others. But since there have been few or no attempts systematically and explicitly to apply the insights of modern philosophy to the most important modern critics, it seems an effort worth making. The essential argument of Chapter I is that the type of justification proper to aesthetic argument is by no means peculiar to it, but has ramifications and analogies in many other fields. This applies to the justification of a particular 'interpretation' of a work of art or literature, and to the justification of a particular emotional 'response'. There are, for instance, close analogies between the way one justifies the interpretation of a rule (pp. 5–8), the way one argues for a particular interpretation of, say, a picture (pp. 28–9), and the way one can rationally persuade someone to take up a particular 'attitude' (pp. 22–25). Several of the critics and aestheticians whose work I discuss have not seen that such 'justification' is of the essence of aesthetic argument, and have sought instead to provide general aesthetic *explanations* analogous to those of science. The account given in this book has, I think, the advantage of preserving the notion that in aesthetics the concept of a personal 'response' is central, while at the same time avoiding the view which is often taken to be a corollary of that – that aesthetic judgement is ultimately 'subjective'.

Chapter I is also intended to provide a general sketch of the philosophical background of the book; compression has, therefore, been unavoidable. I would suggest that any reader who finds the discussion difficult to follow at first reading go on to the later chapters, which are of a more directly literary interest. If he then returns to Chapter I he will, I hope, find its import clearer in the light of what follows it.

In Chapter II I discuss aspects of the theory of value which seem important for aesthetics, and in Chapter IX the possible relations between literary critical and moral judgement. It is argued that those modern critics who are most noted for their insistence on 'moral' criteria in literature use the term 'moral' with a persistent – but at the same time revealing and interesting – ambiguity.

This book is substantially based upon a doctoral dissertation. I am grateful to Caius for the Research Fellowship which enabled me to complete it at leisure. I am indebted to a number of friends for suggestions and criticism, but in particular to Robin Holloway, of New College, Oxford, for reading the proofs and for many helpful suggestions on points of style, and to James Hopkins, of King's College, Cambridge, for criticism which resulted in numerous improvements.

When I began work on this topic my acquaintance with philosophical methods was of the slightest. If I have learned anything since, this has been due in large measure to the interest and encouragement of Renford Bambrough, my Research supervisor, to whom, therefore, is owed my chief debt.

CHAPTER I

Wittgenstein and the Philosophy of Criticism

I. INTRODUCTION

In the *Tractatus Logico-Philosophicus* Wittgenstein writes: "We picture facts to ourselves."[1] Again: "The pictorial relationship consists of the correlations of the picture's elements with things."[2] Later he presents the 'general form' of propositions as "This is how things stand".[3] This 'picture theory' of language can, perhaps, be seen as an extreme statement of assumptions which underly a good deal of philosophy. This view of the relation between language and the world will be likely to lead to the idea that different forms of discourse are distinguished from each other by referring to different types of object. In the *Philosophical Investigations* Wittgenstein rejects the picture theory and with it the search for the "general form of propositions". The notion that "This is how things stand" can be the general form of propositions arises only when "language goes on holiday".[4] Such a paradigm is only plausible divorced from any actual linguistic context, from any "language-game".[5] According to the picture theory the words in a sentence name elements in the world, and the form of the sentence bears a relation of logical analogy to the form of the facts which the sentence depicts.[6] To name is to engage in an activity which is prior to any language-game, and indeed is the precondition of any language being possible. "Naming is so far not a move in the language-game – any more than putting a piece in its place on the board is a move in chess."[7] The setting up of such a purely 'descriptive' paradigm of language (although – as Wittgenstein goes

---

[1] Op. cit., Proposition 2.1. [2] Op. cit., Prop. 2.1514.
[3] Op. cit., Prop. 4.5. When reference is made to this passage in the *Philosophical Investigations* (No. 114) the translation is "This is how things are".
[4] *Philosophical Investigations*, No. 38.
[5] Op. cit., No. 114. [6] *Tractatus*, Prop. 2.16, 2.161, 2.17, 2.171.
[7] *Philosophical Investigations*, No. 49.

on to argue – "This is how things are" is not even being used as a description), the insistence on pure naming as the pre-condition of language, makes the connection between words and things mysterious, private and arbitrary – "some remarkable act of mind, as it were a baptism of an object".[1] An entirely private language would not, on this theory, be impossible.[2]

This 'baptism of an object' is connected with the search for the logically proper name. A favoured candidate for the logically proper name has been the expression 'this', which seems to represent 'naming' as a unique procedure detached from any other activity – "a *queer* connection of a word with an object".[3] Now Wittgenstein argues that naming, far from being the pre-condition of language, is already a linguistic activity, or 'language-game'. There is not *one* relation between name and object named, and we cannot explain naming in terms of 'ostensive definition', if 'ostensive definition' is based upon the analogy of 'pointing'.[4] Pointing itself depends upon a mastery of a language,[5] and cannot be explained simply as a physical or mental procedure. How, in pointing to a piece of paper, do we 'mean' the colour rather than the shape? We may, for instance, screw up our eyes in order to avoid seeing the outline, so that we may be left free to 'concentrate' on the colour. This would be an explanation of 'meaning' in terms of characteristic physical activities or experiences. But none of these experiences constitutes 'meaning' or 'attending to' the colour. Does it follow that 'meaning the colour' is an inward, mental process, of which the physical experiences are outward signs or accompaniments? Wittgenstein rejects this account also: ". . . because we cannot specify any *one* bodily action which we call pointing to the shape (as opposed, for example, to the colour), we say that a *spiritual* . . . activity corresponds to these words."[6] The mental act which is to supply the missing element, like the pure act of 'naming' is an inward 'attending to' an object isolated from any context. Mental acts no more overcome the *logical* difficulties than do the physical accompaniments:

> Just as a move in chess doesn't consist simply in moving a piece in such-and-such a way on the board – nor yet in one's thoughts and feelings as one makes the move: but in the circumstances that we call "playing a game of chess", "solving a chess problem", and so on.[7]

[1] Op. cit., No. 38.   [2] *Philosophical Investigations*, No. 292 and following.
[3] Op. cit., No. 38.   [4] Op. cit., Nos. 34–7.   [5] Op. cit., No. 33.
[6] Op. cit., No. 36.   [7] Op. cit., No. 33.

One fallacy involved here is that the meaning of a word *is* the object to which it refers. Wittgenstein calls this the confounding the *meaning* of a name with the *bearer* of the name.[1] This confusion may account for the 'picturing' aspect of the picture theory, for if words are merely names it is difficult to see how combinations of words could convey information, except by being arranged so as to 'picture' states of affairs – 'how things stand'. Yet if naming is a procedure that comes before any language-game, then naming itself affirms nothing of the objects named, not even that they exist.[2] If the basic particulars to which words have been attached cease to exist, then words lose their meaning. Hence, on such a theory of language, the difficulty of "The present King of France is bald". Logical Atomism also relies on the possibility of naming as the pre-condition of language. It seems that Russell confuses the meaning of a name with its bearer. Strawson says:

> The source of Russell's mistake was that he thought referring or mentioning, if it occurred at all, must be meaning. . . . he confused expressions with their use in a particular context; and so confused meaning with mentioning, with referring. If I talk about my handkerchief, I can, perhaps, produce the object I am referring to out of my pocket. I cannot produce the meaning of the expression "my handkerchief" out of my pocket.[3]

There are further difficulties. If the word 'red' means *this* red patch, then how, on another occasion can it be used to refer to a different red patch?[4] Indeed, how can it be used to refer to the same red patch? Does the concept of 'same' have any place here? If the connection of a name with an object is merely a private determination of the mind to make such a connection, then the mind must make the connection anew every time we wish to use the word. But the result is that we have no reason for saying that the same word is being used to refer to the same object. This is part of Wittgenstein's argument against the possibility of a totally private language: the theory of meaning we have been considering, together with the notion of naming as a

---

[1] Op. cit., No. 40.
[2] Op. cit., No. 46, with a quotation from the *Theactatus*: '. . . everything that exists in its own right can only be *named*, no other determination is possible, neither that it *is* nor that it is *not*'.
[3] Strawson, 'On Referring', *Essays in Conceptual Analysis*, ed. Flew, p. 31.
[4] See E. Daitz, 'The Picture Theory of Meaning', op. cit., p. 71

mental 'baptism', makes a private language not only possible but inevitable.

Now in a system in which sentences are combinations of names, and in which names are merely *connected* with objects, there will be a scale of complexity in which, inevitably, the names will both be and refer to 'simples'.[1] One consequence would be that the command "Bring me the broom!" would really mean (could be analysed into) "Bring me the broomstick and the brush which is fitted on to it!"[2] But why could we not say instead that the second sentence *really* means the first? Why are brush and broomstick more simple objects than broom? A notion of 'simplicity' is being appealed to which is outside of any language-game; simple objects stand, as it were, at the base of language.[3] Wittgenstein points out that the distinction between 'simple' and 'composite' cannot be drawn in isolation from the uses to which sentences are being put. The 'unanalysed' sentence quoted above is likely to be doing something different from the 'analysed' one. The idea that an object could be 'simple' *tout court* goes with the notion that naming is a *pre-condition*, and not a *function* of language.

I shall go on to argue that a number of problems in aesthetics are bound up with the theory of language which, in the *Philosophical Investigations*, Wittgenstein rejects. This can best be shown by a detailed examination of particular critics. I shall try to show that Wittgenstein's work has bearing on such questions as whether our response to works of art is essentially 'emotional' rather than 'rational', whether a work of art can be aesthetically good but morally bad, and whether our judgement of works of art can be 'objective'. To this end it is necessary to say more of the *Philosophical Investigations*.

At one point Wittgenstein asks:

Can I say "bububu" and mean "If it doesn't rain I shall go for a walk"? It is only in language that one can mean something by something. This shows clearly that the grammar of 'to mean' is not like that of the expression 'to imagine' and the like.[4]

The separation of the concept of 'meaning' from that of 'imagining', is of fundamental importance.[5] Certain mental images may regularly

---

[1] See Russell, 'The Philosophy of Logical Atomism', *Logic and Knowledge*, ed. Marsh.
[2] *Philosophical Investigations*, No. 60.
[3] Op. cit., No. 47.
[4] Op. cit., p. 18, note.
[5] Op. cit., No. 691.

occur in me whenever I say "Shut the door!" and mean it; but I cannot 'mean' it if I address my words to a mouse, or if I know that the door is already shut, whatever mental images I may have. Similarly, the person whom I order to shut the door may have the mental image of a door's shutting, but this does not mean that he understands the command; he could take the image as representing my *fear* of the door's shutting. "The picture did indeed *suggest* a certain use to us, but it was possible for me to use it differently".[1] The occurrence of mental images is neither necessary nor sufficient for understanding. A man may interpret a mental picture in various ways, and he may, of course, carry out the order without the interposition of any images whatsoever. ". . . possibly he had a special experience . . . but for us it is the *circumstances* under which he had such an experience that justify him in saying in such a case that he understands, that he knows how to go on."[2] Wittgenstein is here discussing whether knowing how to do a piece of mathematics is a matter of having the appropriate formula in the mind's eye. I may indeed see the symbols of the formula in my mind's eye, but the criterion of my seeing them as the *formula* would be the mathematical application I make of them. Similarly one criterion that the order "Shut the door!" has been understood is that the person to whom the order has been given shut the door. But it is only possible to hear an order *as* an order in a context in which orders are given, obeyed and so on. It would not be possible for there to have been only *one* occasion on which an order was ever obeyed; the act in response to the 'order' could not count as a case of 'obedience'. In the same way to see a group of symbols as a 'formula' depends upon the existence of mathematics, and upon a mastery of the technique of mathematics.[3]

We might not be prepared to say that a child had 'obeyed' a command merely on the grounds of a unique coincidence of a piece of its behaviour with what it had just been told to do. This would not be because we thought it improbable that the child was having the right inner experiences (we do not think it *improbable* that a parrot does not understand the words it utters) but because the general circumstances in which the act could count as 'obedient' might be lacking. Our doubt would not be as to the existence or not of mental (or brain) mechanisms. In the same way, if I am teaching a child to read, I can

[1] Op. cit., No. 139.   [2] Op. cit., No. 155.
[3] I am not here using 'seeing as' as an *explanation* of a 'mastery of a technique'. For Wittgenstein's treatment of that mistake see op. cit., No. 74.

B

make little sense of the question "Which was the first word he *read?*"[1] This question seems plausible (if difficult) only because we know that the experience is different when we 'derive' the words we read in the normal way from the marks on the page from when we arbitrarily try to 'read' a sentence from a mere jumble of signs.[2] It seems possible to ask when the child first had *that* experience, the 'reading' experience. Here again perhaps there is an appeal to an inward mechanism – Wittgenstein brings this out by showing that this would be a possible question to ask of a reading machine: ". . . it would be possible to say: 'The machine *read* only after such-and-such had happened to it – after such-and-such parts had been connected by wires; the first word that it read was. . . .' "[3] If we insist that reading is a matter not only of 'following' the marks on the page, and of uttering the words which in fact correspond to these marks, but also of having certain inward experiences or of employing certain mental mechanisms, then our belief that people do read (and that parrots can't really *talk*) becomes a hypothetical matter, a matter of inference. But in saying that the child is *reading* we are not committing ourselves to any causal hypothesis. We are not, for instance, saying that the marks cause him to utter the words he does; rather they are his *reasons* for uttering them.[4]

It is not simply a well-attested fact that I cannot 'read' a sentence from, say, the series

$$\&8\S \neq \S \neq\!\beta +\% \ 8!\S^* $$ [5]

My capacity to take, or see, the letters as 'intimating' how I should respond is not a matter of a private act invariably but contingently connected with my seeing the letters. This would be to treat the letters as *causes*. Consider, analogously, a mathematical formula and the series derivable from it. There is a temptation to treat either the written formula, or my 'grasping' the formula, as the cause of my continuing the series. The 'formula' occurs to me with characteristic accompaniments – release of tension and so on – and thereafter I always (or nearly always) find I can continue the series. So on 'grasping the formula' I make a prediction which is sometimes falsified by subsequent events.

The fallacy of such a causal account is clear enough. Far from my grasping the formula causing my ability to go on, my ability to go on is the *criterion* of my grasping the formula. The characteristic "Now

[1] Op. cit., No. 157.   [2] Op. cit., No. 169.   [3] Op. cit., No. 157.
[4] Op. cit., Nos. 169, 493.   [5] Op. cit., No. 169.

I can go on!" experiences only *count* as characteristic of grasping the formula, can only be taken as a picture of that, when I have in fact been taught mathematics, have performed calculations of a related sort and so on – when, in short, I have 'mastered a technique'. Even if the actual symbols of the appropriate formula come before my mind's eye, I can only see them *as* the formula in these or similar circumstances.

The most general form of the question involved here is "How am I able to obey a rule?" Wittgenstein again denies that this is a question of causes (or of 'interpretation'[1]). Indeed, if the utterance of a command actually had the effect of physically causing someone to obey it, then his action would not count as 'obedience' at all. If I cannot disobey a rule or command, then I cannot 'obey' it either. Wittgenstein suggests that a sentence which achieved an effect in this way would lose the character of a sentence.[2] The question is rather one "about the justification for my following the rule in the way I do".[3] An arrow can only be seen as 'pointing' in a particular direction when we have mastered certain conventions: we may then find that it does not occur to us to see the arrow except as pointing in that direction, just as we feel irresistibly impelled to see the marks on the printed page as words. "The arrow points only in the application that a living being makes of it."[4] The fallacy of the appeal to mental pictures to explain acts of understanding, meaning and so on was that it assumed that these pictures carry their applications on their face. But no picture can, by itself, compel only one interpretation, and in justifying our interpretation of a particular picture, our response to a particular rule, we should not search for a final self-justifying rule, or for a picture that could be interpreted in only one way.[5]

Wittgenstein compares the sense we have that certain pictures carry only one possible interpretation with our sense that all the possible movements of a machine are in it from the start – "the machine as symbolizing its action".[6] We 'derive' the machine's action from the machine just as we derive words from the printed marks or a mathematical series from a formula. We ignore, for instance, the possibility

---

[1] Op. cit., Nos. 201–202.

[2] Op. cit., No. 493. See also Jonathan Bennett, *Rationality*, p. 17: "For a creature to be correctly said to have a rule, it is necessary that it should be able to break the rule . . ."

[3] Op. cit., No. 217.   [4] Op. cit., No. 454.   [5] See note A, p. 31.

[6] Op. cit., No. 193.

of the parts of a machine bending or melting.[1] But that is not the sort of thing that goes wrong when we think that we 'know the formula' and find, nevertheless, that we cannot continue the series. The feeling "Now I can go on!", the release of breath, the 'flash of insight' which may accompany my grasping the formula may all be false signs; I may have all such experiences and still not be able to go on. But to take this as being like the machine's going wrong would be to take these experiences as *causes*.

I have taken Wittgenstein's treatment of how we obey a rule as central because of its bearing on some important questions in aesthetics. It gives force, for instance, to the idea that there is an internal relationship between a work of art and the 'appropriate' response to it. (There is also a connection here with Wittgenstein's discussion of 'seeing as', which I have mentioned and to which I will return later. He says: "I contemplate a face, and then suddenly notice its likeness to another. I see that it has not changed; and yet I see it differently. I call this experience 'noticing an aspect'."[2] Again: "What I perceive in the dawning of an aspect is not a property of the object, but an internal relation between it and other objects."[3]) On the one hand the work of art does not 'cause' my response. I justify my attitude, I give reasons. On the other hand my response is not the addition of a private feeling (and hence 'subjective'). We cannot *deduce* the correct response merely from a description of, say, a picture; that is, the picture, no more than a rule, does not carry its interpretation 'on its face'. As in the case of 'following a rule' and 'meaning a word' it is the particular context that determines how we are to 'see' the picture. One way of putting it is that the justification of attitudes is neither inductive nor deductive.[4]

The 'feeling' which I add to the picture is the sort of entity which the picture theory of language demands.[5] I have already suggested that the picture theory, with its insistence on 'naming' as the pre-condition of language, leads to the idea that language must be at least partly 'private'. In the same way it leads to the notion that my response to a work of art, if not 'caused' by the work, must be private, or 'subjec-

[1] Ibid.   [2] Op. cit., II, xi, p. 193.
[3] Op. cit., II, xi, p. 212.   [4] See Note B, page 32.
[5] That is, the version of the Picture Theory I have been considering. This is not, in fact, the view of aesthetics taken by Wittgenstein in the *Tractatus*. But any theory which relies on a dichotomy between 'descriptive' and 'evaluative' uses of language – as the picture theory most obviously does – will be liable to lead to such a view.

tive'. We can best see how to deal with this by first considering Wittgenstein's treatment of other mental concepts.

We find the following passage on *intention* in the *Brown Book*:

> Supposing I had made a move in chess and someone asked me "Did you intend to mate him?", I answer "I did", and he now asks me "How could you know you did, as all you *knew* was what happened within you when you made the move?" I might answer "Under *these* circumstances this was intending to mate him".[1]

Returning to the *Philosophical Investigations* we have: "An intention is embedded in its situation, in human customs and institutions. If the technique of chess did not exist, I could not intend to play a game of chess."[2] My 'intending' to perform an action is not an experience which I find to be almost always associated with the action coming about; it is not a form of predicting, any more than is 'grasping a formula'.[3] We may indeed have characteristic experiences when we 'intend'; but we may equally well have no particular experience – when, for instance, we hold to an intention over a period of years. Furthermore, the reason for calling whatever experiences we have 'experiences of intending' (the reason for seeing them *as* experiences of intending) is that they go with intending. If the same experiences went with 'wishing', then they would be 'experiences of wishing'. If it is replied that in that case they are *not* the 'same' experiences, then the attempt to appeal to experiences to distinguish mental concepts has been abandoned, and the experiences themselves depend for their distinction on the concepts. The experiences, in that case "drop out of consideration as irrelevant".[4]

Wittgenstein applies the same analysis to hoping, and to expectation.

> Now suppose I sit in my room and hope that N.N. will come and bring me some money, and suppose one minute of this state could be isolated, cut out of its context; would what happened in it then not be hope? Think, for example, of the words which you perhaps utter in this space of time. They are no longer part of this language. And in different surroundings the institution of money doesn't exist either.[5]

An expectation, like an intention, is 'imbedded' in a situation from which it arises: "The expectation of an explosion may, for example, arise from a situation in which an explosion *is to be expected*".[6] Even if

---

[1] *Brown Book*, p. 147.   [2] *Philosophical Investigations*, No. 337.
[3] Op. cit., No. 195.   [4] Op. cit., No. 293.
[5] Op. cit., No. 584.   [6] Op. cit., No. 581.

I have in my mind the picture of the man I expect entering the door with the money, this would not make my picture a representation of *expectation*; in certain circumstances the mental picture could stand for my fear of his coming, in others for my memory of his having been.

What is it that makes an image a memory image, rather than, say, a day-dream or an anticipation of the future? Well, the image might, for instance, occur in a context in which I am 'trying to remember' something – and so on.[1] The context which determines it as a memory image also makes it appear to have an intrinsically 'memory' character (i.e. a 'property of the object' rather than 'an internal relation between it and other objects').[2] Hume, indeed, suggests that a remembered event differs from an imagined one in that it 'retains a considerable degree of its first vivacity'.[3] The resort to such mythological differences of tone to explain logical differences is bound up with the view of language which Wittgenstein is at such pains to reject in the *Philosophical Investigations*. Even a 'long, long ago' feeling[4] associated with a mental picture is insufficient to establish it as a *memory* picture (unless, of course, the connection is made analytic[5]). For instance we could say that H. G. Wells is sometimes afflicted with 'a nostalgia for things to come'. This might, of course, be a purely critical comment laying stress on certain emotional vulgarities in his work. But there is an actual instance at the end of *The Time Machine*: the final scene is set far in the remote future, on a beach at sunset – in fact the earth has, by then, stopped revolving, and it is perpetually sunset – and all the emotional overtones are of the remote past.

Early in the *Philosophical Investigations* Wittgenstein discusses the difference between descriptive and imperative sentences:

> Now what is the difference between the report or statement "Five slabs" and the order "Five slabs!"? . . . Well, it is the part which uttering these words plays in the language-game. No doubt the tone of the voice and the look with which they are uttered, and much else besides, will also be different. But we could also imagine the tone's being the same – for an order and a report can be spoken in a *variety* of tones of voice and with various expressions of face – the difference being only in the application.[6]

Whether I 'mean' the words as a command depends on the circumstances in which I utter them, not on any mental or physical process

---

[1] *Brown Book*, pp. 182–3.   [2] *Philosophical Investigations*, II, xi, p. 212.
[3] *Treatise*, Book I, Part I, Section III.   [4] *Philosophical Investigations*, II, xiii.
[5] See p. 9.   [6] *Philosophical Investigations*, No. 21.

that accompanies the uttering of them. In arguing that 'meaning' is not a private act of the mind contingently connected with the utterance of certain words I took as an example the fact that I cannot *mean* the command "Shut the door" if I know that the door is already shut.[1] On the one hand one can say "It is impossible in these circumstances to *mean* it even if the utterance of the words is accompanied by those inward experiences that go with commanding". But here again[2] it can fairly be objected that when we know the door is shut it is impossible for us to have the *same* experiences when we utter the words "Shut the door!" as we would have knowing it to be open. But if this is true the impossibility is not a contingent but a necessary one. There is an internal connection between the command and the feelings I am able to attach to the words which express it. At this point the 'inward experience' has become a symbol of a logical impossibility. This is an example of what Wittgenstein calls the tendency to "sublime the logic of our language";[3] elsewhere he says: "When we do philosophy we should like to hypostatize feelings where there are none. They serve to explain our thoughts to us.[4] For instance it seems that we can experiment with some conceptual impossibilities; we can try to 'will' a book to fall off the table. Our incapacity to do this might strike us as 'synthetic *a priori*'. A similar experiment would be to try to say "bububu" and *mean* "If it doesn't rain I shall go for a walk",[5] or to feel proud of the Pacific Ocean,[6] or to find *King Lear* funny.

This last example anticipates the argument, but enough has been said about Wittgenstein's treatment of 'attitudes' to suggest that there is a continuum between a rule's intimating the way I am to go, and a play's intimating the appropriate emotional response. Wittgenstein's discussion of sensations makes the connection still clearer. In his review of the *Philosophical Investigations* Norman Malcolm argues that, according to Wittgenstein, our 'belief' that other people have minds is not a belief but an attitude.[7] I *justify* an attitude of pity towards a man in pain by referring to his pain-behaviour. In so doing am I justifying a belief? "Pity, one may say, is a form of conviction that someone else is in pain."[8] In that sense I can call it a belief; but I am not making an

---

[1] See p. 5.   [2] See p. 9.   [3] *Philosophical Investigations*, No. 38.
[4] Op. cit., No. 598.   [5] See p. 4.
[6] See Philippa Foot, 'Moral Beliefs', *Proc. Arist. Soc.*, 1958–9.
[7] *The Philosophy of Mind*, ed. V. C. Chappell, p. 91.
[8] *Philosophical Investigations*, No. 287.

inference to an inaccessible inward state. The outward expression of pain is not merely contingently connected (perhaps causally) with the inward experience of pain. Similarly we may say that we find it "impossible to believe" that a corpse is in pain; but we could equally well say that we find it impossible to 'take the attitude' to the corpse that it is in pain.[1] The conceptual impossibility is as absolute with both belief and attitude; it is neither a matter of probabilities nor of a subjective emotional response. Belief involves a readiness to act in certain ways (for instance to give the man who is in pain anaesthetic) and the taking up of an attitude involves the readiness to believe certain things (for instance that he *is* in pain – not pretending, etc.).

Is it possible, in certain cases, to doubt whether a man is in pain? We can answer this by taking the opposite example: can we believe that a stone *is* in pain? To ascribe sensations to stones, emotions to trees, and so on seems to be a conceptual impossibility; we cannot, as it were, *locate* feelings in stones:

> Look at a stone and imagine it having sensations. One says to oneself, How could one so much as get the idea of ascribing a *sensation* to a *thing*? One might as well ascribe it to a number! And now look at a wriggling fly and at once these difficulties vanish and pain seems to be able to get a foothold here, where before everything was, so to speak, too smooth for it.[2]

A particular sort of ascription has to be correlated with a particular sort of description: " 'But in a fairy tale the pot too can see and hear!' (Certainly; but it can also talk.)"[3] Similarly we can interpret a dog's behaviour as a sign that he is 'expecting' his master; but we cannot think of him as expecting his master in three weeks' time. The dog's incapacity to form such an expectation rests, among other things, upon his incapacity to use language. Again: "What is the natural expression of an intention? Look at a cat when it stalks a bird; or a beast when it wants to escape."[4] Wittgenstein adds the note: "Connect with propositions about sensations." And, of course, on the model of language set forth in the *Tractatus* to learn the correct use of "I am in pain" is to learn to attach the right words to certain private sensations. The verbal expression of pain has only a contingent connection with the sensation which it expresses (or describes, or names). One man may

[1] Op. cit., No. 284.   [2] Ibid.
[3] Op. cit., No. 282.   [4] Op. cit., No. 647.

always use the word 'pain' or the word 'red' correctly, in that he groans and says he is in pain when he catches his fingers in the door, and can always pick out red objects when asked to do so, but may really, inwardly always feel what we would (if we could 'put ourselves in his place') call 'pleasure' and see what we would call 'blue'. A dog's bark might mean "If it doesn't rain I shall go for a walk".

This is not the place to go into the controversy that has arisen over Wittgenstein's denial of the possibility of a purely private language.[1] It is, however, clear from what has already been said that the idea that it is possible for a man who uses, say, 'red' correctly to *mean* (inwardly) 'blue' rests on the notion of 'naming' and 'meaning' as a private and uncheckable ceremony, and upon a model of language as object and designation. Wittgenstein argues that in this case – if the sensations which pain-language designates are merely conjoined with the pain-language – then "the object drops out of consideration as irrelevant".[2] The strength of Wittgenstein's argument against the possibility of a private language comes out when we see it as integral with the rest of his philosophy. The inward resolution to make certain words signify certain sensations would be a paradigm case of treating *naming* as a pre-condition of language, and not as a move in a language-game.

At one point Wittgenstein says: "Just try – in a real case – to doubt someone else's fear or pain."[3] These 'experiments' would be analogous: try to see the people you pass in the street as automata; try to think of stones as having sensations, forming plans, etc.; try to think of *King Lear* acted as a comedy.

2. WIDER APPLICATIONS

It should by now have become clear that some at least of the central problems of aesthetics have to be seen as special cases of more general philosophical issues. Before concentrating on aesthetic problems more narrowly it is worth discussing to what extent it can be said that Wittgenstein has provided a general account of reasoning.

Wittgenstein often talks of philosophical reasoning as a matter of grasping the relations and differences between different language-games. Sometimes instead of doing this we appeal to feelings, or

---

[1] See *Phil. Inv.*, 243 onwards; Strawson, review of *Phil. Inv.*, *Mind*, 1954; Malcolm, review of *Phil. Inv.*, *Philosophical Review*, 1954; also Ayer, Rhees, *P.A.S. Supp.*, 1954, J. D. Carney, *Mind*, 1960.

[2] See p. 9. [3] *Philosophical Investigations*, No. 303.

objects, to correspond to and explain the different uses of language. Now the attempt to find the 'memory' quality in memory images – the 'long, long ago' feeling for instance – can become less and less crude by becoming less and less empirical. It can be claimed that different mental faculties, rather than different experiences, are involved in remembering from those involved in, say, predicting. Such an insistence on an accompanying process, standing behind our mental acts, an empirical one if such can be found or plausibly suggested, but in default of that a 'transcendental' one, can be seen, in the end, as merely a somewhat mythological way of marking the logical differences. Where characteristic *experiences* are lacking we find it difficult to give any account. On being *guided* for instance:

> But now notice this: *while* I am being guided everything is quite simple, I notice nothing *special*; but afterwards, when I ask myself what it was that happened, it seems to have been something indescribable. *Afterwards* no description satisfies me. It's as if I couldn't believe that I merely looked, made such-and-such a face, and drew a line. But don't I *remember* anything else? No; and yet I feel as if there must have been something else; in particular when I say "*guidance*", "*influence*" and other such words to myself. "For surely," I tell myself, "I was being *guided*." Only then does the idea of that ethereal, intangible influence arise.[1]

In the next chapter I shall suggest that a similar shift is common in theories of evaluation. For instance, the evaluative 'element' to which the value judgement 'corresponds' is defined as, say, a sentiment of approval or disapproval. This is gradually reduced to the claim that all evaluative sentences have an element of 'commendation'; but 'commendation' comes finally to mean no more than 'the defining characteristic of value judgements'.

Now in denying that there can be a 'general form of propositions' which is common to, and the *essence* of, all language-games, Wittgenstein introduces the metaphor of 'family resemblance'.[2] We seek a common feature in respect of which games are games. Finding no such feature we may resort to Platonic Form – a non-empirical entity – in which all games somehow participate. On the other hand we may decide that the only feature games have in common is that they are all called 'games' – which would be a form of Nominalism. The procedure could take the following form: "What all games have in common is that they are all played for amusement." Objections are then raised to this definition – world championship chess, for instance, is not really played for amusement. The rejoinder to this objection might take several forms. First, the definition can be withdrawn, and a better one sought. Secondly, it can be denied that world championship chess is a genuine game. This, as Wittgenstein says, would be to delimit the concept, to draw a line where there was not one before: "Can you give the boundary? No. You can *draw* one, for none has so far been drawn. (But that never troubled you before when you used the word 'game'.)"[1] A third possibility would be so to extend the concept of 'amusement' that it even covers world championship chess (and, perhaps, mathematics and philosophy). But this *is* an extension and as it becomes all-inclusive it becomes uninformative. Now if, as Pears suggests, one general form of the problem of universals is "Why are we able to name things as we do?"[2] then in talking about family resemblances Wittgenstein is saying something apropos the problem of universals.[3] He is showing that there is not any one answer, no 'general form of propositions'. The *general* question "How is language related to the world?" might be satisfied with the account given in the *Tractatus*, for there we have a general answer; but the whole procedure in the *Philosophical Investigations* is so far from giving a general answer as to amount to a dismissal of the question.

It is at this point that we see a further connection between the denial of the possibility of a private language and the rejection of the *Tractatus* theory of language. The idea that the connection between name and object is a determination of the mind which – as I suggested – has to be repeated each time the name is attached to the object, is nominalistic in exactly the way that "the only thing that games have in common is that they are all called games" is. For in the latter case we can have no criteria for saying that *this* is the same object which, according to a linguistic convention, I called a 'game' last time, and therefore should this time. All that is left is my disposition to use the name, and the notion of 'same' ceases to apply.

One way of interpreting Wittgenstein here is to say that it is not possible to state one necessary and sufficient condition for something's being a game; and he gives different examples – reading and walking –

[1] Op. cit., No. 68.

[2] D. F. Pears, 'Universals', *Logic and Language*, II. ed. Flew, p. 52.

[3] See Renford Bambrough, 'Universals and Family Resemblances', *Proc. Arist. Soc.*, 1960–1.

to make the same point about one necessary condition or one *set* of sufficient conditions.[1] Does a similar analysis apply to, say, the problem of the relation between sense-data and physical objects? Wittgenstein says: "Here we have two different language-games and a complicated relation between them. If you try to reduce their relations to a *simple* formula you go wrong."[2] The idea that material-object sentences can be reduced to, or 'logically constructed' out of, sensation sentences is akin to the idea that "Bring me the broom" can, without loss, be analysed into 'Bring me the broomstick and the brush which is attached to it".[3] We cannot, as a phenomenalist might claim, pass deductively from the sensation to the material-object language-game. Nor, on the other hand, is it a matter of inference from the sensations to an object which, say, causes them:

> Does it *follow* from the sense-impressions which I get that there is a chair over there? – How can a *proposition* follow from sense-impressions? Well, does it follow from the propositions which describe the sense-impressions? No. – But don't I infer that a chair is there from impressions, from sense-data? – I make no inference![4]

To appeal to a different object to correspond to the different forms of discourse would, again, be to resort to a symbol of logical differences, to 'sublime the logic of our language'. Sensation sentences have a different use, exist in a different context, are liable to different forms of falsity from material-object sentences. It is difficult not to feel that all this amounts to what we are almost irresistibly tempted to think of as a different object (just as we feel that there must be a special feeling or inward process that goes with reading or intending). It is like being asked to feel ". . . that a mouse has come into being by spontaneous generation out of grey rags and dust . . ."[5]

The passage from one language-game to another, then, seems to be neither inductive nor deductive. We can relate this to Wittgenstein's frequent insistence that philosophy does not explain, does not seek for anything *behind* the phenomena. We do not justify the

---

[1] *Philosophical Investigations*, Nos. 149, 160 and 183.

[2] Op. cit., II, v. p. 180.

[3] See p. 4.

[4] *Philosophical Investigations*, No. 486. See also No. 354 on "the fluctuation in grammar between criteria and symptoms" which "makes it look as if there were nothing at all but symptoms".

[5] Op. cit., No. 52.

material-object language-game in terms of the sensation language-game; they are 'proto-phenomena'. In such cases ". . . we ought to have said: *this language-game is played*".[1] The relation between different language-games can only be seen as a matter of detail – detailed comparisons of differences and resemblances, the finding of intermediate cases and so on. We try to achieve a map of our concepts, to lay our concepts side by side, not to explain one in terms of another, or to assimilate one to another. We "bring particular cases to bear on other particular cases";[2] we do not seek the 'basis' of our conceptual system. This might seem to make our conceptual scheme arbitrary – but in the same sense in which it is sometimes suggested that ethical and aesthetic systems, in default of 'ultimate' justification, are arbitrary. Wittgenstein has a very interesting remark in this connection: "Compare a concept with a style of painting. For is even our style of painting arbitrary? Can we choose one at pleasure? (The Egyptian, for instance.) Is it a mere question of pleasing and ugly?"[3]

Now from the point of view of aesthetics the description of the passage from sensation to material-object language as being neither inductive nor deductive is of the first importance. It seems to allow for discovery which consists neither in the finding of new facts, nor in the drawing of logical implications. John Wisdom calls reasoning which makes genuine discoveries although it is neither inductive nor deductive 'reflective thought'. As a scientific example he cites the familiar story of Newton's 'discovery' of the Law of Gravitation. What Newton saw the possibility of explaining was "the fall of apples *and the like*".[4] We can elaborate this account with the aid of a myth analogous to that of the falling apple. In this version Newton thinks of a cannon-ball's being fired and falling to the earth, then being fired further and further, and landing at a greater and greater distance until at last it is fired beyond the curvature of the globe, in which case it will go on 'falling' without being able to reach the surface again, and will therefore circle the world indefinitely. We then, by analogy, apply this picture to the movement of the moon around the earth, and the earth and other planets around the sun. The movement of

---

[1] Op. cit., No. 654.

[2] Renford Bambrough, 'Principia Metaphysica', *Philosophy*, April 1964.

[3] *Philosophical Investigations*, II, xii, p. 230.

[4] 'Philosophy, Metaphysics and Psychoanalysis', *Philosophy and Psychoanalysis*, p. 253.

the planets has been connected with the fall of apples – or cannon-balls. No new facts have been discovered, but the concept of 'falling' has been enriched by being applied to the whole solar system. The motions of heavenly bodies have been 'explained' by their being connected with those of earthly ones – and a new application has been found for the concept of 'falling'. At the same time an 'explanation' has been provided of what it is for earthly objects to fall by connecting their movements with the movements of the planets.[1]

Now if all reasoning is either inductive (the discovery of matters of fact) or deductive (logical inference) we do not seem entitled to say that anything has been discovered here. No new entity has been located; nor have the logical implications of the concept of 'falling' been worked out so that the movement of planets is, surprisingly, included. A new application of a concept has been shown, the concept has been extended. This is, surely, the discovery of a connection, and not the mere arbitrary insistence on seeing a connection where none had been noticed. The value of such a discovery is not purely its predictive power, but also its explanatory power. A new theory may explain in excess of its tendency to produce new predictions.

We can show more of the nature of 'reflective thought' by taking some account of the claims of psycho-analysis – a discipline which sometimes seems to lie uneasily between art on the one hand and science on the other. It has been argued, by Popper amongst others,[2] that psycho-analysis is not 'falsifiable'. This may be said to take the form of either a 'weak' or a 'strong' thesis. The first, or weak, thesis merely denies that psycho-analysis is truly scientific;[3] the second, or strong, thesis denies that psycho-analysis is a genuine discipline, is genuinely rational, or asserts that it is 'subjective' or even altogether bogus. It seems to me that the two theses are not, in the end, distinguishable, and that any attempt to set up 'falsifiability' as the criterion of science (distinguishing it from metaphysics, Marxism, Freudianism and so on) inevitably involves a limiting notion of what is *fully* rational. Of course, questions about the falsifiability of psycho-analysis may refer to attempts to test (perhaps statistically) the claims made about cures; or they may refer to the whole structure of psycho-analytic theory. For present purposes, however, I have in mind only that type of psycho-analytic 'explanation' that is found in, for in-

---

[1] See Note C, p. 32. [2] *Conjectures and Refutations*, pp. 34–5.
[3] This is, in fact, Popper's position.

stance, Freud's *Interpretation of Dreams*. We can start with some very interesting remarks by Wittgenstein on the subject, which Moore recorded and which preceded the publication of the *Blue Book*.[1]

What would it be like for a psycho-analytic explanation to be falsified? Freud's work on dreams perhaps best shows the relation of that question to another: What would it be like for a literary judgement to be wrong, or for a literary interpretation to be 'far-fetched'? At what point does Empson's discovery of still more ambiguities become 'subjective' or 'arbitrary' – invention rather than discovery? According to Moore, Wittgenstein called psycho-analysis 'aesthetics' rather than science.

> Freud did not give any method of analysing dreams which was analogous to the rules which will tell you what are the *causes* of stomach-ache. ... he had genius and therefore by psycho-analysis could find the *reason* of a certain dream, but ... what is most striking about him is "the enormous field of psychical facts which he arranges".
>
> [Wittgenstein said that] a psycho-analysis is only successful if the patient agrees to the explanation offered by the analyst. ... there is nothing analogous to this in physics; and ... what the patient agrees to can't be an *hypothesis* as to the *cause* – but only that so and so was the *reason*.

It is clear why Wittgenstein should consider psycho-analysis to be more like *aesthetics* than like science. A psycho-analytic interpretation cannot be imposed upon the patient as though it were a causal hypothesis which has been 'proved' by, or which 'explains', the agreed facts of the case. Nor is it simply a logical inference from the agreed facts. The patient is induced to see his behaviour in a different way, or to take up a new attitude. But similarly, the description which emphasizes the connection, or likeness between a cannon-ball's 'falling' and the moon's 'orbiting' cannot be imposed either as a causal hypothesis or a formal 'proof'. The argument might take the form of a comparison of the old description, or picture, and the new one; and the criteria might be those of economy, explanatory richness, elegance and so on – what it would be by no means far-fetched to call 'aesthetic' criteria. Here at any rate is an *analogy* between a scientific 'conjecture' and aesthetic 'insight'. It is true that in literary criticism one does not normally talk of hypotheses and proofs – rather one says, "This is the case; don't you agree?" But this does not mean that these are two

[1] G. E. Moore, *Philosophical Papers* X, *Wittgenstein's Lectures 1930–33*.

quite different procedures, or two quite different forms of reasoning, between which there is *no* analogy.

It seems that there is, at any rate, continuum between the two. Let us take the example of a jigsaw puzzle. If in one room there is a jigsaw puzzle with only one space left, and in another room six pieces, only one of which will fit the space, and if, before deciding which of the six is the right one, one is allowed to see half the space, it would not be far-fetched to call one's choice of one out of the six an *hypothesis* which would be verified or falsified by its fitting or not fitting the space. That part of the space which one saw provided a 'clue'. But similarly, if one were allowed to see the whole of the space, but only briefly, and then had to spend a day in the other room with the six pieces (which, let us say, differ from each other only slightly) it would still be reasonable to call one's final choice an 'hypothesis' which would be verified if the piece fitted. Now there clearly does come a point at which it is no longer usual or correct to use that sort of language. If, for instance, one is sitting directly in front of the puzzle with, say, a large, triangular piece – the last piece in the box and the only triangular one – and the puzzle contains a large, triangular space, the last space in the puzzle and the only triangular one, it would, perhaps, be eccentric to talk about hypothesis and proof; even more so if the piece were held just the fraction of an inch above the space and seen to be about to fit exactly; still more so after the piece has been inserted. At some such point we would claim to be able to see directly that it was the right piece; no intervening connections would be needed. And in the case where we were allowed to see the whole space, but then had to wait before fitting the piece, considerations about the length of the wait – five minutes, or five years? – the shape of the piece – whether simple, like a triangle, or complex – would bear on whether or not it would be strained to talk about an *hypothesis*. One cannot lay down in advance criteria which decide this.

But it seems that we can say that the fact that the piece fits proves that it was the right one. That is, we do not consider the process 'aesthetic' – we do not think that we have to decide to 'accept' that the piece fits. But there is obviously not a rigid distinction. To take another example, there may be two pieces left of identical shape – and two identical spaces. If you insert the pieces in one way, there will be a piece of cow in the middle of the sky and a piece of sky in the middle of the cow. This 'proves' that the pieces are in the wrong place: we would probably not call this 'aesthetic'. But, again, we may have a case in which we have to move a whole group of pieces to another part of the puzzle – otherwise the picture does not 'make sense'. Are we to say that this is of the nature of an 'aesthetic' acceptance of a pattern? Or is it a 'proof'? In both cases the 'decisions' are made on the basis of the gradual building up of patterns of knowledge. There is certainly an intrinsic absurdity about a piece of cow being in the middle of the sky, but the certainty that such a placing is wrong is not of a *different order* from the certainty that one arrangement of pieces 'makes better sense' than another. Nor is it discontinuous with the certainty that a particular triangular piece fits the triangular space into which it is about to be inserted. To take a different example; if you prove that ponds on a certain piece of land drain underground into a lake some miles away by pouring a coloured liquid into the pond and finding it later in the lake, your decision to believe that the liquid travelled underground – rather than that, for instance, a meteorite carrying an identical liquid fell into the lake – is equally 'aesthetic'. The frame of explanation implied by such an account would be too clumsy, ramshackle and 'unnatural'. The account itself would be far-fetched or improbable, just as a dream interpretation by Freud, or a Shakespearian interpretation by Wilson Knight (or, for that matter, a metaphor of Crashaw's), might be far-fetched or improbable.

It is clear that a great deal of reasoning could, on such grounds, be classed as 'aesthetic'. For instance I would show someone that a particular face is 'smiling' by comparing the expression with other expressions, connecting it with behaviour which follows and precedes it and so on. Similarly I do not know that the smile is genuine by inferring that it is caused by a feeling of benevolence, for a man's smile is one of the criteria (not, admittedly, a very important one) of his benevolence. Nor is his benevolence simply a matter of his smiling, and if, on whatever grounds, I become aware that he is malevolent I might interpret his expression not as a smile but as a leer or a smirk. These further facts, or further descriptions, do not 'explain' why the expression is a leer rather than a smile, at least in the sense of providing causal hypotheses; rather they give reasons, or a justification for taking it to be, or seeing it as one or the other. It is clear that any sharp separation here of 'interpretation' from 'sensory perception' is mistaken, since, as new facts come to light I might be prepared to describe what I see quite differently. I might insist that it is not a smile at all. Yet in

c

the same way, as I suggested earlier,[1] when I interpret a sentence as a *command*, or take a series of symbols as a *formula*, I justify my response not by inference to the state of mind of the man who issues the command, nor by a discovery in my own mind of a disposition to obedience, nor (in the latter case) by noticing in myself a "Now I can go on!" feeling, but by being able to refer to a situation in which commands are given and obeyed, and in which there exists – and in which I have mastered – a technique of mathematics.

We cannot, then, set up a sharp distinction between aesthetic reasoning and other forms of reasoning. There is no rigid distinction between hypotheses which are falsifiable in some ideally hard and obvious way, and *interpretations* which can only be shown to be 'farfetched' or 'over-elaborate'. It is not only in aesthetics that arguments aim to persuade us to 'see' in a particular way, without necessarily showing us new facts or deducing consequences from what we already know; and as the measure of the success of a critical argument is that we come to 'see' a picture or poem in a particular way, and as the criterion of the rightness of a psycho-analytical interpretation is that the patient 'accept' it, so in the case of physical hypotheses we have to accept that they *have* been verified or refuted.

3. SOME CONSEQUENCES FOR AESTHETICS AND ETHICS

Wittgenstein's emphasis on the need for the patient to 'accept' the analyst's interpretation for the interpretation to count as successful (and, indeed, for the therapy to be successful) brings out a distinction between an 'aesthetic' and a hypothetico-deductive procedure. Now in ordinary argument we do not talk of a decision to pass from premises to conclusion. Nor, presumably, would a physicist talk of a decision to accept a proof – except, perhaps, in very doubtful cases. Nor does the patient simply *decide* to accept the analyst's interpretation. For the patient's agreement to be real he has genuinely to 'see' his past history in the way the analyst suggests – and a criterion that he really does so is that his emotional attitudes change, or that his behaviour changes. If his emotional attitudes and behaviour remain as before this might well be a reason for doubting whether he really agrees with the analyst's interpretation – even though he may profess that he does. But no 'decision' is needed to bridge the gap between what he knows and how he feels, or between the evidence the analyst assembles and his

[1] See p. 5.

'acceptance' of it. Yet – as we shall see in the next chapter – the notion of a decision as the ultimate factor in any *moral* system has found favour with some philosophers. R. M. Hare, for instance, describes ethical discussion proceeding to ever higher levels of generality until we reach a series of precepts, parables or myths which "characterize a whole way of life",[1] at which point we have to choose which to adopt. I shall discuss Hare more fully later, but meanwhile it is important to realize how out of place the notion of decisions (in this sense) is in literary criticism. A critic might prefer to talk of passing by inevitable stages, and almost insensibly from description to evaluation. The attempt to provide the evaluative 'element' in the shape of a 'decision' or 'pro-attitude' is analogous to the search for some inward process to accompany intention, understanding and so on – another attempt to "sublime the logic of our language".

The emphasis on decision goes with a rigid separation of fact and value. Without anticipating too much the argument of the next chapter it is worth noticing how little such a sharp distinction seems to mean either in psycho-analytic practice or 'practical criticism'. In psycho-analysis there is a gradual rearrangement of the facts as seen by the patient; the aspect of things changes and (ideally, at any rate) behaviour changes, too. This passage from a knowledge of one's condition to a change in behaviour is puzzling only if we remain bound to the idea that the passage from description to evaluation must be either inductive or deductive. Something like a 'decision' seems to be needed to bridge the gap between facts and values. Psycho-analysis, indeed, seems to proceed on the unHumean assumption that Virtue is Knowledge.

Yet this Socratic position is not at all out of place in aesthetics. That is to say, an appropriate emotional response, an appropriate attitude, a correct *valuing*, is a central criterion of genuine aesthetic grasp. If a man has visited all the major art galleries of Europe and yet still derives his highest aesthetic satisfaction from the works of Tretchiakov then there would be at least a *prima facie* case for denying that he had any knowledge of painting – however many pictures he had looked at – and probably for denying that he had seen what there was to see in these pictures. (This brings out, incidentally, a concealed premise in Mill's appeal in *Utilitarianism* to those who are "competently acquainted" with both the higher and lower pleasures as judges of

[1] *The Language of Morals*, p. 69.

which are which; it would be a *criterion* of 'competent' acquaintance that a man who has been exposed to both sorts prefer the higher.) There is no gap here between knowledge and an appropriate aesthetic or emotional or behavioural 'response'; and even if there were it is difficult to see how a 'decision' could bridge it. Similarly it is quite in order in aesthetics to say something like, 'If you really *know* Henry James you *cannot* prefer Marie Corelli'. Or rather, 'You cannot *decide* to prefer Marie Corelli'. For one's 'valuation' of James *is* a matter of knowledge – knowledge of other novels, of literature, of oneself, of 'life'. There is no place for a decision. We consider it virtually impossible for a ten-year-old child (to put the age no higher) properly to appreciate James or Goethe. This is not because he refuses to make the decision to do so, but because he has not sufficient knowledge, or a sufficient sense of bearings. And to say that he has not sufficient 'emotional maturity' is to say something about the amount he knows – although obviously not in a narrowly 'intellectual' sense. The child has to be 'educated' into an appreciation of art and into a proper discrimination.

We cannot 'decide' to change our critical preferences. If, over a number of years, I have come to see that Mozart is a very much greater composer of opera than Verdi, I cannot change my mind at will. Nor is there any point during my initiation into Mozartian opera at which I 'make up my mind' that he is a great composer. After all, how could one 'make up one's mind' in aesthetics? What would it mean? Evolving aesthetic preferences is something like being led unsuspectingly into a trap which closes behind one; one cannot just turn round and walk out again. You cannot decide to jettison great areas of moral and aesthetic knowledge at will any more than you can decide to forget what you know about mathematics or history.

It would, of course, be possible to *come to prefer* Marie Corelli, just as it would be possible for a previously balanced man to come to a paranoid view of politics or a conspiracy view of history, but it is not possible simply to *decide* to take up any such position. And although there is, as Wittgenstein suggests, a logical connection between the patient's acceptance of the analyst's interpretation and the 'success' of the interpretation (both therapeutically and diagnostically) it does not follow that the truth of the interpretation is simply a matter of the patient's decision to accept it, or that the patient's acceptance *causes* the analysis to 'work' therapeutically. In other words the patient's 'acceptance' cannot be characterized only as his taking up an attitude, or becoming ready to act in a particular way, but also involves his coming to 'see' in a new way. Nor is his behaving differently the only criterion that he has come to see or feel differently; he may, for instance, *describe* his own past life, or his present feelings, differently. It is here that there is an analogy with the falling cannon-ball, a criterion of success in that case being the 'cognitive' one – that reasonably independent observers are able to accept it as a suitable, or possible description, are able to see how it 'fits'. Clearly the notion of a 'response' is more central in the psycho-analytic case, as it is in aesthetics, but not in any way so as to introduce any 'irrational' element such as a 'decision'. Later I shall go on to argue that it is difficult to give much sense to the idea of two people 'seeing the same thing' (in, say, a work of literature) but simply 'valuing' it differently.

4. EMOTIONS

It would be true to say that most English criticism since Wordsworth, including what has been called the New Criticism, has been, in its basic assumptions, expressionistic. Works of art have been thought of as conveying, or expressing, or evoking an emotion experienced by the artist. Expressionism, at least in some of its forms, is clearly bound up with the object-designation theory of meaning. As we feel that behind the words a man utters is a mental act of understanding, so we are easily led to think that behind a piece of music, as it were silently accompanying it, is that which it expresses; and what it expresses is what it *means*:

> ... that same illusion possesses us even more strongly if repeating a tune to ourselves and letting it make its full impression on us we say "This tune says *something*" and it is as though I had to find out *what* it says. ... (if) I resign myself to saying "It expresses itself" ... "But surely when you play it you don't play it *anyhow*, you play it in this particular way, making a crescendo here, a diminuendo there, etc." ... Precisely, and that is all I can say about it, or may be all I can say about it.[1]

To say that music 'must have a meaning' may be merely a way of expressing a sense of its structure – and not necessarily the most satisfactory way. When we try to indicate the emotion behind the music, or the poem, we usually end up describing the music or the poem. Or

[1] *Brown Book*, p. 166.

we have the *King Lear* emotions and so on. The emotion can only be described by means of an object. If we turn again to Moore's notes, we find that Wittgenstein has further interesting remarks on this subject. Matters of beauty, he says, are not psychological questions – means to an end, the end of agreeable sensations – but *ends*.

> [Wittgenstein] says that a statement such as "That bass moves too much" is not a statement about human beings at all, but is more like a piece of mathematics; and that, if I say of a face which I draw "It smiles too much", this says that it could be brought closer to some 'ideal', not that it is not yet agreeable enough . . .

Again:

> What aesthetics tries to do, he said, is to give *reasons*, e.g. for having this word rather than that in a particular place in a poem, or for having this musical phrase rather than that in a particular place in a piece of music. Brahms' *reason* for rejecting Joachim's suggestion that his *Fourth Symphony* should be opened by two chords was not that it wouldn't produce the feeling he wanted to produce, but something more like "That isn't what I meant". *Reasons*, he said, in aesthetics are like further descriptions. . . . And he said that the same sort of 'reasons' were given, not only in Ethics, but also in philosophy.[1]

In seeking to name the feelings we find ourselves naming that of which the feelings are supposed to be characteristic. 'Long, long ago' feelings are scarcely an advance on 'memory' (or 'history') feelings.

Looking to the 'feeling' to give meaning to the work of art is like looking to the *thought* in order to understand the sentence. For instance, in trying to decide whether the same negation occurs in "Iron does not melt at a hundred degrees centigrade" and "Twice two is not five" we might try to introspect in order to see what we are thinking as we utter the two sentences.[2] Similarly we often cannot give the feeling or thought of a sentence by replacing it with another one – any more than we can give the meaning of a musical theme by replacing it with another.[3] Having broken down one artificial dichotomy between aesthetic and other forms of reasoning, Wittgenstein goes on to reverse, as it were, the argument by showing that, outside of aesthetics, we often make choices on the basis of 'feeling'. (He is talking of the choice of the 'right' word):

> How do I find the 'right' word? How do I choose among words? Without

---

[1] Moore, op. cit.   [2] *Philosophical Investigations*, No. 551.
[3] Op. cit., No. 531

doubt it is sometimes as if I were comparing them by fine differences of smell: *That* is too . . ., *that* is too . . ., *this* is the right one. But I do not always have to make judgements, give explanations; often I might only say: "It simply isn't right yet." I am dissatisfied, I go on looking. At last a word comes: "*That's* it!" *Sometimes* I can say why. This is simply what searching, this is what finding, is like here.[1]

Again:

The words "It's on the tip of my tongue" are no more the expression of an experience than "Now I know how to go on!" We use them in *certain* situations, and they are surrounded by behaviour of a special kind, and also by some characteristic experiences. In particular they are frequently followed by *finding* the word. (Ask yourself: "What would it be like if human beings *never* found the word that was on the tip of their tongue?")[2]

There is a connection between Wittgenstein's insistence that aesthetics gives *reasons* and his denial that aesthetic argument is primarily "about human beings". We 'justify' the interpretation of a sentence as, say, a command by placing it within a particular context or system, not by inferring to the mental state of the man who utters it, or simply by noticing the 'effect' it has upon its hearers. Similarly, we do not justify an interpretation of a work of art hypothetically – by predicting its effects on people, or guessing at the mental or emotional state of the artist – but by showing its relation to other works, and so on. In other words, the meaning of a work of art is 'given', an interpretation of it is justified, by its 'internal' relations (other pictures, etc.) rather than by its 'external' relations (its emotional 'effect' on particular human beings). I think that this is what Wittgenstein means when he says that aesthetic argument is about 'ends'.

There is a useful discussion along these lines by Errol Bedford.[3] (I shall draw later on another treatment of emotion by Anthony Kenny.[4]) Bedford shows that a fundamental mistake in our talk about emotions is to treat emotion words as *names*. This is, as we have seen, one of Wittgenstein's central arguments. As Bedford remarks, such a view presupposes

. . . a richness and clarity in the 'inner life' of feeling that it does not possess. What evidence is there for the existence of a multitude of feelings

---

[1] Op. cit., II, xi, p. 218.   [2] Op. cit., II, xi, p. 219.
[3] 'Emotions', *Proc. Arist. Soc.*, 1956–7.
[4] *Action, Emotion and Will.*

corresponding to the extensive and subtle linguistic differentiations of our vocabulary for discussing emotions?[1]

Bedford does not, as he could, generalize the point; what evidence is there for the existence of a multitude of different mental processes to correspond to all the differences of meaning and mood of which language is capable? Another point Bedford makes is that ". . . one cannot understand what it is to feel angry without first understanding what it is to be angry".[2] Wittgenstein's remark that an inner process stands in need of outward criteria becomes ". . . being angry is logically prior to feeling angry".[3] In ascribing emotions we take not only behavioural but social context into account. In one context the emotion may be shame; in another, embarrassment. We cannot be 'ashamed' of just anything. But attributions of, say, anger cannot be reduced to descriptions of behaviour; they interpret behaviour. A man's actions are reasons for the ascription of anger. They are not necessary and sufficient conditions for the ascription of anger.[4] This is one feature which distinguishes this account from behaviourism.

5. 'SEEING AS'

One of Wittgenstein's examples – a drawing which can be seen as either a duck or a rabbit – brings together much of his argument in a particularly vivid way. In certain contexts we would see the drawing as a duck, and in certain others as a rabbit.[5] One such context may be the drawing surrounded by obvious drawings of rabbits. But another may be merely: "Don't you see? It's a rabbit!" To quote Strawson's review of the *Philosophical Investigations*:

> If we are to describe the (Duck/Rabbit) experience correctly, we cannot isolate a "pure visual" element in it and say that that, and that alone is the momentary experience; we can describe the experience correctly only by referring to what does not relate to the moment. Experience and interpretation are not merely conjoined.[6]

By stressing 'seeing as' Wittgenstein has brought out important features which the usual 'pure visual' paradigm tends to hide.[7] This

---

[1] Op. cit., p. 282.   [2] Op. cit., p. 283.   [3] Op. cit., p. 284.
[4] Op. cit., pp. 288–9.
[5] *Philosophical Investigations*, II, xi, p. 194.   [6] *Mind*, 1954.
[7] See Hanson, *Patterns of Discovery*, particularly ch. 1, and J. L. Austin, *Sense and Sensibilia*, pp. 100–2.

paradigm gives us an unnecessarily 'cramped' idea of the concept, and leads to our urge to separate the 'pure' seeing from the 'interpretation':

> ... "how is it possible to see an object according to an interpretation?" The question represents it as a queer fact; as if something were being forced into a form it did not really fit. But no squeezing, no forcing took place here.[1]

There is no doubt that the Duck/Rabbit example is of very general application. The interpretation is not merely conjoined with the 'visual' experience; but nor is it *caused* by the lines on the page. Could I see the drawing as a lion? Or would this be merely having an experience unconnected with the drawing? It seems that if the drawing does not 'carry its interpretation on its face' (i.e. if the interpretation does not follow from the basic sense-datum deductively) then my interpretation must be in some sense subjective. So why not see it as a lion as easily as a duck or rabbit?[2] But does the same possibility arise in any case in which we interpret a rule? Remember that "The arrow points only in the application that a living being makes of it".[3] If I interpreted rules irresponsibly, there would be a question whether what I was doing was in any sense obeying a rule.[4] But there is a continuum from clearly obeying a rule, to obeying it eccentrically, and to doing something which cannot count as a 'response to the rule' at all. The paranoid is, as it were, systematically misinterpreting reality; the psychotic has no contact with reality at all. The account which makes the relationship external – a matter of causes rather than reasons – does not solve the difficulty. In the first place, as we have seen, it makes the connection contingent where it is *a priori*; secondly, it would not even be a good causal law. Hume has put the classic objection:

> But tho' the object of love and hatred be always some other person, 'tis plain that the object is not, properly speaking, the cause of these passions, or alone sufficient to excite them. For since love and hatred are directly contrary in their sensation, and have the same object in common, if that object were also their *cause*, it wou'd produce these opposite passions in an equal degree; and as they must, from the very first moment, destroy

---

[1] *Philosophical Investigations*, II, xi, p. 200.
[2] Waismann, 'Verifiability', *Logic and Language* II, ed. Flew.
[3] *Philosophical Investigations*, No. 454.
[4] Op. cit., No. 222.

each other, none of them wou'd ever be able to make its appearance. There must, therefore, be some cause different from the object.[1]

Just as we could find some way of seeing the drawing as a lion, we could probably think up some way in which we could attribute pain to stones. E. M. Forster actually does in one passage:

> How indeed is it possible for one human being to be sorry for all the sadness that meets him on the face of the earth, for the pain that is endured not only by men, but by animals and plants, and perhaps by the stones? The soul is tired in a moment, and in fear of losing the little she does understand, she retreats to the permanent lines which habit or chance have dictated, and suffers there.[2]

Now Forster's lapse into sentimentality here is one way of responding 'irresponsibly'. The context which he has created in which stones 'perhaps' share in the general pain is unconvincing in that it is unserious and not very intelligent. The stones are an excuse for, and not any genuine object of the emotion. Here we have an example of a response's being subjective, and calling it that involves a judgement of value. But is it really surprising that an emotional failure should at the same time be a failure of thought, or that a lapse into sentimentality should at the same time be a lapse into conceptual confusion?

The picture is not related to our response as cause to effect – involving an element of prediction – any more than seeing the formula as the formula and hence knowing how to continue the series is a matter of mental picture and prediction, or than forming an intention (seeing what one is doing as forming an intention) is a matter of predicting one's future action on the basis of an experience. The connection of all this with aesthetic reasoning becomes even plainer when we see how parallel are two remarks of Wittgenstein's: the first to the effect that if God looked into our minds at a particular moment "he would not have been able to see there whom we were speaking of" – i.e. the meaning of our mental images;[3] the second, that one minute of a coronation ceremony, detached from its context, might be cheap and vulgar: ". . . in different surroundings gold is the cheapest of metals, its gleam is thought vulgar. There the fabric of the robe is cheap to produce. A crown is a parody of a respectable hat. And so on."[4]

---

[1] *Treatise*, Book II, Part II, Sect. I.
[2] *Passage to India*, ch. 26.
[3] *Philosophical Investigations*, II, xi, p. 217.
[4] Op. cit., No. 584.

6. CONCLUSION

One of the main effects (for our purposes) of the *Philosophical Investigations* is to destroy the idea (or prejudice) that aesthetic reasoning is essentially unlike other forms of reasoning, or that it is not genuinely rational at all. If reasoning could indeed be exhaustively divided into reasoning about matters of logic and discovering matters of fact – "the abstract relations of ideas, or those relations of objects of which experience only gives us information" as Hume says[1] – then it would be difficult to find any place for aesthetics, which would have to be consigned to matters of taste and psychology. Wittgenstein shows how this model of reasoning is inadequate in very many areas. For instance, in the analysis of mental concepts such as intention, it forces us to hover between making unsound (and anyway irrelevant) inferences to inner states, and behaviourism. It does not even account for philosophical reasoning satisfactorily. Metaphysical theories may be arguments for seeing things in a new way, and, perhaps, for using words in a new way. Similarly – Wisdom draws the comparison – the psychoanalyst may, without discovering new facts, induce a patient to see a pattern in his behaviour for the first time.[2] Nor does the patient deduce that he *must* have, say, hated his father; he comes to see his behaviour *as* manifesting that hatred. He may see a new connection in his feelings between what he had always thought of as love, and what he would be willing to call hatred.

Of course, my account of Wittgenstein has concentrated on the applicability of his thought to the philosophy of criticism, which doubtless involves a distortion of emphasis. I hope, however, that it has become clear that the consequences for aesthetics, and, indeed, ethics, of Wittgenstein's later work are as important and far reaching as they have already been widely accepted to be for, among other things, philosophical psychology.[3]

NOTES TO CHAPTER I

A]   This point was made by Kant: "If (general logic) sought to give general instructions how we are to subsume under these rules, that is,

[1] *Treatise*, Book II, Part III, Sect. III.   [2] See Note C, p. 32.
[3] See Note D, p. 32.

to distinguish whether something does or does not come under them, that could only be by means of another rule. This in turn, for the very reason that it is a rule, again demands guidance from judgement. And thus it appears that, though understanding is capable of being instructed, and of being equipped with rules, judgement is a peculiar talent which can be practised only, and cannot be taught." *Critique of Pure Reason*, A 133, translated by N. Kemp-Smith.

B] It may seem that I am exaggerating the connection between a 'response' and 'obedience to a rule'. See, however, the following passage on "laws of inference" from Wittgenstein's *Remarks on the Foundations of Mathematics*:

> ... the laws of inference can be said to compel us; in the same sense, that is to say, as other laws in human society. The clerk who infers ... *must* do it like that; he would be punished if he inferred differently. If you draw different conclusions you do indeed get into conflict, e.g. with society; and also with other practical consequences.
>
> And there is even something in saying: he can't *think* it. One is trying e.g. to say: he can't fill it with personal content; he can't really *go along with it* – personally, with his intelligence. It is like when one says: this sequence of notes makes no sense, I can't sing it with expression. I cannot *respond* to it. Or, what comes to the same thing here: I don't respond to it. (Op. cit., No. 116.)

c] Another way of bringing out what is involved here is as follows: since induction can occur only over classified instances – instances *of* such-and-such – and since deductions about instances can be explained in terms of class membership (see Strawson, *Introduction to Logical Theory*, Chapter 4), reflective thought involves the redrawing of class boundaries. Popper's insistence on theory as a condition of induction can perhaps be seen as making the point that to be subject to induction, instances must be classified. Bambrough's urging (above) of the logical priority of 'particular cases' can then perhaps be put: if both deduction and induction over cases depend upon the cases being classified, then the assigning of cases to classes by means other than deduction or induction is logically prior. With the priority of classification goes a priority in the justification of a classification.

d] I have emphasized Wittgenstein's point that rules and formulae as well as evaluations can be understood and justified only in a context, in terms of Wittgenstein's apparently separate discussion of the concept of 'seeing as'. This was to stress the important connection of these two topics in aesthetics. Although this can best be shown in the course of such detailed examination of aestheticians and critics as follows, it may be helpful to outline it generally now. It is a commonplace of modern philosophy (see, for instance, Ayer's *The Problem of Knowledge*, Chapter 2, section ix) that sceptical arguments against knowledge of all sorts – knowledge of material objects as well as values – are often based on the fact that the reasons for the knowledge in question do not deductively guarantee it; it is always possible to accept the reasons and consistently, although absurdly, deny the conclusions. Now in the case of material objects there is a certain unreality about such scepticism – the sceptical philosopher knows perfectly well what, in a given case, would count for or against saying that there was a chair in the room. Although there may be a problem in persuading him to see *how* reasons that are neither deductive nor inductive (criteria) can bear on a conclusion, there is no problem in persuading him to see *that* these reasons do bear on the conclusion. Once the first problem is removed the second vanishes. In evaluative arguments, although the logic of scepticism is the same, the doubt may be real, so that the (philosophical) problem of getting someone to see *how* a given set of criteria count towards a conclusion is intertwined with the (critical or aesthetic) problem of getting him to see *that* these criteria are the relevant ones for the conclusion in question. Someone may know a, b, c . . ., and yet not see how a, b, c . . ., bear on C; and someone may know that *if* a, b, c . . . *then* C, and yet not know whether a, b, c . . ., or not even see that such and such was an example of a, b, or c etc. The latter ignorance creates a difficult problem, for it may require not only the enforcing of particular judgements (on the basis of further criteria), but also an introduction to aspects of the whole context in which evaluation takes place. When the two forms of ignorance are combined, they must be remedied together; and that is what I call the problem of getting someone to *see* the criteria *as* criteria – for instance to see the features of the picture as making it a fine picture. Here, at least, the two discussions proceed simultaneously. Furthermore, either may proceed 'extensively' (by comparing the criterial reasoning in question with other examples of the same or different sorts of reasoning, or by comparing the criteria in question with other criteria or other features which are not criteria), or 'intensively' (by, for example, picking out a particularly central criterion, the bearing of which on this sort of conclusion cannot be denied, and the bearing of which on *this* conclusion cannot be denied). The resulting 'seeing as' which is induced by reference to features of the painting in question, to other paintings, to the evaluative context in which paintings are judged, and to the logical context in which valuing takes place, will be a seeing differently, a 'placing' differently on a value 'map', of the painting (or poem, or novel) in question. Although in logic aspects of the problem of persuading someone to see ... as ... can be separated, they are also intertwined. Together with the fact that evaluation, like other forms of reasoning, proceeds as a unity, this means that to separate them in a discussion of a particular critic would in fact be impossible. It is for that reason, and also because the complex change in vision which aesthetic argument induces is so often manifested in a literal seeing and feeling differently, that I discuss the questions together under the concept of 'seeing as'. I hope the resulting cost in clarity and precision of distinction is not greater than I imagine.

CHAPTER II

Values

I. INTRODUCTION

And so saying, he put the bottle into Sancho's hand, who, grasping and setting it up to his mouth, stood gazing at the stars for a quarter of an hour; and having done drinking, he let fall his head on one side, and, fetching a deep sigh, said, "O whoreson rogue! how Catholic it is!" "See", quoth he of the wood, hearing Sancho's phrase, "how you have commended the wine in calling it whoreson." "I confess my error," answered Sancho, "and see plainly that there is no discredit to any body to be called son of a whore, when it comes under the notion of praise."

Don Quixote, Part II, Book I, ch. xiii, trans. Westall.

When we call a motor-car or a chronometer or a cricket-bat or a picture good, we are commending all of them.

R. M. Hare, *The Language of Morals*, p. 118.

In the last chapter I suggested that much of what Wittgenstein says in the *Investigations* has bearing on the traditional problems of evaluation. In this chapter I shall try to develop this theme negatively – by way of bringing out the paradoxes and vacuities to which certain other (more or less traditional) accounts succumb. A more positive note will, I hope, emerge in the discussion of particular critics.

It might be well to recall one's initial surprise on hearing of the distinction between facts and values. In a state of philosophical innocence one is not usually aware that in 'making a value judgement' one is doing anything unusual; but when the logical differences between describing and evaluating have been pointed out for the first time the peculiarities seem monstrous and the difficulties overwhelming.

Many of these difficulties arise from taking the 'descriptive' as the paradigm of language. Language ultimately has meaning because of a 'correspondence' of (say) its basic terms with facts in the world, and of its structure with the structure of the facts. (That, at any rate, is the doctrine of the *Tractatus*, which, as I suggested, brought out the presuppositions of such theories in an extreme form.) The difficulty immediately arises of how certain sorts of discourse can have meaning. When I say "X is my intention" what is the feature, or quality, or tone of X which makes it (assuming that 'X' gives a description) the picture of a state of affairs which I *intend* to bring about, rather than one which I remember, or fear? If I am not referring to a quality of X then perhaps I am referring to a feeling I have in respect of X – a feeling of *intention?* In that case, on such a model of language, I am naming an essentially private inner state. I have already examined Wittgenstein's treatment of this method of distinguishing different 'language-games' by means of an alleged difference of subject matter. When we can find no empirical feature to account for differences we resort to 'mental' differences – differences of 'attitude' and so on – or to some other non-empirical feature. In this way we symbolize *logical* differences.

Various formulae have been advanced to mark the distinction between the 'descriptive' and the 'evaluative' uses of language. P. H. Nowell-Smith, for instance, in adopting the traditional distinction between the theoretical and practical sciences declares that the purpose of the former is "to enable us to understand the nature of things, whether the things be stars, chemical substances, revolutions, or human behaviour". Practical discourse on the other hand "consists of answers to practical questions, of which the most important are 'What shall I do?' and 'What ought I to do?' "[1] Descriptive language, then, presents the object as in itself it really is; evaluative language expresses an attitude to the object – perhaps with an eye to some action or other. Some such distinction seems common to very many theories of evaluation. I shall examine some typical formulae and the muddles to which they lead, and then try to show how these muddles have a common origin in a mistaken view of language.

It is generally admitted that such a sentence as "Housman's poetry is sentimental" can have evaluative force. It is also generally admitted that such a sentence describes. Perhaps what makes it evaluative is the purpose for which it is used? This is undoubtedly the correct answer, but we may not find it very informative. So we try various formulae. "It expresses the speaker's feeling." But so does "President Lincoln has been assassinated!" It evokes an emotion in the hearer; so does the statement about Lincoln (different emotions in the breasts of Northerners and Southerners). Perhaps, then, it "tends to guide choice".

[1] *Ethics*, p. 11.

This may, of course, be true; but does not a B.B.C. weather forecast tend to guide choice? Or a B.B.C. news bulletin? All language is used to some purpose, and very much of it tends, in some way or other, to influence behaviour. If one were to ask the Director-General of the B.B.C. why he goes on putting out news bulletins, he could certainly not appropriately answer "To make the crops grow faster", or, "I just felt like it"; if he replied, "I do so in order to enable people to choose responsibly in social and political matters", he would at least be speaking relevantly.

Perhaps evaluative language is more overtly choice-guiding, or more overtly and intentionally seeks to evoke or express emotion? To guide choice or express emotion might be its central endeavour. For example "Joseph Stalin, for twenty-five years Dictator of the Soviet Union, died today" would tend to be evaluative, whereas "Joseph Stalin, for twenty-five years First Secretary of the Soviet Communist Party or Chairman of the Council of Ministers of the U.S.S.R., died today" would be purely descriptive. Here we are aware of lines leading off to two theories of evaluation – the 'imperative' and the 'emotive'. According to these two theories the first sentence would be analysed as "Dictator! Ugh!" or as "Don't ever allow yourselves to come under the sway of dictators!" Both theories would analyse the second sentence as "First Secretary . . . (no discernible reaction demanded or to be expected)".

But 'dictator' has a different *meaning* from 'First Secretary . . .'; so we have not the same situation presented first in a context of evaluation and secondly in one of neutral description, but two different situations.

A further move of the same sort would be to claim that 'dictator' relates the situation more clearly to human interests than does 'First Secretary'. In so far as we can be clear about this the suggestion seems to be that some human interests are more human and more interesting than others. We have, then, human interest (1) – that is, mathematics, philosophy and so on, and human interest (2) – that which is to our advantage or disadvantage. Hare is relying upon such a distinction when he remarks[1] that we have no concept of a 'good wire-worm'. This would seem to mark the lack of human interest (2). Yet surely the fact that we have the concept of a wire-worm marks the presence of human interest (1). Can a coherent account be given of the distinction between human interest (1) and human interest (2)? We are obviously

[1] *The Language of Morals*, pp. 127–8.

D

back again at the original, and unsatisfactory, distinction between the neutral, contemplative attitude to the world and the 'evaluative' attitude (the world as 'something to be manipulated'). The fact that the primitive distinction we have made relies upon the notion of what is of *advantage* shows that we are already assuming a judgement of value; 'advantage' is not being used purely descriptively. It was, of course, to be expected that a blanket-phrase of such facile generality as 'human interest' would only 'explain' value judgements at the price of circularity.

Can we attempt another distinction? Evaluative language, we might say, is bound up with our pragmatic, everyday affairs; purely descriptive, 'scientific' language is a more sophisticated affair – perhaps, historically, a later development. However, are not our aesthetic interests very often – particularly when they concern highly formal art (music for instance) – sophisticated, specialized in the same way? Yet are not aesthetic judgements matters of value? To avoid this difficulty we would have to invoke yet another distinction – between the 'moral' and the 'aesthetic', the moral certainly being a matter of value, the aesthetic only doubtfully so. There is a full-blooded statement of this view by Stuart Hampshire[1] who argues that works of art are 'gratuitous', whereas in a moral situation some course of action is *demanded*. Works of art, therefore, are not capable of being evaluated. This indeed is a logical conclusion of the form of reasoning which seeks to locate the evaluative 'element' of value judgements in 'human centrality'.

The separation, in this way, of the aesthetic and the moral gives rise to at least as many problems as it attempts to solve. The aesthetic attitude is to be looked upon as purely contemplative, detached from our everyday interests. We are not now trying to distinguish between the descriptive and the evaluative, and then, within the evaluative to distinguish between the aesthetic and the moral; for the same reasons which seemed to demand the separation of the evaluative, including the moral, from the descriptive are here seen to require the separation of the evaluative, including the aesthetic, from the descriptive.

Can we perhaps drop the idea of an 'aesthetic' mode and seek to distinguish only between descriptive and moral-evaluative language? The descriptive is presumably to be separated from the moral-evaluative in terms of the moral-evaluative's greater relevance to 'human

[1] 'Logic and Appreciation', *Aesthetics and Language*, ed. Elton.

purposes'. But surely there is good reason to separate the aesthetic from the descriptive on the grounds of the aesthetic's greater relevance to '*human* purposes'? Should we then reduce the aesthetic to the moral rather than to the descriptive? The descriptive then is separated from the evaluative on the grounds of the descriptive's lack of relation to human purposes; but these were exactly the grounds on which the aesthetic was distinguished from the moral in the first place.

All this, of course, is something of a caricature. It does, however, seem clear that the basic confusion lies in the attempt to define descriptive language in such a way that it lacks all of the characteristics of language, and then to give a definition of evaluative language which really states the necessary conditions for any language whatsoever. And behind this is the idea that there is the sort of 'correspondence' between propositions and facts which might theoretically be expressed in terms of a 'general form of propositions'. The opposite view is put by Wittgenstein when he describes different language-games as 'proto-phenomena', and by Austin when he remarks: "The total speech act in the total speech situation is the only actual phenomenon which, in the last resort, we are engaged in elucidating."[1]

The emotivist and imperativist accounts, whatever absurdities they lead to, have at least the virtue of making genuine claims. They may misinform but they do offer genuine criteria for distinguishing between evaluative and descriptive language. Now when an empirical feature which is intended to be the 'essential element' which marks and explains a logical difference fails to fulfil its role (is found to be, say, neither necessary nor sufficient), the usual move, as I tried to show in the previous chapter, is to resort to something non-empirical. One example of this is "Evaluative language commends", or "The essence of evaluative language is that it has a commendatory element". Now if 'commendation' does not mean something incorrect – like 'choice-guiding', or 'emotion-evoking' – what does it mean? What probably happens is that 'commendation' starts off with a quite positive meaning – it may mean something like 'choice-guiding' or 'recommendation'. Then confronted with cases (for instance, "Housman's poetry is sentimental") where we can only talk about recommending or choosing in a very strained way, and where anyway our grounds for "choosing not to re-read Housman often" are the low value we set upon sentimental poetry, it retreats into vacuity. If we still insist that the difference

[1] *How to do Things with Words*, p. 147.

between the critical statement and, say, "The earth is five hundred million years old", is that the former 'commends', which, however, does *not* mean that it 'guides choices' or 'evokes emotions', or anything else which can be shown not to cover all cases, then has not 'commends' come to cover both favourable and unfavourable evaluation, and come to mean no more than 'evaluates'? And of course the only 'essential' distinction between evaluative and descriptive language is that the latter describes and the former evaluates. We are, again, merely choosing an eccentric way to mark a logical difference, "subliming the logic of our language".

This does not mean that guiding choice, evoking emotion are irrelevant to the distinction between description and evaluation. It would, indeed, be surprising if they were – if only because of the frequency with which one or another has been singled out as the essential distinguishing feature. In one sense the mistake lies in looking for an over-simple formula; but behind this is the deeper mistake – the search for a difference of subject matter (extra emotional or mental elements and so on) to correspond to a different use of language.

2. FROM DESCRIPTION TO EVALUATION

The only recourse of a man who refused to accept the things which counted in favour of a moral proposition as giving him a reason to do certain things or to take up a particular attitude, would be to leave the moral discussion and abjure altogether the use of moral terms.

Philippa Foot, 'Moral Arguments', *Mind*, 1958, p. 510.

If the view of language rejected in the *Philosophical Investigations* is as widespread in traditional philosophy as Wittgenstein suggests (the book begins with a quotation from St Augustine) then we should expect moral philosophers to be preoccupied with the problem of the relation between ethical statements and things in the world. If ethical (or aesthetic) statements do not refer to states of affairs in the way that descriptive statements do, then perhaps they are not genuine propositions at all. This is exactly the preoccupation we do find. In the *Enquiry Concerning the Principles of Morals* Hume says (the italics are mine):

But in moral deliberations we must be acquainted beforehand with all the objects and all their relations to each other, and from a comparison of the whole fix our choice or approbation. *No new fact to be ascertained; no new relation to be discovered.*[1]

So Hume decides that we add a sentiment of approval; this provides the extra fact which is necessary if the ethical proposition is to have an object. The point is made more explicitly in the *Treatise* (my italics):

> The vice entirely escapes you, as long as you consider the object. You can never find it, till you turn your reflexion into your own breast, and find a sentiment of disapprobation, which arises in you towards this action. *Here is a matter of fact; but tis the object of feeling, not of reason. It lies in yourself, not in the object.*[2]

But as "no process could have the consequences of meaning" so no sentiment could have the consequences of evaluation. Hume is here being ambiguous, as we can see by comparison with a rather more guileless passage in Mill's *Utilitarianism*. In speaking of the ultimate sanction of the Principle of Utility he says:

> The internal sanction of duty, whatever our standard of duty may be, is one and the same – a feeling in our own mind; a pain more or less intense, attendant on violation of duty, which in properly cultivated moral natures rises, in the more serious cases, into shrinking from it as an impossibility.

Later he says: "Undoubtedly this sanction has no binding efficacy on those who do not possess the feelings it appeals to. . . . On them morality of any kind has no hold but through the external sanctions."[3] We see in these two passages of Mill the consequences of the reduction of ethics to psychology. The moral 'feelings' in us may be difficult to break through, but there would be nothing logically odd in asking why we should obey them, or whether they are the right feelings to have. But it *is* logically odd to ask "Why should I do what is right?" or "Why should I do my duty?" It is a question not of the psychological but of the evaluative force of 'right' and 'my duty'. Mill has, in fact, put the 'internal sanctions' on the same logical level as the 'external sanctions'. We cannot use evaluative language (except in an 'inverted commas' sense) without committing ourselves in various ways. Hume has described his 'sentiment' as being one of 'approbation'. If 'approbation' does not mean 'pleasure' or 'satisfaction' but rather 'approval' then the only characterization of the sentiment that is being offered

---

[1] Op. cit., Appendix I.
[2] Op. cit., Book III, Part I, Sect. I.
[3] Op. cit., Part III, 'Of the Ultimate Sanction of the Principle of Utility'.

is that it is a favourable judgement of value. Of course in using a term like 'favourable' a flavour of the 'emotive' seems to be retained – an 'inner process' seems to be guaranteeing a judgement of value. But there is no independent criterion of whether a sentiment is favourable or not. A favourable sentiment would be one of 'approbation' and an unfavourable sentiment would be one of 'disapprobation'. If I said "I take pleasure in what you are doing but I disapprove of it" then my pleasure would not count as a sentiment favourable to your action. The sentiment, then, does not define the judgement as being one of approval or disapproval, but is itself defined by the judgement's being one of approval or disapproval. But the judgement can *only* be defined by means of the 'sentiment'. We are therefore left in the curious position of not being able to distinguish between approval and disapproval – which is another reason for saying that a 'process' cannot have the consequences of valuing.

To search for the evaluative 'element' which corresponds to the 'value judgement' is analogous to the attempt to isolate the mental events which are supposed to accompany and account for 'meaning', 'intending' and so on. 'Commendation' is different only in that it is vacuous. "Where our language suggests a body and there is none: there, we should like to say, is a spirit".[1] For 'spirit' we can substitute 'commendatory element' or 'pro-attitude'; for 'body' we can substitute 'feeling of approval' or 'command'.

If the passage from description to evaluation is not in the nature of an inductive inference, then is it deductive? In the last chapter I discussed the reasons we have for denying that the passage from one language-game to another is either inductive or deductive. A description of a picture does not entail a value judgement about it. It would be possible to agree to the description but deny the evaluation without contradiction. Similarly it is not deducible from his behaviour (or reducible to his behaviour) that a man intends, or understands, or is angry about something. Is it, therefore, something 'over and above' his behaviour? Are value judgements 'over and above' descriptions? We should recall the objection to the idea that we could without loss analyse "Bring me the broom" into "Bring me the broomstick and the brush which is attached to it".[2] Is the first sentence a 'logical construction' out of the second? To suppose that it is is to have a notion of 'simplicity' and 'complexity' which is somehow absolute and prior to

[1] *Philosophical Investigations*, No. 36.   [2] See p. 4.

any system of language. We can recall again Wittgenstein's remark: "Here we have two different language-games and a complicated relation between them. If you try to reduce their relations to a *simple* formula you go wrong."[1]

It would be appropriate at this point to pay some attention to two theories which seem at first sight to be at opposite extremes from each other – those of R. M. Hare and Philippa Foot. Despite their apparent differences they both suffer from the insistence that the passage from description to evaluation must be a matter either of induction or deduction, and consequently from a tendency to over-simplify the relationship.

Hare argues that since an evaluative conclusion cannot be entailed by descriptive premises, and since we justify our value judgements by more general principles from which they follow, we must, if we are finally to justify our value scheme, come to an assertion of principle at the highest level of generality. ". . . the statement of the characteristics of the man (the minor or factual premise) *together with* a specification of a standard for judging men morally (the major premise) entails a moral judgement upon him."[2] If we are asked for a complete, ultimate justification of a particular moral decision we specify as completely as possible its consequences and the principles under which it is to be brought, and we point also to the consequences which lead from the observation of these principles.

> Thus, if pressed to justify a decision completely, we have to give a complete specification of the way of life of which it is a part. This complete specification it is impossible in practice to give; the nearest attempts are those given by the great religions, especially those which can point to historical persons who carried out the way of life in practice.[3]

If our questioner is indecent enough to demand "But why should I live like that?" then all we can do is to "ask him to make up his own mind which way he ought to live; for in the end everything rests upon such a decision of principle".[4]

The obvious objection to this is that the ultimate 'decision' is, in that case, arbitrary. Hare is very short with this objection:

> To describe such ultimate decisions as arbitrary, because *ex hypothesi* everything which could be used to justify them has already been included in

---

[1] Ibid.
[3] Op. cit., p. 69.
[2] Hare, op. cit., pp. 145–6.
[4] Ibid.

the decision, would be like saying that a complete description of the universe was utterly unfounded, because no further fact could be called upon in corroboration of it. This is not how we use the words 'arbitrary' and 'unfounded'.[1]

The question is not how we use the words 'arbitrary' and 'unfounded' but how we use the words 'description' and 'decision'. Can we attach any sense at all to the notion of 'a complete description of the universe'? I can, perhaps, say that in *Anna Karenina* Tolstoy gives a completely satisfactory description of a particular sort of predicament – but I do not literally mean that it could not possibly be improved on in any way. We may for all practical purposes call many descriptions 'complete' but this does not involve the claim that no further fact could corroborate or count against them. If by 'complete description of the universe' Hare just *means* 'a description such that no further fact could count for or against its completeness' then he does not seem to be using 'description' in any normal sense. Apart from this difficulty the analogy – if it is to base itself on how we use these words – is false. It would indeed be odd to call a description arbitrary just because everything supports it, but it would not be odd to call a decision arbitrary because it cannot be justified. Hare's own analysis makes it necessary, for a decision to be rational it should be subsumable under a principle – the ultimate decision of principle would not be the sort of decision he has previously been describing at all. It is a necessary postulate, a piece of logical mythology. It is not a decision in the previous sense – just because it cannot be subsumed under a principle. In speaking of justifying a decision in terms of giving a 'specification of the way of life of which it is a part', Hare recognizes the role I have been attributing to context in justification; he is right also in thinking that we frequently justify something by subsuming it under something more general. Yet he seems not to see that 'subsuming under a principle' is only a non-circular justification in so far as it consists in 'giving a more nearly complete specification'. As it is, the final decision carries its own justification with it – like the mythical final picture which carries its interpretation on its face, or the final self-interpreting rule. But the most fundamental objection is that this is not how we use the word 'decision' – a point I discussed in the last chapter, and to which I shall return.[2]

Against Hare, Mrs Foot argues that values are *entailed* by descrip-

[1] Op. cit., p. 69.   [2] See Note A, p. 57.

tions. She argues that it is impossible arbitrarily to attach just any emotion to any situation. "It is logically impossible to warn about anything not thought of as threatening evil, and for danger we need a particular kind of serious evil such as injury or death."[1] She goes on to claim that it is equally impossible to attach just any valuation to any situation. ". . . there is no describing the evaluative meaning of 'good', evaluation, commending, or anything of the sort, without fixing the object to which they are supposed to be attached."[2] The conclusion is that where the value is greatly different the concept is different. In so far as another tribe or nation has a *very* different concept of 'good daughter' or 'good father' from ours, they have a different concept of 'father' or 'daughter'.[3]

Are we to look upon Mrs Foot's arguments as merely a straightforward revival of Naturalism? The answer is, I think, that in most respects Mrs Foot's conclusions are based upon an analysis which is both much more subtle and more nearly correct than that which underlies most traditional forms of Naturalism, but that in one central respect it fails – and fails in the way in which naturalistic theories classically fail.

In *Moral Beliefs* Mrs Foot explicitly invokes the *Philosophical Investigations*, Nos. 253–315, where Wittgenstein argues, among other things, how sensations, expectations and so on cannot be ascribed to just *any* objects (such as, respectively, stones or dogs), and how it is logically, not merely empirically, impossible that stones should feel or dogs expect their masters in three weeks' time. Similarly the evaluative significance of such concepts as 'rude'[4] is not merely attached to the sort of behaviour which 'rude' describes. To describe a number of 'rude-making' characteristics and then deny that the behaviour so characterized *is* rude would be senseless. And so to describe it *is* to evaluate it.

But at one point Mrs Foot allows an exception which may seem to undermine her whole position;[5] she allows that "a little rudeness is sometimes in place", which, if 'rude' is being used with its full evaluative force, and not in an 'inverted commas' sense, is a contradiction.

[1] 'Moral Beliefs', *Proc. Arist. Soc.*, 1958–9, p. 88.
[2] Op. cit., pp. 85–6.
[3] 'Goodness and Choice', *Arist. Soc. Supp.*, 1961, pp. 50–1.
[4] 'Moral Arguments', *Mind*, 1958.
[5] This was pointed out to me by M. K. Tanner.

Compare "To be rude is sometimes good" with "To be bad is sometimes good". Obviously the latter is a contradiction, and, if the evaluative force of 'rude' is entailed by the description, so is the former. Now a similar exception is allowed when she discusses the sorts of object of which, the sorts of situation in which, one can be 'proud'. We cannot possibly be proud of the Pacific Ocean – *unless we devise a context which enables us to be.* " 'But in a fairy tale the pot too can see and hear!' (Certainly, but it can also talk.)"[1] Similarly, we would expect any dog in a fairy tale who expected his master in three weeks' time to be able to talk about such things.

The significance of these exceptions is obvious. Mrs Foot has not produced a description which entails a valuation – any more than anyone has ever produced a series of statements about sense-data which entail an assertion about a material object, or a series of descriptions about someone's behaviour which entail that he has a mind, a consciousness. Just because we do not think that a man's intention is something merely conjoined with his behaviour, we are not therefore forced to think that it is nothing but his behaviour. Fresh evidence could always turn up to make us withdraw our ascription of a particular intention. Although all the evidence we give is a ground for the conclusion, we have not stated the necessary and sufficient conditions such that the conclusion is entailed. In so trying to reduce evaluation to description, Mrs Foot is making essentially the same mistake as Hare. He thinks that value judgements have to be deducible from evaluative plus descriptive premises, while she believes that they have to be deducible from descriptive premises. This may seem an important difference, and in a way it is; yet we are, surely, seeing merely two sides of the same coin.

At this point we might as well examine the 'Naturalistic Fallacy' as analysed by Moore, and see its relevance to the discussion so far. In *Principia Ethica*[2] Moore says:

> ... it is a fact, that Ethics aims at discovering what are those other properties belonging to all things which are good. But far too many philosophers have thought that when they named those other properties they were actually defining good ... This view I propose to call the 'naturalistic fallacy' and of it I shall now endeavour to dispose.

Moore's argument is that to call a car 'a good car' is not equivalent to

[1] See p. 12. [2] Chapter 1, Part 10.

describing its 'good-making' characteristics. "This is a good car" cannot *mean* "This car has an engine of —— performance, strong bodywork, accurate steering, great seating capacity, easy manœuvrability, etc." (we could substitute exact specifications for 'great', 'easy', and so on), because the car could lack any of these features and still be a good one, or possess them all and still not be good. Or rather, we could accept that all the features described are present, and yet, without contradiction, deny that the car is a good one. We might, for instance, say, "Yes, but it shows a tendency to vibrate at speeds of over fifty miles an hour". This would be new evidence against the judgement that it is a 'good' car. And, for instance, large seating capacity is not *essential* to a car's being a good one.

Yet because none of the features we have mentioned is essential to a car's being a good one, it does not follow – as Moore thinks it does – that all are irrelevant. ". . . one thing may be a matter of other things without being formally definable in terms of them."[1]

For a car to be good is a matter of all the characteristics we have mentioned, but it is not definable in terms of them. The mistake of Naturalism – and of Mrs Foot – is to think that it is so definable. The parallel confusion of anti-naturalists is to believe that if goodness cannot be defined in terms of a finite set of features then it is something altogether different from them.[2] Yet if a man says that a particular object is 'a good car' because it is a total wreck and will thus serve as a barricade against an armed force's advancing down the road, then he is not talking about its goodness as a *car* but as something else. If we state that it has features A–N (i.e. good-making features) it will be absurd to deny it is good, although not contradictory. To 'commend' a particular object is not to add to it some mysterious mental attitude (compare again Wittgenstein on how we "concentrate on the colour rather than the shape", how we 'expect' someone, etc.[3]) any more than 'being proud' consists in adding 'pride' to any situation; nor, again, can we ascribe feelings to stones. As we would have to think up a special context to allow it to be logically possible to be 'proud' of the Pacific Ocean, so also would we to make it logically possible for us to 'commend' it.

---

[1] Wisdom, review of Waddington's *Science and Ethics*, *Philosophy and Psychoanalysis*, p. 103. See also 'Metaphysics and Verification', op. cit., pp. 80–3.

[2] See Note B, p. 58.

[3] See pp. 2, 9.

There are two further, connected, reasons for denying that 'good' can be defined in terms of its criteria. The first is that if 'good' is merely a shorthand for the criteria of goodness, 'good' can never be used with commendatory force. Accordingly 'This is a good clock' cannot *mean* 'This clock keeps time correct to -nth of a minute' because if it did mean that we could not, in uttering the first sentence, 'commend' the clock. We would be doing no more than saying 'This clock keeps time correct to -nth of a minute' in slightly fewer words. This argument is, however, at least partially false. To say 'This clock keeps time correct to -nth of a minute' *can* be a way of 'commending' the clock, can be used with evaluative force. In such a case 'This is a good clock' will mean 'This clock keeps time correct to -nth of a minute' if, first, it is clear that accuracy of time-keeping rather than a beautiful appearance is the desirable characteristic, and when, secondly, the remark is uttered in circumstances which make it a judgement of value. These circumstances might include: that you choose on hearing it to buy this clock rather than another, or that you feel proud or pleased that you have bought it, or that you mentally compare it with another you own which is markedly less accurate, or that when it comes to wear out you buy another of the same sort, and so on.

The second, more powerful reason for denying that the meaning of 'good' is analytically identical with its criteria, is connected with this. Even though one sentence may, in particular circumstances, properly be said to mean the same thing as another, in the sense that the one sentence about the clock may (*in these circumstances*) be replaced by the other, it does not even here follow that 'good', as used on this occasion, has a meaning analytically identical with its criteria. For 'This is a good clock' could, in different circumstances, mean something like 'It only needs to be wound up every two months'. In both cases 'This is a good clock' would be uttered with reference to centrally clock-like excellences, but the excellences would be different in each case. The criteria of goodness would be different in each case; and they would be still more different as between, say, a good claret and a good poem. Now when the criteria are as different as they are in the case of the claret and the poem, can we say that 'good' is being used in the same sense of the claret and the poem, or is it simply "a homonym with as many punning meanings as the situations it applies to"?[1] The latter would seem (unwittingly) to be implied by Ethical

[1] See Urmson, 'On Grading', *Logic and Language*, II, p. 176.

Naturalism with its insistence that 'good' is no more than the sum of its criteria. If we drop that insistence, however, there seems no good reason why we should be forced to choose between 'good' as being used in the *same* sense of a good claret and a good poem, and 'good' simply as a pun or a homonym. That would be rather like being forced to choose between Realism and Nominalism: either 'game' is applicable to games because they all have something in common – and hence 'game' is applicable in the same way to all games – or else the only thing that games have in common is that the term 'game' is, by convention, applied to them.[1] Yet both clarets and poems can really be good, which is to say 'good' really classifies them, is a genuine universal and not a pun. But 'good' is not used in the same sense of both. Perhaps it is used, if not in the same sense, at any rate in an analogous sense? Or perhaps it is what Waismann would call a vague or 'open-textured' concept.[2] Both these suggestions have their point, but neither is entirely satisfactory. The notion of 'family resemblance' is probably more useful. When I call a claret 'good' I may mean that it is 'fruity', or that it has body, or that I find myself frequently wanting to drink more of the same, that I am prepared to recommend other people to drink it, that I would choose it rather than another and so on. When I call a poem 'good' I may imply that it has richness or complexity of texture, that I frequently find myself coming back to it without boredom, that I would prefer to read it rather than certain other poems. There are obviously analogies between the two cases as well as differences. These analogies and differences extend not only to the 'descriptive' features picked out in each case, but also the *circumstances under which* these features are picked out. For instance, even if I mention a feature X which a claret has in common with a poem, I might, in the first case, be picking out this feature in the context of recommending someone to put down a cellar of this vintage, and in the second case I might be inducing someone simply to 'see' that the poem has this feature by comparison, say, with another which has not – but with no eye to any future *action*, but only to future attitudes, or, indeed, present attitudes.

What I am saying here amounts to a modified form of Naturalism. With a word like 'good' the 'family resemblances' are between the criteria of application; with words like 'dangerous', 'flourishing' and

[1] See Renford Bambrough, 'Universals and Family Resemblances', loc. cit.
[2] 'Verifiability', *Logic and Language*, I.

'rude' (on which Mrs Foot concentrates) there are also 'family resemblances' among the 'objective' features.

Now to say that 'good' is used in the same sense of claret and poems in that there is an element of 'commendation' common to both cases is either a sort of Realism (all games and all good things have each something in common – perhaps a relation to something else) or else 'commendation' is simply being used to depict the existence of the classification, so that when it is said that the element common to all value judgements is 'commendation' this is like saying that games all have something in common – that they are all games. ('One might as well say: "Something runs through the whole thread – namely the continuous overlapping of the fibres."[1]) 'Commendation', like 'pro-attitude', 'human interest' and so on, has simply become coterminous with the concept it is meant to explain – another 'sublimation' of the logic of our language.

In Chapter I, I tried to bring out the analogies between justification of attitudes, justification of interpretations (my taking this group of symbols as a *formula*) and justification for my 'seeing' something in a particular way ('seeing as'). The type of reasoning by which we induce someone to 'see' or 'interpret' in a particular way is analogous to that by which we induce someone to 'feel' in a particular way, and, indeed, ethical argument may in many cases be as much a matter of inducing someone to 'see' as to 'feel' (hence the relevance of the comparison with psycho-analysis). Wisdom puts this very well:

> It is the same with ethical statements ... his attitude must be altered by *rational* persuasion. And this is done by drawing attention rhetorically to the features of what we are talking about, insisting upon how different it is from this, how like to that, passing insensibly from the purely factual through the semi-factual, semi-critical to the critical predicate at issue. Only this mixture is proof and the name of it is rhetoric.[2]

There is no sharp distinction, in the relation between premises and conclusion, between arguments to 'see' and arguments to 'feel' in a particular way. To bring this out further we may take a passage from Bernard Mayo's *Ethics and the Moral Life* which assumes a rigid distinction of just this sort:

> Take a factual statement, such as that Hitler persecuted the Jews. If I

[1] *Philosophical Investigations*, No. 67.
[2] 'Note of Ayer's *Language Truth and Logic*', *Philosophy and Psychoanalysis*, p. 246.

produce all the relevant evidence, documents and witnesses, it would be absurd for somebody to ask, "Why is all that a reason for saying that Hitler persecuted the Jews?"; but if I give my reasons for saying that Hitler was wrong to persecute the Jews, it does always make sense to ask, 'Why is that a reason?' It seems as if moral reasons can always be challenged, whereas factual ones cannot, beyond a certain point.[1]

Yet this very example is one where, if someone could see no force in our arguments that what Hitler did was wrong, we would be at a loss to know whether he had the same concepts as we have. 'If that is not wrong, what is?' is the essential rejoinder. But this rejoinder is no different from one we would make to someone who said, "I don't call *that* 'persecuting' ". Now supposing he were to give reasons for his refusal to call Hitler's treatment of the Jews 'persecution' – suppose, for instance, he were to produce documents which showed that there really was a body corresponding to the 'Elders of Sion' who really were – in collusion, say, with the Bolsheviks – plotting to enslave the German People: then could he not rightly say, "It wasn't *persecution* – it was self defence, and punishment for treason"? Undoubtedly he could. And this is not a merely far-fetched example; after all is this not what Hitler (assuming his sincerity) really did believe? Of course this belief is absurd – of course paranoia is absurd, but paranoia can as well operate in the realm of facts as can moral blindness in the realm of values. A paranoid, we might say, is one whose belief is 'unfalsifiable'. There is no 'certain point' (when philosophers say 'certain point', we can be sure – to adapt Moore's remark about the philosopher's use of 'really' – that they mean that the point is very uncertain: otherwise they could, perhaps, say *when*) beyond which it becomes 'senseless'[2] to go on questioning. It does not follow that certainty is impossible. In other words it does not follow that I have failed to answer the question 'Why is it so close today?' if I merely explain that the day is cloudy, and do not go on to explain why there are clouds, and in short give a history of the universe. ". . . an explanation serves to remove or to avert a misunderstanding – one, that is, that would occur but for the explanation; not every one that I can imagine."[3] Similarly[4] we can go on demanding rules to tell us how to apply this one. There is no

---

[1] Mayo, op. cit., p. 47.

[2] By which Mayo must mean something like 'contradictory' if it is to have the force he intends it to have.

[3] *Philosophical Investigations*, No. 87.   [4] See Note C, p. 59.

point at which the questioning becomes contradictory – except in the sense that the questioner may be demanding evidence of a certain kind and then, when it is given, refusing to count it as evidence.

3. ENDS

In *Ethics* P. H. Nowell-Smith suggests that the most a moral philosopher can do towards justifying the moral principles he advocates is to paint pictures of various types of life in the hope that the one he recommends will be found to be the most attractive:

> ... the type of life you most want to lead will depend on the sort of man you are. Decisions and imperatives do not follow logically from psychological or biological descriptions; but the sort of life that will in fact be satisfactory to a man will depend on the sort of man that he is. Generalization is possible only in so far as men are psychologically and biologically similar.[1]

Perhaps the most extraordinary thing about this way of talking – as of Hare's characterizations at the highest level of generality – is that ethical argument is held virtually to end just where aesthetic argument would begin. Given Hare's or Nowell-Smith's structure of ethics, argument about ends (in the sense of ultimate ends) becomes a highly problematic and vague affair. Yet we recall that (according to Moore) Wittgenstein said that aesthetic arguments are about *ends*. Now Hare really makes it impossible to argue about ends. The Original Decision which he is impelled to posit stands in relation to ethics as the Newtonian God to the universe – an entity the sole function of which is to set the whole system in motion. It is, I think, by comparison with critical argument that the artificiality of the whole scheme becomes most apparent. Critical persuasion consists overwhelmingly in inducing people to 'see' in a particular way, and little meaning can be given to the notion of 'seeing the same facts but valuing them differently'. It is here that Wittgenstein's treatment of 'seeing as' is most relevant, for it breaks down the over-narrow idea of 'fact' upon which Hume's analysis of evaluation depends, and also dispenses with the artificial distinction of 'aesthetic' from other forms of reasoning which goes with it. It is no doubt platitudinously true that men cannot 'see', and hence value, things in the same way unless they are in some basic sense similar (although exactly what Nowell-Smith means by 'psycho-

---

[1] pp. 319–20.

logically and biologically similar' is obscure – 'psychological' similarity is a vague enough concept), but critical arguments do not proceed on any hypothesis about human similarity. Nowell-Smith's remarks could be interpreted as having reference to what Wittgenstein says about the need for agreement in judgements,[1] but aesthetics does not move out of the realm of reason-giving into the realm of causal hypotheses. Nor does philosophy; it is significant that at some point both Nowell-Smith and Hare feel forced (the former admittedly in a very tentative way) to abandon the language of ethical reasoning and resort to a bio-psychological and a psychological hypothesis respectively.[2] To try to introduce, say, 'biological' differences into ethical reasoning is on a level with introducing causal explanations into an account of human action.[3]

In the first chapter I used the example of psycho-analysis to illustrate Wittgenstein's treatment of 'seeing as', and to undermine the exaggerated notion of choice which we find in Hare. In psychoanalysis there is an extension of what can fairly be called ethical *reasoning* into areas where previously 'rational persuasion' was thought to come to an end.[4] I do not claim that the comparison of ethical with aesthetic argument results in a comparable extension. But if we take literally Nowell-Smith's talk about painting pictures of various types of life, and ask ourselves how we in fact judge pictures, then we see that his (and Hare's) accounts not only have little bearing on aesthetic reasoning, but are also defective as accounts of ethics at those points where it most resembles aesthetics. It is no good being told to judge the quality of a man's emotional states or his motives by reference to a further end which we are then supposed just to make up our minds to find attractive. The 'quality' of a picture of life is just the sort of thing that is judged in the way we judge a man's emotional states or motives, or in the way we judge a picture or poem. It is here that the dichotomy between judgement in terms of intrinsic qualities and judgement in terms of consequences becomes most troublesome. It would obviously be absurd to judge works of art in terms of consequences. That Hitler found ideological inspiration in the music of Wagner is indisputable – but it does not follow that Wagner's music is bad. Indeed, if an institution which we considered wicked constantly succeeded in expressing itself in works of art of the highest

[1] *Philosophical Investigations*, No. 242.   [2] See Note D, p. 59.
[3] See Melden, *Free Action*, ch. 3 and 4.   [4] See MacIntyre, op. cit., p. 93.

value, then this could be a reason for revising our view of its wicked-ness. (It is not an accident that the artistic manifestations of Fascism were banal in the extreme.) Similarly, we might admire a man's charac-ter even though it led to disastrous results – as James II is described in *1066 and All That* as "a Good Man but a Bad Thing". On the other hand there is an obvious correlation between our incapacity to admire certain states of mind and our awareness of their constant ten-dency to produce disastrous results. It is not *always* misguided to justify one's condemnation of a work of art on the grounds of its social or moral consequences.

However, if 'consequences' is interpreted narrowly the absurdity remains, because whether a consequence is good or bad is itself a matter of valuing. It is useless at this point to argue that we know that certain consequences would be, say, biologically disastrous, or that certain forms of life would obviously be intolerable. Every good anti-naturalist knows that values do not 'follow logically' from (or, as I have put it, 'are not entailed by') biological or psychological descrip-tions. So although suicide would, as an ethical ideal, lead to the des-truction of the race, it is not thereby rendered impossible to adopt (certain of the Manichaeans did in fact adopt it). By stressing the simi-larity between ethical and aesthetic judgement we can avoid the dis-tortions which a concentration upon choice and consequences leads to. If I object on ethical grounds to sentimentality I may well be judging its internal relations with other qualities, and not its consequences; I will be doing something in the nature of analysis, not of prediction. An objection to sentimentality on aesthetic grounds will almost cer-tainly be an 'analysis' in this sense. Indeed if I try to round off a piece of 'practical criticism' by mentioning that this poet's work has in-duced a nihilistic attitude to life in many young men, then I would quite likely find myself accused of resorting to 'non-aesthetic' or 'moralistic' or 'political' criteria. It is always the case that if a serious work of art contradicts certain of our ethical criteria then there is a *prima facie* case for reconsidering our ethical criteria. In close criticism of a text one shows what sentimentality involves, or goes with (rather than what it leads to), by way of giving those 'further descriptions' which Wittgenstein said was the essence of aesthetic argument. I shall return to this point later. That is, the argument does not rest on the discovery or prediction of matters of fact, but in our seeing the object 'in a new light' through seeing its relations to other objects. In this sense Freud shows us the reasons of certain human 'norms'. He does not judge certain neurotic states to be undesirable with reference to a human ideal which has been arrived at 'scientifically'; rather he shows what neurosis is in detail and so gives us the possibility of much greater insight into our values than we had before.[1] It is true that Freud hoped that both the theory and practice of analysis would eventually be given a biological validation, and that this was part of the confusion of cause and reason which Wittgenstein points out, but his work is in no more need of such underpinning than is, say, our language of mental activity in need of a satisfactory theory of the brain.

In the first chapter I suggested[2] that 'How do I obey a rule?' is the most general form of a number of the problems treated in the *Philosophical Investigations*. Wittgenstein shows that this is not a matter of causes but of 'the justification of my following the rule in the way I do'. The justification of attitudes came under the same analysis – there was a parallel between trying to see people as automata, trying to regard stones as sentient beings and trying to see *Lear* as a comedy. We cannot just choose to do any of these things – we have to invent a context which would make it possible. To describe a crown as "a parody of a respectable hat" (to use Wittgenstein's example) would be a move to induce a different attitude to it, to persuade people to see it differently. Now some changes in our value scheme would require such an elaborate rearrangement of our way of seeing the world as to be virtually impossible. We may not agree with Aristotle (and Mrs Foot) that we can deduce ethics from a functional definition of man:

> Is it likely that joiners and shoe-makers have certain functions or specialized activities, while man as such has none but has been left by Nature a functionless being? Seeing that eye and hand and foot and every one of our members has some obvious function, must we not believe that in like manner a human being has a function over and above these particular functions?[3]

Our concept of man is not that precise;[4] but could I hold forth as my

---

[1] I do not wish to suggest that Freud was mainly a moralist. Clearly his thought can only be understood with reference to his theory of mind. As MacIntyre says – *The Unconscious*, p. 13 – Freud never offered a non-theoretical account of psycho-analysis. [2] See p. 7.

[3] Aristotle, *Nicomachean Ethics*, Book I (Penguin translation).

[4] Nor, indeed, are our concepts of eye, hand or foot. Mrs Foot's mistake lies not just in suggesting a definition of *man*, but of looking for definitions in general.

human ideal one who was lame, blind, deaf, dumb, and mentally defi-
cient? For us to be able to 'admire' such a man just for those characteristics we would surely in some sense have to have changed our
concept of what a man is. It is certainly true – as Mrs Foot says – that
we cannot choose what will count as a benefit or harm to human
beings. If she is also arguing that it would be logically impossible to
count certain things as beneficial in the sense that we would have to
alter our concept of man in order to do so, then it seems to me that she
is right in this also. But this should not be exaggerated; many revolutionary changes in ethics involve a change in our picture of what man
is – as do similar changes in art and literature. Mrs Foot stresses the
logical connection between such changes and changes in values which
Hare's preoccupation with choice obscures. Unfortunately she makes
ethical change virtually impossible – whereas Hare makes it arbitrary.
We can recall here a remark of Wittgenstein's which I have already
quoted and which bears on the ultimate justification of a 'conceptual
scheme': "Compare a concept with a style of painting. For is even our
style of painting arbitrary? Can we choose one at pleasure? (The
Egyptian for instance.) Is it a mere question of pleasing and ugly?"[1]
This steers a course between the Scylla of Mrs Foot's Naturalism and
the Charybdis of Hare's Prescriptivism. We can be rationally per-
suaded to alter our way of looking at the world not only by the discovery of new facts but by what Wisdom calls 'rhetoric'. Wisdom gives
a vivid example of what he means by rhetoric in *Gods*[2] where he
describes how disputes about the existence of God can cease to be
experimental and become arguments about the appropriate attitudes
in respect of the 'same' facts. He argues that 'interjections' – such as
'beautiful', 'divine' and so on – have a logic, and arguments about
them are genuine arguments. In order to alter what a person sees – and,
hence, what he feels – when he is looking at a picture, we may put
another picture beside the first one. In this way we enable him to see
something in the first picture which – although he saw everything
there was to be seen – he had not noticed before. Hume is right in
saying that there are 'no new facts to be ascertained' – in the sense
that there is no part of the canvas which is hidden; but it does not
follow (*a*) that the new element is an 'attitude' which we arbitrarily
or subjectively contribute to the painting (the sort of attitude it is being
guaranteed by some aesthetic equivalent of 'benevolence'), or (*b*) a

[1] See p. 17.   [2] Wisdom, op. cit., pp. 154-5.

non-natural quality which we intuit in it (Moore). Nor does it follow –
as Mrs Foot seems to hold – that (*c*) there is nothing 'extra', and that
to describe *is* to value. What we see new in the 'dawning of an aspect'
is not a new fact, but nor is it deducible from the facts already before us.

4. CONCLUSION

If the sketch I have given of certain sorts of value theory is correct
then it should have bearing on the work of the various critics and
aestheticians whose work I am about to examine. Indeed a major purpose of this book is to show that chronic aesthetic disputes are a
sub-class of more general philosophical questions. We shall find that
of the two critics discussed primarily for the account they give (or the
method they exemplify) of how judgements of value are established –
Yvor Winters and F. R. Leavis – the second is nearer to Mrs Foot,
and the former (although he manages to be naturalistic as well) to
Hare. The discussion in the first chapter is more germane to those
critics and aestheticians – notably T. S. Eliot, Langer, Osborne and
Murry – whom I consider chiefly for what they have to say about the
place of emotion in our response to works of art or literature, but there
are consequences for evaluation here, too.

We shall see that the naturalist is right in holding that pleasure,
usefulness, 'organic configurational unity', 'significant form', intelligence, intensity and so on are all part of our reasons for valuing
highly works of art. He is wrong in thinking that he can construct
from all these activities incontrovertible standards of value. The idea
that criticism is irrational if it does not, in the last resort, appeal to
a priori standards is one of the most frequent confusions into which
critics and aestheticians fall.

NOTES TO CHAPTER II

A] There are two relevant examples of analysis of aesthetic arguments on the same line as Hare's. One, by René Wellek, is discussed
in Chapter VIII. The other is by Pepita Haezrahi. Like Hare, Haezrahi
sees evaluative argument as proceeding to the more and more general
and hence *having* to come to some sort of stop.

Thus, let us assume that our argument runs: "a is a good X, the Lac
d'Annecy is a good Cézanne." Why? Because "Cézanne is a good painter

and the Lac d'Annecy is a good painting." Why? – because "painting is good." Why? Leaving aside therapeutic, pedagogic, moral and religious answers which would take us outside the field of aesthetics in an obvious way, we should have to answer "because painting is an art, and art is good." Why? Because, "it is beautiful." Here having reached an ultima thule the argument has to stop. The basic proposition "Beauty is good because it is beautiful," tautologous as it is, is the underlying basic assumption which from a psychological point of view is most necessary to all aesthetic enquiries. If we did not care about beauty there would be no theory of beauty and no aesthetics.

'Propositions in Aesthetics', *Proc. Arist. Soc.*, 1956–7, p. 186.

If we always argue to the general we are clearly always likely to hit upon a tautology or a vacuity when we wish to reach an 'ultima thule'. In this case 'caring about beauty' is the evaluative premise to which we finally appeal. But there is no need for such a 'basic assumption' to guarantee the finality of the argument. How do we know whether we do, or should, care about beauty unless we know whether we do, or should, care about Cézanne? 'Beauty is good because it is beautiful', if it has sense at all (can Beauty be beautiful?), is hardly a tautology. But "If we did not care about beauty there would be no theory of beauty and no aesthetic" comes close to being one.

Haezrahi is, of course, trying to show that aesthetic judgements are absolute within a particular framework (p. 180) and rely on criteria internal to their particular 'kinds' (pp. 189–90). If one wishes to make values objective (in a certain sense) and deducible, from general principles, this is a good move to make. Other people's value schemes derive from different tautologies (or 'decisions') so that one's own can be objective but not dogmatic.

B]   See Paul Edwards, *The Logic of Moral Discourse*, p. 120, on 'nice-making' characteristics:

    I. The niceness belongs to, is 'located' in, the steak, not in me or my feelings.

    II. the niceness of the steak is *not* identical with any one or any one set of nice-making characteristics.

    III. although niceness is objective there is no feature or set of features to which one can point and say "This is niceness".

    IV. nevertheless niceness is not something distinct from or over and above these features – it *disjunctively* refers to an indefinite set of them.

In the same way Edwards argues that the features to which moral judgements refer are not 'non-natural'. From this he goes on to suggest – as I have argued in these two chapters – that there is often a close analogy between the methods of settling scientific and moral disputes. However, he later weakens the force of this by asserting that 'fundamental moral judgements' – those, that is, for which no further reason can be given – have no descriptive content, but only an emotive one. One example he gives is, "Regardless of consequences, it's just *wrong*". (Op. cit., p. 183.)

c] See John Hospers: *Explanation*, in *Essays in Conceptual Analysis*, ed. Flew.

> Question 1. Why did the water pipes break?
> Explanation: They always do when the temperature falls to below 32 degrees.
> Question 2. Why do they break when the temperature falls . . . etc.?
> Explanation: Because water expands when it freezes.
> Question 3. Why does water expand when it freezes?
> Explanation: Here we try to answer in terms of the structure of the water molecule.
> But to say that we have not explained (1) until we have explained (3) is grossly to underestimate the number of phenomena for which we do have perfectly satisfactory explanations. Thus we *do* have explanations for (1) and (2), and our having them is *not* contingent upon having an explanation for (3) (op. cit., pp. 102–3).

Each answer is a *complete* answer to the particular question. As for 'ultimate questions' – "Why does anything do anything?" – these are hardly genuine questions.

> . . . to explain is to explain *in terms of something*, and *ex hypothesi* there is no longer something for it to be explained in terms of, then the request for an explanation is self-contradictory: it demands on the one hand that you explain X in terms of a Y while insisting simultaneously that there is no Y (p. 117).

The application to aesthetic arguments is plain.

d] David Pole suggests (*Conditions of Rational Enquiry*, p. 57) that 'decision' is a psychological, not a logical fact – although Hare seeks to make it a logical one. Logically such a 'decision' adds up to saying "There is no reason".

Pole also points out that – as my own argument suggests – Hare's concept of 'decision' is a *pis aller* in what is, in all essentials, a positivistic system:

> ... the initial problem is plain; it is simply to find room for ethics between the fork of the analytic/synthetic dichotomy: and the solution comes with the doctrine of imperatives. The main positivist edifice is left to stand; the project is rather to find a way of accommodating morals without seriously disturbing it.   Op. cit., p. 43.

CHAPTER III

Art and Feeling 1 – Some Aestheticians

1. INTRODUCTION

English criticism since Wordsworth has been involved in a dilemma. It has taken the poem as, in some sense, the vehicle of the poet's feeling. The poem has value in that it expresses a valuable feeling – but the excellence of the poem is the only guarantee of the value of the original feeling. Because English critical theory has been bound up with a (philosophical) terminology which assumes only a contingent connection between inner states and their outward expression it has not been able to solve the problem of the dichotomy between 'objective' and 'subjective'. It has often seemed that a choice has to be made between, on the one hand, accepting that our response to literature (or at any rate imaginative literature) is subjective, and, on the other, looking for a 'scientific' account which will give a psychological or even neurological description of what happens when a person reads a poem. The most resolute attempt to put criticism on a scientific basis was made by I. A. Richards. A possible – if selective – view of the history of critical theory from the nineteenth to the mid-twentieth century is to see it as a series of attempts to solve the objective–subjective dichotomy – and a series of failures to do so resulting from an inadequate and even mistaken philosophy of the emotions.

There are two twentieth-century aestheticians – Susanne Langer and Harold Osborne – who bring this conflict to the surface in an unusually clear way. Their attempts at a solution result in theories which, superficially at least, are as mutually contradictory as could be, but which, at a deeper level, have their most important premises in common. The assumptions which they share are, as we shall see, those very ones which my argument in the first two chapters has sought to undermine. The third aesthetician I discuss – Clive Bell – occupies a sort of half-way position between the other two in that he attempts to give an 'objectivist' account of art but is unable to avoid the orthodox language of Romantic expressionism.

2. SUSANNE LANGER

By 'feelings' I refer to the sorts of things which people often describe as thrills, twinges, pangs, throbs, wrenches, itches, prickings, chills, glows, loads, qualms, hankerings, curdlings, sinkings, tensions, gnawings, and shocks.

> Gilbert Ryle, *Concept of Mind*, pp. 83–4.

Art is the creation of forms symbolic of human feeling.

> Susanne Langer, *Feeling and Form*, p. 40.

It is impossible in a small compass to do justice to the sweep and brilliance of Mrs Langer's writings on the philosophy of art.[1] For our purposes, however, it will be sufficient to concentrate upon her attempt to show (*a*) that art has *meaning*, and (*b*) that its 'meaning' is a matter of its relation to human feeling. Mrs Langer illustrates well some of the moves described in Chapter I, and at the same time provides a transition to the discussion, in later chapters, of particular critics.

Mrs Langer's 'New Key' is a theory of symbolism which is based upon the *Tractatus Logico-Philosophicus* of Wittgenstein.[2] She insists upon a fundamental dichotomy between 'sign' (or 'symptom') and 'symbol'; this distinction is intended both to refute irrationalist or emotivist theories of art, and at the same time to explain how art is both rational *and* of an essentially emotional nature – and hence significant for human beings.

It is worth starting with some more quotations from the *Tractatus*.

2.2   A picture has a logico-pictorial form in common with what it depicts.

2.154   The pictorial relationship consists of the correlations of the picture's elements with things.

2.17   What a picture must have in common with reality, in order to be able to depict it – correctly or incorrectly – in the way it does, is its pictorial form.

4.014   A gramophone record, the musical idea, the written notes, and the sound-waves, all stand to one another in the same internal relation of depicting that holds between language and the world.

---

[1] This account is based upon *Philosophy in a New Key, Feeling and Form, Problems of Art*, and *Philosophical Sketches*.

[2] There is also a derivation, via Cassirer, from Kant. Langer quotes *Tractatus* 4.0311, 4.015 and 4.0141 (*Phil. N.K.*, p. 79).

According to this view of language sentences have meaning in so far as they stand in a relation of logical analogy to things in the world. If the world is to be described it must be described in language, and this is only possible if there is a conformity between the structure of the world and the language wherein we symbolize the world. That which is not expressible in language is not 'possible'. That is to say, whatever we think of, we think within the context of a language, of a 'grammar'; we cannot *dissociate* the objects of thought from their 'grammar'. Thought is not necessarily a mental matter; it is essentially a *symbolization*. The correlation of our symbols with what they symbolize is the essence of thought – and thus the dualism between thought and the world is obliterated. Things 'in themselves' prior to their 'grammar' are ineffable; they have no status before they are made into facts by taking their place within a system of language.[1] Logic, therefore, precedes experience. "The grammar of a symbol determines the range of its applicability: . . . the possible logically precedes the actual."[2] The possible is that which exists within the logical space of our language. That which can be expressed must be capable of existing – although it need not exist. Although we can deny that our logical space contains any facts, we cannot conceive of a fact's existing outside of a logical space.

For a proposition to depict a state of affairs it must have something in common with the state of affairs. What it has in common is "the logical form of representation".[3]

Mrs Langer reproduces this theory of language in *Philosophy in a New Key*. "A proposition is a (symbolic) picture of a structure – the structure of a state of affairs."[4]

> . . . denotative symbols . . . symbolise the very different but *analogous* configurations of denoted things. A temporal order of words stands for a relational order of things. . . . A sentence is a symbol for a state of affairs, and pictures its character.[5]

It is not difficult to see to what theory of art this view is likely to lead. If meaning is a matter of a symbol's depicting something, works of art, if they are to have meaning, must be symbols, must depict states of affairs. A straightforwardly mimetic theory, according to

[1] This account is indebted to Alexander Maslow's *A Study in Wittgenstein's Tractatus.*
[2] Op. cit., p. 25.
[3] *Tractatus,* 2.2.
[4] *Phil. N.K.,* p. 68.
[5] Op. cit., p. 73.

which works of art imitate actual or possible objects in the world, presents difficulties, the most obvious being that a great deal of art – and especially music – is not in any normal sense imitative. But an even more fundamental difficulty is that the mimetic theory does not explain artistic meaning or significance. Art object A may resemble natural object B, but it does not follow that B is the 'meaning' of A. After all, natural object B may resemble natural object C, but we do not say that C is the 'meaning' of B. Here we might adapt a remark of Wittgenstein's: no resemblance could have the consequences of meaning. And the argument is not changed – although it may easily seem that it is – where C is not a natural object but a feeling or emotion, or is in some such way importantly related to human beings.

We can look upon the various forms of expressionism[1] as attempts to meet these two difficulties. If works of art can be shown to reflect some central or essential human reaction to the world, we would seem to have gone a long way in explaining how they can have meaning and why they are valuable. Mrs Langer embraces a sophisticated form of expressionism. Works of art are not 'expressive' in the way that a cry of pain expresses one of Ryle's thrills, twinges or pangs. Such manifestations are 'signals' or 'signs' rather than symbols. On the other hand, Oedipus's or Gloucester's cries of pain on the stage are true symbols; they "serve . . . to let us develop a characteristic attitude towards objects *in absentia* . . . to refer *to* them, think *of* them, talk *about* them".[2] The symbolic transformation of experience is the essence of rationality, for through it a form can be "at once an experienced, individual thing and a symbol for the concept of it, for *this sort of thing*".[3]

Works of art do not *name* elements in one's inner life of feeling. That is, they are not denotative. Art, therefore, is not a true language. Wittgenstein says in the *Tractatus*:[4] "There is also the inexpressible. It makes itself manifest. It is the mystical." For Mrs Langer Art *is* the expression of the 'inexpressible'. Art has *connotation*; it expresses those areas of human experience – "the inner life of feeling" – which lack a conventionally assigned verbal notation. Works of art express feelings

---

[1] This is, of course, to talk very schematically. I do not take 'mimetic' and 'expressionist' to be exhaustive, nor homogeneous categories. Abrams deals well with the varieties of literary theory in *The Mirror and the Lamp*.

[2] *Phil. N.K.*, p. 31.

[3] Op. cit., p. 89.   [4] *Tractatus*, 6.552.

by reproducing their form; works of art stand in a relation of logical analogy to feelings. For instance, of music Mrs Langer says:

> The upshot of all these speculations and researches is, that there are certain aspects of the so-called 'inner life' – physical or mental – which have formal properties similar to those of music. . . . So the first requirement for a connotative relationship between music and subjective experience, a certain similarity of logical form, is certainly satisfied.[1]

Again:

> . . . the import of artistic expression is broadly the same in all arts as it is in music – the verbally ineffable, yet not inexpressible law of vital experience, the pattern of affective and sentient being.[2]

Art 'reveals' the forms of feeling in the same way that, according to the *Tractatus*, logic 'shows' the form of discourse, which discourse itself cannot state. Carnap had 'translated' Wittgenstein's "There is also the inexpressible" as "There are also sentences which are not sentences", but for Mrs Langer the 'mystical', although not capable of being expressed in sentences, can be 'articulated' in works of art. She gives several reasons why great areas of human experience are not expressible verbally; visual forms, for instance, "do not present their constituents successively but simultaneously, so the relations determining a visual structure are grasped in one act of vision". Visual forms are, therefore, "too subtle for speech. A language-bound theory of mind . . . rules [them] out of the domain of understanding and the sphere of knowledge."[3] The forms of feeling "defy linguistic projection".

We can appreciate some of the motives behind Mrs Langer's theory by examining her attacks on 'positivistic' analyses of art. For instance, Carnap, seeking (not uncharacteristically) to distinguish literal, factual propositions from others, writes:[4]

> Many linguistic utterances are analogous to laughing in that they have only an expressive function, no representative function. Examples of this are cries like "Oh, oh" or, on a higher level, lyrical verses.

Mrs Langer attacks this view with some panache:

> At best [on the positivist analysis] human thought is but a tiny, grammar-bound island in the midst of a sea of feeling expressed by "Oh, oh," and

[1] *Phil. N.K.*, p. 228.   [2] Op. cit., p. 257.
[3] *Phil. N.K.*, p. 93.   [4] *Philosophy and Logical Syntax*, p. 28.

sheer babble. The island has a periphery, perhaps of mud – factual and hypothetical concepts broken down by the emotional tides into the 'material mode', a mixture of meaning and nonsense.[1]

The main part of Mrs Langer's reply to Carnap is the distinction between Sign and Symbol. Art does not merely exhibit or evince feelings, it gives insight into them. Music, for instance,

> ... is not stimulation of feeling but expression of it; ... not the symptomatic expression of feelings that beset the composer but a symbolic expression of the forms of sentience as he understands them. It bespeaks ... what he *knows about* the so-called 'inner life'. ...[2]

The threshold over which symptoms have to cross in order to become symbols is very low. Displacement activities are, for example, symbolic.

> The great contribution of Freud to the philosophy of mind has been the realisation that human behaviour is not only a food-getting strategy, but is also a language; that every *move* is at the same time a gesture.[3]
> ... ritual and compulsive acts are ... expressive behaviour ... symbolic presentations rather than practical measures ... spontaneous transformations of experience.[4]

The mere 'repeatability' of experiences involves the power of abstraction – which is the power of symbolization. If we recognize an experience as one we have suffered before, this means that we have abstracted its essential 'form'.

This theory of symbolism is of vast scope, and here we can but give a brief sketch of its main outlines. Art, Religion, Ritual, Myth – all have meaning, are important, and, in some sense, true. We cannot ascribe literal, representational truth to art and myth, but to see them as mere emotional symptoms does not do justice to the sort of meaning we feel them to have. Instead we can look upon them as the very categories through which we apprehend our experience. And this is not confined to Art, Ritual and Myth; *all* our experience of the world comes to us 'interpreted', under the light of the categories of the human mind – or, as Mrs Langer would say – of the human 'Spirit'. Intuitions, in the Kantian terminology, logically involve concepts; or, in the language of the *Tractatus*, only that which has a place in our discourse can be said to be either possible or impossible.

[1] *Phil. N.K.*, p. 87.   [2] *Feeling and Form*, p. 28.
[3] *Phil. N.K.*, p. 51.   [4] Op. cit., pp. 50–1.

There is an immediate and obvious objection to Mrs Langer's theory. How do we *know* that works of art stand in a relation of logical analogy to forms of feeling? Have we any way of becoming acquainted with these 'forms' apart from their artistic (or religious or mythical) expression, so that we can compare them with the works in which they are said to be instantiated, and so decide whether they have been satisfactorily realized? Clearly we cannot; the essence of these forms is that they are ineffable. They cannot be described since for anything to *be* a description it must have a form in common with what it describes. To attempt to describe a form would be a category mistake.

As sheer 'events' in themselves, before they have been formulated as 'facts' in our grammar, have no status, or as the 'manifold' has no status before it has been brought under our categories, so the feelings are, as it were, *noumena*, sheer things-in-themselves, before they have been instantiated in works of art. And, like *noumena*, their function is explanatory; *only if* art expresses human feeling can it be said to be valuable and to have meaning. But for it to have such meaning *is* its value – good art is to be defined as art which is fully and successfully expressive.[1] Only if art expresses the essential patterns of human sentience is it significant.

There is clearly no way of inferring the forms from the artefacts which express them, and vice versa. Mrs Langer, however, denies that our acquaintance with them is a matter of inference.[2] We do not *infer* them but *perceive them through* the artistic symbols. The forms are *constitutive* of our experience and are therefore not empirical but transcendental. Works of art unite the subjective life with the objective world; thus man knows himself *in* the world. The emotional implications of such a philosophy have been well expressed by Cassirer:

> In this sense each new "symbolic form" – not only the conceptual world of scientific cognition but also the intuitive world of art, myth and language – constitutes, as Goethe said, a revelation sent outward from within, a "synthesis of world and spirit", which truly assures us that the two are originally one.[3]

All this is a far cry from Ryle's thrills, twinges, pangs, throbs, curdlings and sinkings. Mrs Langer has enormously extended the "inner life of feeling", and the metaphysical justification of it that she

---

[1] See Note A, p. 84.   [2] *Problems of Art*, p. 25.
[3] Ernst Cassirer, *The Philosophy of Symbolic Forms*, Vol. I, p. 111.

provides is very dubious. But, in any event, is it really necessary? Is this the only way to give significance to art? That Mrs Langer's theory is not really explanatory is shown in the archetypically metaphysical answer she gives to the crucial question, "How is the import of a work known?" Her answer[1] is, "... by the basic intellectual act of *intuition*".[2]

Mrs Langer has offered what we can call a 'profound' account of art. By this I mean that she is not satisfied with the more or less detailed descriptions we can give of the effect on us of works of art, and wishes to provide an 'explanation' at a deeper level. It is useful to divide 'profound' accounts of human behaviour into two main sorts. On the one hand there is that element in Freud's thought which consists in describing the facts in such a way that we become compelled to put an interpretation on them quite at odds with the conventional interpretation. A man's affectionate behaviour is 'really' the expression of intense envy, and so on. In this sense the reality can be quite unlike the appearance. But such extreme cases are not discontinuous with cases where we look again at a picture and see what we had missed before.

Another sort of 'profound' account is offered by Hobbes. Hobbes's attempt to show that human motives are not what they may appear to be is partly based on empirical evidence –

> Let [an objector to Hobbes's system] therefore consider with himself, when taking a journey, he arms himself, and seeks to go well-accompanied; when going to sleep he locks his doors; when even in his house he locks his chests ... Does he not there as much accuse mankind by his actions, as I do by my words?[3]

– partly on a determined revision of concepts – "*Grief,* for the calamity of another, is PITY; and ariseth from the imagination that the like calamity may befall himself; and therefore is called also COMPASSION"[4] – but primarily upon a causal account of human behaviour. The reasons we usually give for actions are fictitious – the real explanation is to be found in the two causal principles of pride and fear, which themselves are to be explained in terms of desire/aversion, which in its turn is to be reduced to the motion of particles. Egocentricity is built into this model and any account of our motives which tries to pretend otherwise is false.[5] The aim is an entirely

[1] See Note B, p. 84.   [2] *Feeling and Form*, p. 375.
[3] Hobbes, *Leviathan*, Part I, ch. 13.   [4] Op. cit., Part I, ch. 6.
[5] See Richard Peters, *Hobbes*, pp. 176–7.

deductive system. Ethics is to be deduced from psychology, psychology from physiology, and physiology from physics.

Now in offering a profounder account of human behaviour than – as he thinks – our usual descriptions can give, Hobbes is producing something radically discontinuous with such descriptions. In this he is doing something quite different from Freud (at least from the somewhat bowdlerized Freud I have presented). We can challenge a Freudian interpretation on the grounds that it is an inadequate description of the situation; and this, in principle, is the way in which we can challenge a critical judgement. But this is not how we can challenge any of Hobbes's ethical assessments, since they are supposed to be true in virtue of the fact that they are valid deductions from the ultimate causal premises.

The question is, whether Mrs Langer's account is like a *critical* description of a work of art, and, if not, whether this vitiates her theory. It is clear that she believes that if a work of art can be shown to be connected in the way she describes with human feeling then its meaning and value have been established. This is, of course, influenced by the *Tractatus* view of meaning: the 'meaning' of a work of art must be some entity which it names – or, on Mrs Langer's theory, to which it stands in a relation of logical analogy. It would be well to recall the remarks in the *Brown Book* which I quoted in Chapter I, where Wittgenstein suggests that, having described the 'surface' features of a tune – its rhythm, phrasing, intervals – we have said what it 'means'. Similarly, asked why a particular piece of music is good, I describe it, compare it with other pieces by the same composer, with pieces by other composers and so on. All this would be giving reasons why it was good. I am not required, at some point, to clinch the matter by adding triumphantly: "And also it articulates a form of human feeling, and, since good art is all fully expressive art, it is good." On Mrs Langer's theory we know by intuition that an artefact expresses feeling, and hence *deductively* that it is a good work of art.

This idea that works of art are *symbols* having something in common with what they symbolize is used to *explain* rather than to describe our aesthetic response[1] and is pursued by Mrs Langer to

---

[1] A distinction employed by MacIntyre (op. cit.), which, in its application to Freud, comes from Wittgenstein's lectures as recorded by Moore. (See Chapter I, pp. 19-21.) The distinction should not be made sharper than it is: an *aesthetic* explanation is in the form of a *description*.

extravagant lengths. Architecture, for instance, ". . . creates the sem-
blance of that world which is the counterpart of the Self. It is a total
environment made visible."[1] Similarly, sculpture is ". . . an illusion
of kinetic volume, symbolizing the self or centre of life".[2] This is
rather far-fetched and is the inevitable result of deciding that art has
meaning and then looking for the meaning it has. The meaning is
thought of as an entity – in this case, a form of feeling.

Even if it could be shown that works of art have the relation to
forms of feeling that Mrs Langer thinks they have, it would not follow
that they had been given meaning. To continue the comparison with
the *Tractatus*, artefacts in her theory have the form 'This is how things
stand' – the 'general form of propositions'. That is to say, they are
'not a move in any language-game'. Neither a proposition nor a piece
of music can have meaning simply by possessing a form analogous to
that of a state of affairs. Meaning depends on a convention – the imperative aspect of "Shut the door!" does not depend on inner imperative feeling, but upon the convention in which orders are given,
obeyed and so on.[3] Mrs Langer's attempt to establish a natural, non-
conventional form of meaning rests on the assumption that meaning
is an extra entity. The objections to such a theory have already been
discussed in Chapter I and there is no need to go over the same ground
here. Perhaps the position could be characterized in a slightly different way. Mrs Langer has made the meaning of works of art hypothetical – we find that they are connected with an inner state, and this
gives them meaning. We can compare this with the discussion in
Chapter I of how I see a certain mathematical notation *as* a 'formula'.[4]
The notation does not 'correspond' to an inner state of 'knowing the
formula'; nor is my recognition of it as a formula a prediction that I
will be able to apply it. Rather it is that, in virtue of my mastery of a
mathematical technique, I can see how it fits within a mathematical
system, can see it *as* the formula. The notation *as the formula* (rather
than as, say, a random series of signs) is the *intensional* object of my
understanding – just as, when I see the 'duck' aspect of the duck/rab-
bit drawing, the duck is the intensional object of my seeing.[5] Now it

---

[1] *Feeling and Form*, p. 98.   [2] Op. cit., p. 101. See also Note C, p. 84.
[3] See p. 5.   [4] See pp. 6–7.
[5] This derives from G. E. M. Anscombe's article 'The Intentionality of
Sensations', *Analytical Philosophy*, 2nd Series, ed. Butler. I retain the more
common spelling – 'intensionality' – except when quoting Miss Anscombe.

is not a hypothetical matter that *Oedipus Tyrannus* is horrifying – the horror is not a feeling we simply contribute; it is not shown to be horrifying just because it usually goes with feelings of horror in the audience. Even if the connection between object and emotion is made as close as Mrs Langer tries to make it, we still do not have a logical connection. We justify our response to *Oedipus* by pointing to its 'surface' features, comparing it with other works and so on. This, we might say, shows how we 'locate' horror in the play. The justification is in the form of a description of the play. For a play to be horrifying or sad a description of it which brings out horrifying or sad features would have to be plausible. No appeal to forms of feeling will make any difference when such a description is implausible; nor would any appeal to causes make Hobbes's description of human motives more compelling than it is in its own right.

Mrs Langer's tendency to give hypothetical rather than critical accounts of art is noticeable throughout her work. The aesthetician is more like a scientist than like a critic; he discovers 'laws' which 'explain' why art is important to human beings. For instance she gives a biological explanation of comedy. Comedy is basically *happy* because it embodies "the rhythm of sheer vitality".[1] There is a similar explanation of laughter: "Laughter, or the tendency to laugh . . . seems to arise from a surge of vital feeling . . ." This is reminiscent of Hobbes's account of laughter as "sudden glory". Do we feel that anything has been explained? When Freud explains the funniness of jokes he does not produce causal or metaphysical hypotheses – he gives *reasons*. In the same way the critic gives reasons why *Lear* is sad. Compare "I raised my arm because chemical processes x, y and z took place in my brain". This would not be a correct description of why I raised my arm, but it might be a correct description of *why my arm rose*. An account in terms of reasons cannot be reduced to one in terms of causes.[2]

The same objections apply to the idea that in relating works of art to forms of feeling we have established their value. It would never be impossible to say "I realize that this work embodies a form of feeling, but I think it is bad". That works which embody form of feeling x are good is a *critical* matter and cannot follow merely from the fact that they do embody it. Mrs Langer's way of dealing with this is simple: it is the *essence* of a work of art that it embodies a form of

[1] *Feeling and Form*, pp. 331–2.   [2] See A. I. Melden, *Free Action*, loc. cit.

feeling. If it fails to do so it is not a bad work of art – it is not a work of art at all.

Behind Mrs Langer's urge to make it the aesthetician's task to give metaphysical or quasi-scientific explanations of art is the belief that only in this way can we establish an objective, rational relationship between art and human beings. Now someone who shares this belief may very well take a different way out of the dilemma. He may wish to give an 'objective' account which gives up the idea of a pre-established harmony between art and human beings, and concentrate instead on the intrinsic features of works of art in themselves. The two aestheticians whom I shall now examine both attempt to give a 'non-relational' account.

3. CLIVE BELL AND HAROLD OSBORNE

To the question – 'Why are we so profoundly moved by certain combinations of forms?' I am unwilling to return a positive answer. I am not obliged to, for it is not an aesthetic question.

Clive Bell, *Art*, p. 59.

Clive Bell is an extraordinarily muddled aesthetician; this has been pointed out often enough. The theory of "Art as Significant Form" has been dismissed as irrefutable, demoted as a suggested 'linguistic revision', and explained away as an attempt to reform the Victorian and Edwardian taste for pictures that tell a story. More can, perhaps, be salvaged from his theory than that.

Critics of Bell have been too eager to point out that there are many art-forms to which his theory does not apply. *Macbeth*, for instance, is not valuable purely on account of its 'formal' properties. It is true that Bell carries his theory to extremes, and commits some astonishing confusions on the way. We may, however, take a more sympathetic view in the light of the following passage: "How inferior is my normal state of mind at a concert. Tired or perplexed, I let slip my sense of form, my aesthetic emotion collapses, and I begin weaving into the harmonies that I cannot grasp the ideas of life."[1] What Bell is asserting is that formal qualities are meaningful in themselves. His attempt to explain all art 'non-relationally' is, as it were, the obverse of Mrs Langer's attempt to explain it 'relationally'. He does, of course, constantly talk of the 'aesthetic emotion'. This is both the

---

[1] *Art*, p. 31.

characteristic feature of our response to works of art, and the means by which we recognize them as works of art.[1] The 'aesthetic emotion' is variously defined. At one point[2] it is the 'thrill' of apprehending pure forms; at other times it seems to be a sharing in the emotion of the artist.[3] Yet again, significant form is a means of glimpsing 'ultimate reality'[4] and the aesthetic emotion is one felt "for reality revealing itself through pure form". Yet – as quoted at the beginning of this section – Bell denies that he knows why 'certain combinations of forms' move us. This is an ungenerous denial, for a few pages earlier[5] he has offered an inclusive – although, unfortunately, entirely circular – account:

> . . . the reason why some forms move us aesthetically, and others do not, is that some have been so purified that we can feel them aesthetically and that others are so clogged with unaesthetic matter . . . that only the sensibility of an artist can perceive their purely formal significance.

The confusion increases when we remember that at the beginning of the book Bell seeks to found aesthetics upon the experienced emotion: "The starting point for all systems of aesthetics must be the personal experience of a peculiar emotion."[6] Yet this emotion – if we may take his most common formulation and ignore the fact that he contradicts it *passim* – is in respect of the apprehension of significant form. The critic can, however, point out significant form descriptively: "To be continually pointing out those parts, the sum, or rather the combination, of which unite to produce significant form, is the function of criticism."[7] But criticism is entirely subjective "since my only data is the individual experience of a particular emotion".[8] Only the emotion tells one that one is in the presence of a work of art, and the characteristic of a work of art is significant form; therefore only the emotion tells one that one is in the presence of significant form. Yet the emotion is *in respect of* significant form – i.e. significant form is the cause of, or the reason for, the emotion.

Bell has involved himself in these muddles because he is unable to think the concept of significant form through. It clearly started off as an attempt to show that the significance of a work of art is not to be deduced from its relation to 'centrally human' interests, but is a matter of the work itself. He even goes so far, at one point, to compare the

[1] Op. cit., p. 7.   [2] Op. cit., p. 53.   [3] Op. cit., p. 49.
[4] Op. cit., p. 54.   [5] Op. cit., p. 55.   [6] Op. cit., p. 6.
[7] Op. cit., p. 9.   [8] Op. cit., p. 8.

relation of the work of art to the artist with that of the pure mathematician to a piece of mathematics.[1] Now nobody wishes to posit pure
mathematical, philosophical or judicial emotions to explain the interest
a mathematician takes in his work, or a philosopher in the arguments
he produces, or a judge in the opinion he writes. Similarly, there are
no special 'furniture emotions' which account for my caring about
the chairs and tables in my room. The interest I take in their arrangement is, to some extent, 'aesthetic'. But what of my refusal to hang the
tables and chairs from the ceiling? What of my mere sense of the objects
as being in the room?[2] Bell says that the question, "Why are we so profoundly moved by certain combinations of forms?" is not an aesthetic
one. This is quite true.[3] Similarly, the question, "Why are lawyers
interested in the Law" is not a legal question. "Why do human beings
have interests?" is perhaps not an intelligible question at all. At any
rate, unless we are prepared to consider in detail why we are interested
in this particular matter, this particular art-form, this particular writer,
this particular poem, this particular image – we cannot even make the
first gestures towards answering it. General answers of the sort given
by Mrs Langer and Clive Bell are nearly always vacuous. "Human
beings respond to works of art because works of art embody the
fundamental forms of human feeling. The forms of human feeling are
those features of a work of art in virtue of which we respond to it.
Ergo, we respond to works of art because we do." But why do we
respond to, what is the significance of, *this* work of art, *this* form of
art? Why we value 'certain combinations of forms' is probably not an
aesthetic question – at least it is hard to see how it could be – but
"Why is *this* picture of Giotto good?" *is*. We do not have to know
why we respond to forms in order to know why we respond to *this*
one. It is not a hypothetical matter at all. People were not lamentably
ignorant of why they raised their arms until the physiologists and
chemists discovered the exact mechanism. But Eliot's Hamlet *may* not
have known why he was *so* disgusted; a psycho-analyst *might* have
helped him to discover why. Similarly, Eliot may have helped Edwardian critics to see why Pope and Dryden were, after all, great poets.
Not least, Clive Bell may have helped people to see why Cézanne is a
great painter.

Despite all these muddles, Bell is right in seeing that the significance

[1] Op. cit., p. 25.　　　　　　　[2] See Wittgenstein, *Investigations*, 602, 603.
[3] See Note D, p. 87.

of works of art cannot simply be something the audience contributes. The 'response' of the audience to the work must in some sense be defined by the description to be given of the work. It does not follow that works of art cannot be of emotional significance. Mrs Langer thinks that the emotional significance of art must be a matter of its relation to fundamental forms of feeling. A theory taking Clive Bell as its point of departure would try to show that the formal and emotional qualities of art are related even more closely than Mrs Langer thinks.

Such an attempt has, in fact, been made by Harold Osborne. The basis of Osborne's aesthetic is the search for definition. He insists that either one begins with a definition of what the object of aesthetic enquiry is, or one is condemned to a merely random investigation – guided by conventional prejudice or by "the linguistic habits of mankind".[1] This definition is to be at once about the nature of art, of beauty and the principles of criticism. One of the remarkable things about Osborne is his refusal to distinguish between the three. This refusal is, as we shall see, bound up with the search for definition. Briefly, works of art are beautiful objects, and their beauty is their value.

Osborne's argument has a fairly impressive completeness and symmetry. By virtue of the definition of a work of art, that an object *is* one must be deducible from the description of it; that it is beautiful is deducible from the same description and in virtue of the same definition; that it is good is deducible from the same description and in virtue of the same definition. For Osborne, the only alternative to such a deductive system would be an 'empirical' – by which he means totally random – shuffling of the data. Osborne believes that if one cannot provide what Moore calls an *analysis* of what one is doing, then one does not – in a very straightforward sense – know what one is doing.

> . . . criticism has ever lacked its own philosophy, without which research must continue always inconclusive, having no touchstone or relevance nor any criterion to distinguish failure from success. . . . every formulation of doctrine . . . inescapably implies theoretical assumptions which belong to the province of aesthetics. . . . as long as aesthetics remains inchoate criticism must needs be muddled and confused.[2]

[1] *Theory of Beauty*, pp. 12–13.   [2] *Aesthetics and Criticism*, p. 6.

I have already suggested why it is possible to recognize members of a class without being able to define the conditions of a thing's being a member of its class.[1] Yet Osborne clearly thinks that anything short of such a definition is not knowledge at all. In fact he takes the predictable position: if works of art have no one feature common and peculiar to works of art, then they are not related in any real way, but only by linguistic convention.[2] In Chapter II I discussed how this is likely to lead to a naturalistic theory of value – and, as we shall see, Osborne's refusal to separate the philosophy of criticism from the practice of criticism is part of the same confusion. He attacks, for instance, Leavis's account of evaluation as follows: "Whenever two things are compared in judgement they are estimated in relation to some common property or properties which one thing is alleged to possess in greater or equal degree than another."[3] Again:

> ... unless the critic defines his norms of judgement clearly and without ambivalence, either by verbal description or ostensively, the judgements which he utters will be strictly devoid of meaning, they will be no more than empty ejaculations.[4]

The symmetry is clear; in default of a defining common property there are no classes – Nominalism; in default of a prior principle of value, which states what all valuable objects of a certain sort have in common, there are no objective value judgements. If evaluation is a matter of 'estimating in relation to some common property' then the value judgement follows directly from the presence of the property. If the common property is the defining property of the object, then the value judgement follows deductively from the definition of the object – which is Naturalism. We shall see that Osborne's theory is thoroughly naturalistic.

Beauty, then, is defined as "the property in virtue of which works of art are judged to be good works of art".[5] Osborne declares that such a definition is 'pragmatic' – ". . . unless this, or some such definition, is accepted and is found to work, aesthetics will never become more than an empirical study of the linguistic habits of mankind."[6] How, on this sort of analysis, such a definition could be found to work or not to work – except in virtue of a prior definition – is obscure, but the point need not be pursued here. It is essential for

[1] pp. 14–15.   [2] Ibid.   [3] *Aesthetics and Criticism*, p. 33.
[4] Op. cit., p. 35.   [5] *Theory of Beauty*, p. 12.   [6] Op. cit., pp. 12–13.

Osborne to arrive at some sort of definition in order that conclusions can follow from it deductively. For him all reasoning that is not deductive is random. The definitions he finally arrives at are meant to be the only ones from which a coherent aesthetic could be deduced.

That beauty is the defining feature of works of art is a *formal* assertion; the content still has to be filled out. Osborne examines Hedonism, Realism and Expressionism and finds that none of them are necessary and sufficient for works of art. Again, he says:

> Works of art serve many functions in human society. They may be devotional objects, instruments of social, religious or political propaganda, incentives to morality, pleasant relaxation from the more strenuous occupations of life, a means to the ventilation of intellectual or pecuniary snobbery, or objects of barter. But none of these functions is peculiar to works of art and none of them seems necessary or common to all works of art.[1]

Hence Osborne concludes that all these qualities are *irrelevant* to an object's being a work of art. This is carrying the demand for a definition that shall state necessary and sufficient conditions to its logical – and absurd – conclusion. As Bernard Williams says, "... I cannot (on these criteria) commend a sports car for its speed, because there are such things as aeroplanes".[2] Now if Osborne rules out all the normal qualities of works of art as irrelevant, the common property he finally discovers is liable to be a rather peculiar one. In fact it turns out to be 'organic configurational unity'. The mechanism whereby such definitions can be made to cover all works of art has already been discussed[3] and will be examined again later. It suffices to point out that the only reason why 'organic configurational unity' is less obviously implausible than, for instance, 'tendency to produce relaxation', is that it is more vague. It has no immediate advantage over significant form.

Osborne's next move (logically) is to explain the relation between the work and its audience. Now he rigorously denies what he calls 'relational' theories of art. All such theories are 'subjective';[4] the argument is, briefly, that 'relational' theories assert a merely *fortuitous* connection between the work and the emotional or other effects we experience in its presence. If the only thing works of art have in common is the response of the audience – for instance 'synaesthesis'[5] –

[1] Op. cit., p. 18.   [2] Review of *Aesthetics and Criticism*, *Mind*, 1958, p. 410.
[3] See pp. 14–15.   [4] *Theory of Beauty*, pp. 73, 75.
[5] A term used by I. A. Richards.

and if there is no common 'non-relational' element in the works of art in respect of which this is experienced, then there is no intrinsic connection between our response and the object towards which it is directed.[1] Again Osborne is seeking for deductive certainty; what he calls 'appropriateness'[2] of response is a response that can be deduced from the description of the object, such that it would be contradictory to assert that two people see the same object but respond differently to it. Osborne is here approaching, but not arriving at, the position which I have suggested is the correct one – that the description under which someone sees an object is logically connected with his 'response', and that his 'response' is a *criterion* of the description under which he sees it.

Osborne achieves his deduction in a way which accords satisfyingly with the schema I set out in the first chapter. There is, he says, a characteristic 'aesthetic' response.[3] At first sight this would seem to contradict his insistence upon a non-relational account of art. This, however, is not the case. This response just *is* the apprehension of organic configurational unity. Osborne had started with what looked like an empirical account of the aesthetic emotion.

> ... when we are engaged in aesthetic activity, sight, hearing and imagination are exercised for themselves alone, our powers are strained to their fullest tension and beyond their full so that the capacities themselves are vitalized and enlarged . . .[4]

This does not avoid the difficulties of 'relational' theories. We could have all these experiences as the result of a drug, and not in connection with any external object – let alone a work of art – at all. The "unique kind of mental activity" still has to be correlated with ". . . its proper object – a non-relational property in things of beauty."[5] This property must "render certain reactions appropriate" just in virtue of itself,[6] but Osborne seems not very sure what the 'rendering appropriate' is. At one point, for instance, he talks as though he is putting forward an empirical hypothesis: ". . . we should reasonably expect that the contemplation and appreciation of this special kind of complex unities might involve some special mental features which do not otherwise occur."[7] But this is merely a confusion: Osborne's whole procedure is calculated to issue not in empirical hypotheses but in

---

[1] *Theory of Beauty*, pp. 70–75.   [2] Op. cit., p. 90.
[3] Op. cit., pp. 4, 22, 66–7, 70, 92, 159, 166, etc.   [4] Op. cit., p. 4.
[5] Op. cit., pp. 66–7.   [6] Op. cit., p. 90.   [7] Op. cit., p. 92.

definitions. To suggest that, *as a matter of fact*, certain experiences are conjoined with certain types of objects is to fall into 'subjectivity'.

The connection must – on Osborne's premises – be *necessary*. A less hypothetical-sounding account is the following: "A work of art is a successful work of art in so far as it achieves an organization of perceptual material into a single organic whole from which emerges a new and unique perceptual quality in awareness."[1] It is still not clear whether the connection is necessary; but it becomes clearer in the following passage: ". . . enhancement of the vivacity of awareness, intensification and invigoration of consciousness, depend upon the apprehension of very complex configurational unities."[2] Although Osborne does not succeed in being completely clear about this, we are, I think, entitled to draw the only conclusion that his method logically allows, which is that the essential property of a work of art and our response to it are to be defined *in terms of each other*. That is, organic configurational unity is that quality, our response to which, *just in so far as* it *is* a response to organic configurational unity, is one of heightened perception, vivacity and so on. Conversely, a response of heightened perception, vivacity, etc., is definable as the response to organic configurational unity. Osborne has certainly achieved a necessary connection between the two, but only at the expense of defining each in terms of the other. He believes that by this means he has solved the "hitherto insoluble antimony between 'subjective' and 'objective' beauty".[3] Reduction to identity is certainly a short and easy way with antinomies – but hardly solves anything. To find a necessary connection between the subjective or psychological and the objective – or 'non-relational' – aspects of art is, for Osborne, the central problem of aesthetics. In this he is in the company of Mrs Langer. Osborne does not obliterate the subjective aspect of art (not that this would remove art from a position of 'central human significance' – as we shall see) but he *reduces* it to the objective. Similarly he reduces the objective to the subjective. He does, then, obliterate the distinction, but does not, as he thinks, solve the antinomies.

The conclusions for evaluation follow with a satisfying rigour. The aesthetic response is not, as the expressionists would maintain, a re-creation of the artist's emotion; it is merely an acute perceiving.[4] Sometimes Osborne thinks that the contemplation of a work of art develops

[1] Op. cit., p. 125.　　　　　　　　[2] Op. cit., p. 159.
[3] Op. cit., p. 162.　　　　　　　　[4] *Aesthetics and Criticism*, p. 168.

into an emotion – with the emotion as something separable from the acute perception.[1] But normally he maintains his reductionist position – that the emotion *is* the contemplation. Now with the distinction obliterated between the work of art as it is in itself and our response to it, how do we account for differences in value judgement? Do not critics sometimes 'see the same thing' but value it differently? This, of course, is one of the classic objections to Naturalism. Osborne's reply is perfectly consistent with the rest of his argument. Critics who disagree do *not* see the same thing; therefore, they do not *really* disagree. A trained person sees far more of the features of a work than does a novice; the difference even adds up to a different *gestalt*. This is the effect, for instance, if one sees a part not in relation to the whole: ". . . you have not only changed the character of the whole but you have changed every part and relation. And this change is as 'real' as the change of sensation when red light is switched to blue."[2] Discrepant judgements, then, are never genuinely contradictory, for those who arrive at them ". . . will always be judging unlike sets of sense-impressions and genuinely contradictory judgements must be about the same thing."[3] This, again, is obviously close to the notion of 'seeing as', or at least as close as Osborne's premises allow him to come. However 'seeing as' helps to show how genuine disagreements about values are possible, whereas Osborne's account really rules out any possibility of rationally persuading someone to 'see' differently. This reductionist analysis is completed with ". . . to be fully aware of a work of art is to be sensible of its beauty and the two things cannot be severed."[4] Elsewhere he softens the force of this:

> It may be that no two competent critics who had experienced precisely similar actualisations of a work of art would ever disagree about its beauty, and if we exclude the variable idiosyncrasies of personal emotion there are strong *a priori* reasons for thinking that this may be so. But if it is so, we could never know it. Because when two critics seem to disagree about the beauty of any one work of art we can never know whether they have experienced the same or rather different works of art.[5]

This is confused; on Osborne's analysis the only sense in which we could 'never know' would be that in which it has been alleged that we can never know what goes on in other minds – which would be a

---

[1] Op. cit., p. 251.　　　　　　　　　　[2] *Theory of Beauty*, p. 131.
[3] Op. cit., p. 128.　　　　　　　　　　[4] Op. cit., p. 132.
[5] *Aesthetics and Criticism*, p. 233.

position of general scepticism. Osborne tends to slide from the empirical to matters of definition without being in the least aware of it: "The *value* we assign to beauty derives from its power to awaken and exercise our dormant capacities of awareness."[1] This sounds like a (vague and dubious) statement of fact. Later he suggests that there is a value *feeling* which attaches to heightened vitality.[2] Again, he says: "This is why the experience of beauty is valued. It is valued because it makes us more vividly alive than we otherwise know how to be."[3] All this gives his theory of art the flavour of the empirical. Yet if value judgements are made in respect of the essential property of works of art,[4] then the presence of the property entails the value judgement. The structure of his argument – although he never makes this clear – is that to say that a work of art is good is to report an experience of heightened vitality, etc., which in turn entails the apprehension of Beauty, which in turn entails the apprehension of a work of art. Thus, to say that this is a good work of art is to say that it is a work of art – which, as we have discussed it in the last chapter, is Naturalism. Conversely, if we wish to deny that an ostensible work of art is good, we have to deny that it *is* a work of art at all – which is the conclusion of expressionists such as Mrs Langer and Collingwood.[5]

Thus Osborne succeeds in avoiding the morass of merely empirical investigation. He succeeds in establishing absolutely certain connections between the essential property of Art (Beauty), our response to it and the value we assign to it. He attains this by the simple expedient of defining them all in terms of each other. For aesthetics this is a Pyrrhic victory. It is to achieve the 'gravid maturity'[6] of total certainty by a short cut which seeks to by-pass the 'fecund adolescence'[7] of careful examination. It is a sobering thought that Osborne could have achieved an equally cogent series of deductions had he defined art as Significant Form, or The Apprehension of Permanence Amid Change, or The Holding of a Mirror up to Nature, or almost anything else.

4. CONCLUSION: THE STRUCTURE OF THE ARGUMENTS

It could fairly be asked why I have devoted so much space to an examination of these aestheticians only to arrive at such apparently

---

[1] *Theory of Beauty*, p. 126. [2] *Op. cit.*, p. 163.
[3] *Aesthetics and Criticism*, pp. 228–9. [4] *Op. cit.*, p. 33.
[5] See Collingwood, *Principles of Art*, Book III, p. 282. See also Note E, p. 87.
[6] *Theory of Beauty*, Introduction, p. 1. [7] Ibid.

negative conclusions. The answer is that, apart from being interesting in their own right (Mrs Langer's work, for instance, is fascinating in its generality and brilliantly original) they show in an unusually clear form the logical results of certain philosophical assumptions. They clearly have a great deal in common despite their real differences. Osborne believes that if we are to try to establish the value and meaning of art by referring to the response of the audience we are left with a gap between the objective and the subjective. And this is quite true – at least according to the traditional empiricist account of the emotions. If the connection between an emotion and its object is only contingent there is no logical reason why any particular type of emotion should be attached to any particular type of object – no reason why we should not feel pity for stones or fear of capital letters. We can relate this back to the question discussed in Chapter I – 'How do I obey a rule?' Wittgenstein shows that obedience to a rule is not a matter of an inner state's corresponding to the appropriate outward actions; no inner state could count as obedience to a rule outside of a context or convention in which rules are given and obeyed. It would not, for instance, be possible to obey a rule privately. The outward behaviour would be the criterion, and the only possible characterization, of this 'inner process'. We justify a claim that a particular response counts as obeying the rule in terms of such conventions. For instance a child learning mathematics who always squared a number where he should multiply by two would be consistently misinterpreting a rule. Between this and the merely random scribbling of numbers there is a continuum. No one response by itself would count as rule-guided even if it happened to be right. We do not make an inference to an inner state, nor do we appeal to causes. If we did, it would be possible to ask of a child learning to read 'which was the first word he *read*?', and I have already suggested why this would not be an intelligible question.[1] Now Mrs Langer wishes to make our response a matter of inference to an inner state, the inner state being guaranteed by a sort of synthetic *a priori* correlation of works of art with forms of consciousness. I am not sure that this commits her to a *causal* account, but she is certainly not leaving room for the giving of reasons – for justification. Justification would consist in setting out, in some detail, the structure of the concept in question. In deciding whether a parrot which recites a sonnet of Shakespeare understands the words it utters we would

[1] See pp. 5–6.

look to its other conversational habits and, indeed, to its general behaviour, rather than to the structure of its brain (not that that could *never* be relevant). We are not faced with a hypothetical question about the presence of a soul, or the size of the brain. The justification of a response to a work of art is of the same sort – which is to say that it is a critical matter which cannot properly be described on the model of scientific explanation.

Osborne, in his quite justifiable anxiety to avoid the appeal to inner states, tries to abolish the notion of a 'response' altogether. For him the rule or picture "carries its interpretation on its face"[1] – which means that the idea of an 'interpretation' has no place. Yet no picture can compel a particular interpretation: "The arrow points only in the application that a living being makes of it." We justify how we see or respond to a rule or a picture by pointing to a context, to a background. Interpretation is not 'subjective', for it involves 'placing' within a context, and does not merely record a 'determination of the mind' to see the facts in a particular way. Osborne thinks that a 'response' would consist in adding something subjective to the work before one. Here he is essentially at one with Mrs Langer – except that she believes that she can guarantee her responses by presenting them as general laws of human nature. Osborne does not see – any more than does Mrs Langer – that the response is a matter of seeing the facts in a particular way, and that we cannot lay down in advance criteria which tell us when a way of seeing the facts becomes subjective. But if *all* interpretation were subjective – as he seems to think – then most of our psychological concepts would become impossible. How do we decide that a particular act expresses intention, or that a particular mental image is a memory image, except by interpreting them as such, seeing them as such, in the light of a particular background or context? If facts are as hard and uninterpretable as Osborne thinks, then the only explanation of psychological concepts would be in terms of the inner feelings we attach to the facts: a memory image would be distinguished by its 'vivacity' or by a 'long long ago' feeling from, say, an expectation of a future event. And this, of course, would be to land us in exactly the abyss of subjectivity – of the individual 'response' to the facts – which Osborne wishes to avoid.

One way in which we should *not* try to distinguish between 'relational' and 'formal' accounts is to claim that the former, unlike the

[1] See p. 7.

latter, gives art a place of 'central human significance'. I shall return to this point in a later chapter. For the time being it is sufficient to point out that Osborne's preoccupation with 'objective' qualities and Bell's preoccupation with 'formal' qualities arise from the recognition that we cannot go very far in defining the value and meaning of art in terms of our response to it, since our response is itself to be described in terms of the works to which it is a response. If it is true that the description of the intrinsic qualities of a *single* work of art gives us no sense of why it is significant for human beings unless in some sense we know why art in general is significant, it is equally true that our sense of the value of art will be constituted of our experience of individual works. The arguments of the previous chapter against Hare apply also to a Hareian aesthetic. If we take care of the 'objective' qualities of works of art, then the human significance will take care of itself.

NOTES TO CHAPTER III

A]   On good art as successful expression: Hospers argues that even if the expression theory is true, bad art shows all the symptoms of the expression of emotion that good art does. 'The Concept of Artistic Expression', *Proc. Arist. Soc.*, 1954–5, p. 320.

B]   This point is taken up by Margaret Macdonald in a review of *Feeling and Form*:

> ... what feeling is related to the pattern of virtual time which is a Mozart symphony and how does this differ from that conveyed by a Beethoven quartet? If the answer is, we know by intuition or that the feelings differ as the works differ, does this say more than that the works differ, which is indisputable? There must be more to say of the relation of feeling to art if the assertion of a connection is not to be pointless or merely personal.
>
> *Mind*, 1955, p. 549.

c]   We find many examples of this kind of analysis in Kenneth Burke. In *Counterstatement* we are told that a 'crescendo' in art is the objectification of a psychic sense of crescendo. ('The Poetic Process', op. cit., p. 57.) Burke applies the analysis not only to *forms* of art but to particular writers. A work of art is a symbol which

> "attracts us by its power of formula, exactly as a formula of history or

science. If we are enmeshed in some nodus of events and the nodus of emotions surrounding these events, and someone meets us with a diagnosis (simplification) of our partially conscious, partially unconscious situation, we are charmed by the sudden illumination which this formula throws upon our own lives. Mute Byrons (potential Byrons) were waiting in more or less avowed discomfiture for the formulation of Byronisms (the ramifications of the symbol) and continued enchanted. And thus, the symbol being so effective, they called the work of Byron beautiful. By which they meant that it was successful in winning their emotions."

Op. cit., p. 73.

Now we need not deny that Byron may in some sense have had an audience waiting for him. The objection to Burke's account is that he believes this to be the *only* explanation, the *essential* explanation of the power and significance of literature. Like Mrs Langer he makes the passage from the work in itself to its significance for the reader by means of subsuming it under a category already existing in the reader's mind. This 'explanation' is little more than an inflated way of asserting that Byron *is* important to some people – unless we are to take it as an account of why *particular* people at a *particular* time were so ready to respond to him. Later (p. 77) Burke claims that a symbol 'applies to life' by "serving here as a formula for our experiences, charming us by finding some more or less simple principle underlying our emotional complexities . . ." This formula or principle is meant to be analogous, in its simplifying power, to scientific theories. Again Burke, like Osborne and Mrs Langer, is trying to explain the significance of this simplifying power for us by means of a general formula: we are 'charmed' by seeing our emotions articulated. We are again being offered a general, quasi-causal explanation of the significance of art. Our being 'charmed' is taken as the basic evaluative premise which makes the essential connection between the work and ourselves. Yet are we necessarily 'charmed' when we find our emotions articulated for us? To assume, at this level of generality, that we are, is surely to assume what is certainly a vague, and possibly a doubtful *hypothesis*. The value we assign to art is not, however, an *hypothetical* matter at all. The basic confusion of this sort of theory is to imagine that it *is*.

The examples from Burke can be multiplied almost endlessly. Literary form is "an arousing and fulfilment of desires . . ." ('Lexicon Rhetoricae', op. cit., p. 157.) Later there is a generously inclusive explanation of the 'appeal' of the various forms: "Form, having to do with the creation and gratification of needs is 'correct' in so far as it gratifies the needs which it creates." (Op. cit., p. 175.)

Burke thinks that he has provided criteria of relevance – as well as criteria of meaning and value; irrelevant material is material included for its own sake, rather than to fulfil the demands of a form, and to 'satisfy expectation' (op. cit., pp. 182–4). The symbol is the "Verbal-parallel to a pattern of experience" (p. 193), stirs "remote depths" (pp. 196–7), and is an "emancipator of emotions" (p. 197). Now these 'inward processes' certainly stand in need of 'outward criteria'; whether a particular 'symbol' gratifies needs, fulfils expectation and so on, is to be decided by way of deciding whether the symbol *is* successful, or 'correct'. To say something about the one is to say something about the other. We do not decide that a work of art is successful by intuiting an inner state for which it stands; but nor does the palpable success of a work of art, its palpable 'significance', guarantee a connection with an inner state. (The same point is discussed in Chapter VI.) We must avoid the idea that criticism is a matter of *inference*. There would be no way of measuring whether a form gratified the needs which it created unless we already *knew* whether or not it was 'correct'.

Like Mrs Langer, Burke works out an elaborate system of literary forms, each allegedly corresponding to some aspect of the psyche – Syllogistic Form, Qualitative Progression, etc. His analysis becomes extremely Kantian (and here we have another connection, via Cassirer, with Mrs Langer) when he discusses 'minor forms' – contrast, comparison, metaphor, series, bathos, chiasmus, etc. These forms are "based upon our modes of understanding anything" (*Counterstatement*, p. 179). The forms of art are the modes of organizing experience – largely *inner* experience – as Kant's categories organize experience.

In *The Philosophy of Literary Form* Burke proposes to examine the 'symbolic act' – what the poem 'does' for the author (pp. 62–3). For instance, he uses biographical material to interpret a poem by Coleridge (pp. 79–86). We can compare this with a psycho-analyst's use of his knowledge of his patient's life to support and check his interpretation of a dream. This sort of investigation into what the poem 'does' may genuinely develop into an unusually profound account of what the poem 'means'. We have here a real method of checking our interpretations – not by any inference, but by a greater grasp of the relevant context. (I discuss this point further in Chapter VII.) The concept of 'symbolic act' is a considerable advance on his earlier orthodox expressionism.

We find another attempt to explain, in terms of categories, the meaning of art in J. Crowe Ransom:

> To what [in music] do our feelings respond? To music as structural composition itself: to music as manifesting the structural principles of the world; to modes of structure which we feel to be ontologically possible, or even probable.
>
> 'Criticism as Pure Speculation',
from The Intent of the Critic,
ed. Stauffer, p. 116.

We are again being pushed towards an ultimate – i.e. *unquestionable* – major premise – the 'structural principles of the world'; we can scarcely ask for more than that! This must, however, go the way of all such explanations (leaving aside its looseness and superstitiousness).

D]

> In every experience, even in science, there is feeling. No discourse can sustain itself without interest, which is feeling. The interest, or feeling, is like an automatic index to the human value of the proceedings – which would not otherwise proceed.
>
> J. Crowe Ransom, op. cit., p. 96.

E]   On the connection between the search for a definition of art and the attempt to derive evaluative criteria from such a definition, see W. E. Kennick, 'Does Traditional Aesthetics Rest on a Mistake?', *Mind*, 1958.

One defect of this article is that it leans heavily upon an over-simple distinction between such objects as, say, *knives* which are 'defined by their function' and works of art which are 'gratuitous' (op. cit., pp. 327, 334). Kennick allows that definitions of the 'essence' of art can be useful as slogans. (*Vide* Chapter VIII, p. 28.)

CHAPTER IV

Art and Feeling 2 – T. S. Eliot

I. EMOTION AND OBJECT

It has been said that each of these poems has a purpose. Another circumstance must be mentioned which distinguishes these Poems from the popular Poetry of the day; it is this, that the feeling therein developed gives importance to the action and situation, and not the action and situation to the feeling.

Wordsworth, *Preface to the Lyrical Ballads.*

This remark of Wordsworth can be seen on the one hand as the baptism of expressionism in the form more or less in which it has continued to dominate English criticism, and on the other as the bestowing on it of its original sin and most tenacious confusion. For if, in place of the various criteria of 'reality' which the mimetic theory assumes and supplies, we appeal to the emotion which the poetry evokes in the audience, or expresses for the poet, then we find ourselves asking *what* emotion is being expressed, whether it *ought* to be attached to this action and situation, and what criteria we have for deciding whether the emotion was *worth* expressing. Coleridge, Arnold and I. A. Richards all attempted to solve these difficulties and, as I have suggested, one way of seeing the development of critical theory in English in the latter part of the nineteenth and the first half of the twentieth century is as a series of attempts to bridge the gap between the poet's inner state and the external world. (I shall say more of this in a later chapter.) In T. S. Eliot we have a critic who returns again and again to the problem, without, as we shall see, satisfactorily solving it, or, indeed, avoiding very deep confusions. In some of his writings – especially in his famous doctrine of the 'objective correlative' – Eliot brings out in an extreme form the logical consequences of Wordsworth's assertion.

It is not at all easy to be clear what Eliot means when he talks about 'emotion', and yet many of the difficulties of his criticism – his theory of artistic creation and communication, his various pronouncements

88

about the relation between art and 'life', and between poetry and 'belief', and even his doctrine (if it can be so called) of 'impersonality' – seem to revolve round this concept. Of the many paradoxes one associates with Eliot perhaps the most extraordinary is that the 'classicist in literature' should believe that poetry expresses not thought but its "emotional equivalent".[1]

Let us start, however, with what appears to be an extremely 'objectivist' account of the reader's response to a poem: "The poet does not aim to excite – that is not even a test of his success – but to set something down; the state of the reader is merely that reader's particular mode of perceiving what the poet has caught in words."[2] Again: "And Dante helps to provide a criticism of M. Valery's 'modern poet' who attempts 'to produce in us a state'. A state in itself is nothing whatever."[3] Again: "The end of the enjoyment of poetry is a state of pure contemplation from which all accidents of personal emotion are removed."[4] The reader is responding 'impurely' to poetry who is "unable to distinguish the poetry from an emotional state aroused in himself by the poetry, a state which may be merely an indulgence of his own emotions."[5] The sentimental attitude is the opposite of the artistic: "The sentimental person in whom a work of art arouses all sorts of emotions which have nothing to do with that work of art whatever, but are accidents of personal association, is an incomplete artist."[6]

We have here several types of theory; first there is a particular view of the 'end' of poetry – "a state of pure contemplation"; secondly a value judgement about sentimentality in art; and thirdly a logical doctrine – "the state of the reader is merely that reader's particular mode of perceiving what the poet has caught in words". There is no reason to suppose that Eliot is aware of the variety of arguments he is using, and it is, anyway, not easy to separate them. For the time being I shall concentrate on the 'logical' aspect which is summed up in the remark I have just quoted and in the assertion that "A state in itself is nothing whatever".

If we talk of works of art as 'arousing' or 'evoking' emotions, and if in so doing we use causal language – which is almost inseparable from 'affective' theories – we fall into a major difficulty. How do we

---

[1] 'Shakespeare and the Stoicism of Seneca', *Selected Essays*, p. 135.
[2] 'Dante', *Sacred Wood*, p. 170.
[3] Ibid.   [4] 'The Perfect Critic', op. cit., pp. 14–15.
[5] Ibid.   [6] Op. cit., p. 7.

say *what* emotion a work of art does, or should, arouse? One possible solution would be to say that works of art 'fit' certain human states. This is, essentially, Mrs Langer's theory; it also seems to be Hume's:

> ... beauty is such an order and construction of parts as either by the *primary constitution of our nature*, or by *custom*, or by *caprice*, is fitted to give a pleasure and satisfaction to the soul. ... Pleasure and pain, therefore, are not only necessary attendants of beauty and deformity, but constitute their very essence.[1]

Hume is using 'fitted' ambiguously. On the one hand there is at any rate the feeling that an evaluative element is being slipped in; beautiful things *should* give pleasure rather than pain. On the other hand we have a causal law, the force of which is destroyed however by the appeal to the primary constitution of our nature *or* custom *or* caprice. By the time we have reached 'caprice' it is difficult to see that 'fitted' retains even any causal force. Apart from this ambiguity it is clear that a causal theory of our response to works of art cannot establish logical connections, and that the supposition of a pre-established harmony between the work and our primary constitution etc. is an illicit way of arriving at such connections. Pleasure and pain become the 'necessary' and 'essential' attendants of beauty and deformity.

Alternatively it might be allowed that our response is subjective. For instance, someone who is asked what emotions he experienced when he watched *King Lear* might reply "boredom". Or he might say, "I felt sad because I was reminded of my grandfather." The play might have been the occasion of both these emotions, but neither of them would be appropriate. They would be 'irresponsible' reactions.[2] Both responses could be occasioned by the play. In this account the work of art and the emotions we have in respect of it are merely 'conjoined' – as, on the same account, our 'experience' of the lines on the page which make up the Duck/Rabbit drawing is merely conjoined with our interpretation of it *as* a duck or a rabbit.

What is required is a justification of our response. The play is the object not the cause of our response,[3] and what we justify is an attitude. I have already (in the first two chapters) said something of the logic of such justification, and it is clear that no new principle is involved; being proud of the Pacific Ocean, attributing feelings to stones, and

---

[1] *Treatise*, Book II, Part I, Sect. VIII.   [2] See pp. 29–30.
[3] See Wittgenstein, *Philosophical Investigations*, 476.

finding *King Lear* funny are all on the same footing. We have to devise a context which would make such odd responses possible. However much my breast swells and my shoulders straighten at the thought of the Pacific Ocean, this does not, of itself, constitute pride. If I happened (personally) to own it, or if as a human being I were boasting to Martians of the superior grandeur of the earth (although even here the silliness of such boasting would be not unrelated to a conceptual strain), then I could feel proud of it.[1] But the same sensations could go with an entirely different emotion.

Eliot is bringing out something of the logic of emotion words in saying that the reader's state is merely his "particular mode of perceiving what the poet has caught in words". To describe his emotions he would have to describe the object of his emotions.

No criterion of value follows immediately from this. It does not follow, for instance, that poetry should not be such that it tends to evoke irrelevant associations. It is true by definition that if the associations are irrelevant then it is not the poem alone that is being contemplated. It would *prima facie* be possible to value most highly that poetry which is so incomplete, so uncontrolled that the reader's response to it is inevitably highly 'creative' or sentimental. The badness of that sort of poetry does not follow directly from any theory of emotion; nor does it immediately follow that the 'end' of poetry is to produce in the reader a state of 'pure contemplation'. Such conclusions cannot follow from matters of logic.

2. ARTISTIC CREATION

It is hard to see how Eliot's theory of the perception of works of art consorts with what he says about their production. Let us take a formulation which connects both theories:

> The only way of expressing emotion in the form of art is by finding an 'objective correlative'; in other words, a set of objects, a situation, a chain of events which shall be the formula of that particular emotion; such that when the external facts, which must terminate in sensory experience, are given, the emotion is immediately evoked.[2]

[1] See for instance Hume, *Treatise*, Book II, Part I, Sect. VI.

[2] 'Hamlet and His Problems', *Sacred Wood*, p. 100. This passage is ambiguous. It may be that the emotion is only being evoked in the artist. However, a later passage where Eliot talks of the state of mind of Lady Macbeth walking in her sleep being communicated "by a skilful accumulation of imagined sensory impressions" suggests that the emotion is evoked in the spectator.

This is a theory both of what it is for a poet to 'express himself', and of how the audience understands him. The notion of an 'objective correlative' is elaborated in *The Use of Poetry and the Use of Criticism*:

> I suggest that what gives (certain imagery) such intensity . . . is its saturation . . . with feelings too obscure for the authors even to know quite what they were. . . . Why, for all of us, out of all that we have heard, seen, felt in a lifetime, do certain images recur charged with emotion, rather than others? . . . an old woman on a German mountain path, six ruffians seen through an open window playing cards at night in a small French railway junction where there was a water mill: such memories may have symbolic value, but of what we cannot tell, for they come to represent the depths into which we cannot peer.[1]

The writer, then, knows that the image he chooses properly represents his state of feeling because it *evokes* the feeling which it is meant to symbolize. Indeed this is what it *is* for certain images to have 'symbolic value'. Yet, we remember, "The poet does not aim to excite . . . but to set something down" and ". . . the end of the enjoyment of poetry is pure contemplation". There is, then, a complete disparity between the writer's creation and understanding of his own work, and the reader's response to it. For the reader the evocation of emotion is of no importance; for the writer it is of the first importance. The obvious difficulty here is that whereas for the writer the test of the rightness of the image he uses to objectify a feeling is the evocation of the feeling – which comes to the same thing as saying that the *meaning* of the image is the emotion it evokes – there is no such test available for the reader. The reader can only 'perceive' what the poet has 'caught in words'. But the poet is only able to 'perceive' what he is saying by seeing the words of the poem *as* the formula of this particular emotion. The words or images have meaning only in that they are such a formula. The *reader* has no way of knowing whether the emotion they evoke in *him* is the right one since he has never previously made the connection between the feeling state and the image which stands for it; he has, therefore, no way of knowing what the poet means or whether the meaning he (the reader) assigns is the right one.

But is the author really in any better position? Can we say that a particular image has 'expressed' or 'objectified' a particular emotion merely because it recurs frequently to his mind, seems to have 'symbolical value', to 'represent the depths of feeling into which we can-

[1] Op. cit., p. 148.

not peer'? Do we not – to adopt Eliot's language – require the image in some way to illuminate the 'depths' and not merely to stand for them? If, for instance, an obsessional neurotic devotes great care to avoiding the joins of paving stones we should certainly say that his action had a symbolic value for him, even that it 'expressed' an unconscious state of mind. But the whole point of this action as an expressive gesture is that it is 'displaced'; it distorts or hides – by being a substitute for – some state of mind that may be utterly unlike anything that is naturally suggested by the avoidance of joins, and which is linked with it only by the most tenuous and metaphorical connection. Part of what we would say is that the neurotic has not properly 'objectified' his state of mind; he has, as it were, to unpack his obsessive behaviour, to give, eventually, an account of whatever it is that his behaviour symbolizes. In doing this he will gradually trace a connection between the action and the unconscious state. Now if we regard the analyst's relation to the patient as analogous to that of the reader to the poet we see that in one sense the analyst is at a disadvantage in comparison with the patient – for the patient experiences the compulsion, whereas the analyst does not. Yet, in another sense, they are in the same position, for the patient no more than the analyst knows *what* the compulsion is. The action is a private symbol, even for the patient, and he can only communicate it – as he can only understand it – by tracing more and more connections which will eventually explain what it means.

It is clear that according to the theory of the 'objective correlative' we learn to identify emotions by associating them with objects. There seems to be some sort of causal relation between the emotion and the object which calls it forth – the most explicit confusion of cause and object we have yet met with. There is no intrinsic connection between the emotion and the object, between the inward state and its outward expression. The images the poet uses stand for, and name, certain private, subjective states. His knowledge that the 'expression' is correct is in the nature of a causal law, an inference. But is there any way of knowing that the inference is correct? The connection between the emotion and the object which expresses it is an essentially private act of the poet, an inward 'baptism'. As Kenny, paraphrasing Wittgenstein, says:

> If the names of emotions acquire their meaning for each of us by a ceremony from which everyone else is excluded, then none of us can have

any idea what anyone else means by the word. Nor can anyone know what he means by the word himself; for to know the meaning of a word is to know how to use it rightly; and where there can be no check on how a man uses a word there is no room to talk of 'right' or 'wrong' use.[1]

The theory of the 'objective correlative' rests squarely on the notion of a private language, and on the view of emotion words as standing for private states. The poet can have no grounds for saying that the image evokes the original emotion because there is no criterion for deciding whether it is the same or a different emotion – which means that the concept of 'same' does not apply.

The case of the obsessional neurotic is important because it seems to suggest the possibility of a disparity between emotions and their expression, such that the connection between the two is only contingent. Emotions are, however, necessarily attached to objects; if I am afraid, I am afraid *of* something, if I am shocked I am shocked *at* something – whereas I can be cold or hungry without any particular object being involved.[2] Now the psycho-analyst investigates the context in which the patient's action can have the symbolic weight it seems to have; he does not seek the *cause* of the emotion – a point to which we shall return.

Wordsworth also, in the passage quoted, assumes that the connection between object and emotion is contingent – "the feeling . . . gives importance to the action and situation, and not the action and situation to the feeling". But it cannot be that the importance the neurotic attaches to his obsessional action gives importance to the action. When there seems to be a disparity between feeling and object, or when the feeling seems to lack an object, we may try to discover 'unconscious' beliefs etc. which might account for the disparity. I can no more simply 'mean' something profound when I use banal language than I can mean "If it doesn't rain I shall go for a walk" when I say "Bububu".[3]

3. IMPERSONALITY

Eliot's remarks about the 'impersonality' of art form, perhaps, the most confusing part of his critical theory. In the first place words like 'personal' and 'personality' are capable of such a variety of meaning that it is impossible to say whether art should be 'impersonal' unless one specifies exactly how the word is being used.

[1] *Action, Emotion and Will*, p. 13.   [2] Op. cit., pp. 60–2.   [3] See p. 4.

In 'The Perfect Critic'[1] Eliot writes:

> . . . in an artist these suggestions made by a work of art, which are purely personal, become fused with a multitude of other suggestions from multitudinous experience and result in the production of a new object which is no longer purely personal, because it is a work of art itself.

In a lecture called 'The Modern Mind'[2] he denies that the poet simply communicates an experience. The final poem may so differ from the original experience

> as to be hardly recognisable. The 'experience' . . . may be the result of a fusion of feelings so numerous, and ultimately so obscure in their origins, that even if there be communication of them, the poet may hardly be aware of what he is communicating; and what is there to be communicated was not in existence before the poem was completed.[3]

In 'Tradition and the Individual Talent' Eliot speaks of the poet's mind as a 'medium' in which the fusion of feelings takes place. "The poet's mind is, in fact, a receptacle for seizing and storing up numberless feelings, phrases, images, which remain there until all the particles which can unite to form a new compound are present together."[4]

Eliot connects this with a denial that the poet expresses his 'personality':

> The point of view which I am struggling to attack is perhaps related to the metaphysical theory of the substantial unity of the soul: for my meaning is that the poet has, not a 'personality' to express, but a particular medium, which is only a medium and not a personality, in which impressions and experiences combine in unexpected and peculiar ways.[5]

These impressions cease to be merely personal when they have been 'fused' into new wholes. In some way this fusion is at the same time a 'transformation'; the private experience becomes public, impersonal.

It is worth noticing, in passing, how deceptive the form of the argument – one might almost say how deceptive the appearance of argumentation – is here. As one reads, one is under the impression that Eliot is giving factual information about the creation and understanding of works – that he is suggesting an empirical theory. But if we look more closely we find that that is not the case. The suggestions from multitudinous experience combine, we are told, to form a new

---

[1] *Sacred Wood*, p. 7. [2] *The Use of Poetry and the Use of Criticism*, p. 138.
[3] See Note A, p. 103. [4] Op. cit., *Sacred Wood*, p. 55. [5] Op. cit., p. 56.

object 'which is not purely personal'. Why is it not purely personal? 'Because it is a work of art itself.' Now Eliot has been talking very much in quasi-scientific, mechanical language. There is a 'fusion' which 'produces' a work of art; the 'because' in 'Because it is a work of art itself' sounds as though we are carrying on the causal, mechanistic language. Yet if we are, then it is clear that it is the 'fusion' that is the cause of the work of art, not the work of art that is the cause of the fusion. But we have obviously left the language of a causal mechanism behind; 'because' gives not a cause but a reason. It states, furthermore, not an empirical fact, but an insistence upon certain definitions of 'art', 'personal' and so on. We could never find a 'personal' work of art; it would either be not 'really' a work of art, or not 'really' personal. The 'fusion' does not *produce* a new object – we must adopt the language of reasons here too – rather the 'new' object is a redescription of the elements out of which it is 'made'. Again the 'fusion' is not a *process*; we say that elements are 'fused' when we are prepared to describe them as a 'work of art'.

It seems possible that we might decide that many of Eliot's theories are 'matters of definition'. I do not propose, at this point, to do more than suggest the possibility in the light of what has just been said. Of course, there is just as much point in arguing about non-empirical as about empirical theories; to show that, say, the 'expressionist' theory of art is non-empirical is not a short and ready way of disposing of it. But Eliot is almost certainly mistaken as to the nature of his own theories, and this is probably the key to most of the more baffling aspects of his criticism – particularly the doctrine of impersonality.

To revert to 'impersonality': if we set aside the analogy of the catalyst, it is not at all easy to see what Eliot is saying. The choice we are being offered between the poet as 'expressing his personality' and the poet as 'a medium in which impressions can combine' seems spurious. The way a man talks, the behaviour which characterizes him, the images characteristic of his poetry – all these are part of his 'personality'. It need have nothing to do with any 'metaphysical doctrine of the substantial unity of the soul'. Presumably Eliot is struggling to oppose the idea that experiences are valuable just in that they are expressions of personality – an idea connected with the belief that 'the soul' is the place where 'genuine poetry is made'.[1] The experiences presented in the poem have to be valuable in their own right – not just

[1] Matthew Arnold, 'Thomas Gray', *Essays in Criticism*, 2nd series.

because they are the experiences of an unusual person. But even if the poet is a 'medium' in which impressions combine, he will still be expressing his 'personality' if the images – and, indeed, the opinions – he produces are sufficiently individual or eccentric.

Eliot also seems to mean by the 'personal' the inarticulate, the subjective; experience is depersonalized by being objectified; it is objectified when a public symbol is found for it, and that symbol is successful in that it evokes the inarticulate emotion – the "swarms of inarticulate feelings".[1] In being objectified the private, personal experience is transmuted: "It is not the . . . intensity of the emotions . . . (that counts) . . . but . . . the pressure under which the fusion takes place . . ."[2] It is this 'intensity' which determines the greatness, the success of a work of art. "The episode of Paolo and Francesca employs a definite emotion, but the intensity of the poetry is something quite different from whatever intensity in the supposed experience it may give the impression of."[3]

This is extremely confusing. Clearly, if the intensity of the poetry is quite different from the intensity of the actual experiences or emotions out of which it is made, there can be no place for a doctrine of an 'objective correlative' in which the object 'evokes' the original emotion. In an article entitled 'The Critical Ideas of T. S. Eliot'[4] Ants Oras suggests that there is no contradiction between the theory of the objective correlative and Eliot's other view that "the poet does not aim to excite" – and also, by implication, no contradiction between the objective correlative and the idea that personal emotions are 'transmuted' into works of art:

> The actual meaning of this denial of excitement as an aim of the poet appears to be that mere excitement, excitement not produced by means of an 'objective correlative', is not his object. This would accord with the deprecation of emotion 'however intense – in the crude living state'.

Ants Oras believes that Eliot's thought is consistent throughout; but this seems to be a denial of a clear contradiction, as well as a failure to see the real force of Eliot's 'denial of excitement'. A view of the reader's emotion as merely his 'particular mode of perceiving' the poem

---

[1] 'Ben Jonson', *Sacred Wood*, p. 105.
[2] 'Tradition and the Individual Talent', op. cit., p. 55.
[3] Ibid.
[4] *Acta Universitatis Tartuensis*: Humaniora xxvii, 1932, pp. 17–18.

must contradict a view of the poem as awakening in the spectator an emotion similar to the poet's – an emotion distinct from the poem, and for which the poem stands.

In the same article Mr Oras suggests that the idea of 'transmutation' of emotion is related to the Freudian theory of 'sublimation'.[1] Now the Freudian theory has its own difficulties: some of its immediate plausibility, for instance, depends upon a metaphor of 'psychic energy' which can be 'displaced' into various activities. However, since the parallel is illuminating, we might return to the case of the obsessional neurotic. We can say that the action has an intensity in his own ex- perience – but, as a symbol, 'means' little to anybody else. There is a disparity between the emotional material and the symbol that is made out of it; the 'public' significance of the symbol bears almost no rela- tion to its 'private' intensity. We use *public* criteria to judge whether it is an 'intense' symbol. The episode of Paolo and Francesca has an intensity of its own as a public image – an intensity which can to a large extent be explained by a description of the episode. It is an intensity which is intrinsic. The reader does not have an emotion apart from his understanding and following the episode; his emotion is his interest in the story, his attention to the details of the verse – his "particular mode of perceiving what the poet has caught in words". Now are we to say that the emotions of the neurotic have not been 'transformed' whereas those of Dante have? Perhaps we should say this: the image chosen by the neurotic is connected with a context which is unconscious. If the context – the memories, wishes, fears and so on – were drawn into consciousness, we would come to understand what the symbol means. The emotional charge of the symbol would be resolved into a set of associations, and the patient's emotion would then be his 'mode of perceiving' these associations and could be described in terms of them. In this sense the emotion is being 'trans- formed' into a public object; but it is not being replaced – rather its essential structure is being revealed. The relation of the symbol to the unconscious state is not that of paper money to a bank's deposit of gold, but that of the tip of an iceberg to what is below the water.

What sort of transformation or transmutation can have taken place in Dante's mind? Can we use this sort of language about normal mental processes? If I had invented and told the story either of Ulysses or of Paolo and Francesca, would my mind have 'digested and trans-

[1] Op. cit., p. 73.

muted the passions which are its material'?[1] If this is so, there seems no good reason why a judge delivering an opinion or a philosopher producing an argument could not be said to be digesting their passions. For the organizing power involved in Dante's rendering of Cantos xxvi and v is intellectual as much as anything else. It is as natural to give an account in terms of perceptions and ideas as in terms of passions. Indeed, Eliot says: "The *Agamemnon* or *Macbeth* is equally a statement, but of events. They are as much works of the 'intellect' as the writings of Aristotle."[2] If someone asks me why I told a particular story, expressed a particular opinion and so on, I should give reasons which would be publicly understandable. There would be no question of transmuting anything: the reasons given, my description of my 'interest' in the story, of my 'belief' in the opinion would, as it were, be on the same level as the telling of the story, the expressing of the opinion. There is a sense in which my interest in the story *is* distinct from my 'mode of perceiving' it: I may be looking round for, trying to think of something to illustrate a particular point (or for a musical phrase to fill a particular gap) when the story (phrase, argument) suddenly 'comes'. Eliot says of Canto xv of the Inferno (Brunetto Latini):

> The last quatrain gives an image, a feeling attaching to an image, which 'came', which did not develop simply out of what precedes, but was probably in suspension in the poet's mind until the proper combination arrived for it to add itself to.[3]

A great deal of thought 'comes', does not 'develop simply' out of what precedes; we cannot predict it, or, as it were, think it before we have thought it. But if we can trace the relevant connections between the new thought and the thoughts which preceded it – can answer, that is, various 'Why?' questions – then we have found the reason[4] why the new thought 'came'. In a sense, a tension, a search for a thought has been 'transformed' into the thought itself.

This same image underlies Eliot's discussion of *Hamlet*. According to Eliot *Hamlet* communicates an emotion 'in excess' of the presented

---

[1] 'Tradition and the Individual Talent', *Sacred Wood*, p. 54.
[2] 'The Possibility of a Poetic Drama', op. cit., p. 65.
[3] 'Tradition and the Individual Talent', op. cit., p. 55.
[4] As distinct from the *cause* of the thought. Eliot again sounds very much as if he is giving a pseudo-mechanical *causal* explanation.

situation. We might say that Ernest Jones's[1] psycho-analytical investigation of the play seeks to explain Hamlet's disgust – suggests the sorts of answer which Hamlet would give if asked (under analysis!) why he feels such physical disgust at Gertrude's marriage. To say that Shakespeare has failed to transmute a personal experience into a work of art is to say that he could not answer these questions; and it is also to say that we, the audience, are unable to locate precisely the peculiarly insidious glamour that we may find in *Hamlet*. It is not that there has been no transmutation of the original experience into the symbol, but that the connections between the symbol and the original situation – that is, the context of the symbol (the symbol is part of the situation; it does not stand for it) – have remained unconscious. Again the failure is not causal; it is a gap in the chain of reasons.

If Shakespeare had re-written *Hamlet* so as to bring out clearly the 'Oedipal situation' that Ernest Jones claims to find in it, would we say that the revised version was more 'impersonal' than the first? If a man who suffers from strong feelings of disgust, which are apparently provoked by his mother, discovers that the 'excess' emotions are bound up with situations of which – up to this time – he has been unconscious, would we say that in discovering and articulating these situations he has made his feelings more impersonal? We might just as well say that they have become more *personal*, have been more fully integrated with his adult personality. A person dominated by violent pressures which are discontinuous with his normal consciousness is to that extent not responsible for his actions. If the pressures become too great, his personality may disintegrate. In coming to understand these pressures he re-establishes the connections with the rest of his personality; there is, if anything, an extension, a filling out of personality.[2] This is just another example of the looseness of words like 'personal' and 'personality'; but it has bearing on Eliot's view of the relation between artistic experience and experience in 'life'.

Similarly, Eliot says that Coleridge has not 'used' the imagery in *Khubla Khan*. Here again, if we leave aside the image from chemistry (or alchemy) of 'transmutation', then we are talking about gaps or incompleteness in the poem itself; Coleridge has not fully worked out his idea. But he has only left some 'emotion' untransmuted to the same extent that someone has who leaves out a vital step in an argument. In

[1] Op. cit.
[2] Freud, *Interpretation of Dreams*: "Where Id was, there shall Ego be."

fact Eliot does apply the idea to thought: "Certain works of philosophy can be called works of art: . . . Mr Russell's essay on 'Denoting': clear and beautifully formed thought . . . (*not*) . . . what is not clear, but . . . is an emotional stimulus."[1] An 'artistic' philosopher, like Bergson, is both less of an artist and less of a philosopher. Bergson, Eliot would say, has not fully 'worked up' his interests into an objective statement.

4. POETRY AND BELIEF

We see at once that Eliot's theory of the relation between poetry and belief is closely connected with his view of the relation between ordinary experience and the work of art. Poetry offers the 'emotional equivalent' of thought. Dante is not writing philosophy; nor is he producing the Thomist philosophy decorated with poetic imagery. He is making poetry out of a philosophy – just as poetry is made out of emotional experience. Aquinas' philosophy has become a datum – "almost a physical modification". The contemplation of Aquinas' philosophy is capable, like any other experience, of being transmuted into poetry.[2] Eliot sees that to carry this theory too far would lead to an impossible situation; he admits that he ultimately prefers Dante to Shakespeare because Dante has 'a saner view of Life', and also that a dislike of Shelley's beliefs is involved in his dislike of Shelley's verse. Conversely, it is a defect in Lucretius's beliefs that they are incapable of being so fully assimilated into life that they can be properly transmuted into poetry.

In several places Eliot expresses disagreement with I. A. Richards's theory of poetry; yet it is clear that he is not far from Richards. Like Richards he distinguishes the poetic from other uses of language as expressing 'emotion' rather than fact. By an odd reversal of his theory of emotion being transmuted into an 'objective correlative' he now believes that thought can be transmuted into feeling. "In Chapman especially there is a direct sensuous apprehension of thought, or a recreation of thought into feeling, which is exactly what we find in Donne."[3]

The discussion of emotion suggests why talk of transmutation of emotion into thought, or of thought into emotion, or of 'the emotional equivalent of thought' is misleading. The problem of the way in which

---

[1] 'The Possibility of a Poetic Drama', *Sacred Wood*, pp. 66–7.
[2] See Note B, p. 103.
[3] 'The Metaphysical Poets', *Homage to John Dryden*, p. 29.

H

we adjust to the beliefs of a poet is, admittedly, difficult (although René Wellek dismisses it as a purely psychological matter of no critical interest)[1] but it is no solution to try and cut the Gordian knot by divorcing the experience of poetry from the experience of ordinary life. The problem of the nature of poetic belief is part of the general problem of the relation of art to 'life'.

5. ART AND 'LIFE'

One logical conclusion of Wordsworth's assertion that the feeling gives importance to the situation, and not vice versa, is the view that the materials of poetry have to be usable for emotional purposes. That is Coleridge's position in the *Biographia Literaria*,[2] and it is the grounds on which Eliot, to say nothing of Winters, Murry, Carnap, and others, distinguishes poetry from prose (and, perhaps, 'statement' from 'pseudo-statement'). The corresponding view is that the tests of poetic value are essentially distinct from any question of the truth or intrinsic adequacy of the materials 'used'. In the Preface to *The Sacred Wood* Eliot says:

> And certainly poetry is not the inculcation of morals, or the direction of politics . . . or an equivalent of religion. . . . And certainly poetry is something over and above, and something quite different from, a collection of psychological data about the minds of poets, or about the history of an epoch; for we could not take it even as that unless we had already assigned to it a value merely as poetry.

I shall try, in a later chapter, to show that this insistence that poetry cannot be reduced to morality, politics, and so on, is linked with the attempt to locate the essence of poetry in its 'formal' qualities, which in turn is a product of the view that poetry is fundamentally emotional (Clive Bell's vacillation between an extreme formalism and an appeal to the aesthetic 'emotion' is relevant here). The lack of any intrinsic connection between emotion and object – which, as we have seen, the theory of the 'objective correlative' assumes – makes the connection between poetry and the materials out of which it is made, between art and 'life', obscure to the point of incomprehensibility. Eliot characteristically wavers between preferring Dante to Shakespeare because

---

[1] 'The Criticism of T. S. Eliot', *Sewanee Review*, Vol. 64, 1956, p. 417. "It is not susceptible of a theoretical solution and does not concern the theory of criticism."

[2] See for instance *Biographia Literaria*, p. 211 (Everyman edition).

Dante has a basically saner view of life and asserting that a test of the adequacy of a view of life is its capacity to be made into poetry. Aestheticism and didacticism are certainly deeply intertwined in Romantic criticism, and Eliot is, perhaps, not to be blamed for failing to achieve an adequate relation between them. Wordsworth attempted to replace the criteria provided by the neo-classical mimetic theory of art with an insistence on the emotional importance of poetry, but he was unable to appeal to a philosophy which could show that emotions too have their logic, and are subject to objective tests. While I would hesitate to say that the equivocations and confusions which beset English Romantic criticism on the subject of the relations between art and reality are the result simply of conceptual mistakes, there is no doubt that they can to a great extent be explained in terms of them.

Clearly what is needed is a demonstration that poetry can be both emotional *and* rational. One critic who has made a major attempt to demonstrate this is Yvor Winters, whose work will be the subject of a later chapter.

NOTES TO CHAPTER IV

A] Hospers produces a *reductio ad absurdam* of this way of talking:

> Because the artist, while expressing his feeling, is clarifying it to himself, he cannot before expressing it state what he is going to express; therefore he cannot calculate in advance what effects he wants to produce and then proceed to produce them. If he could, he would have no need to express, since the emotion would be already clear to him.
>
> 'The Concept of Artistic Expression',
Proc. Arist. Soc., 1954–5, pp. 314–15.

Collingwood indeed argues (*Principles of Art*, p. 109) that an emotion cannot be known until it has been expressed. Hence the form of the composition cannot be known in advance, and poetry, being art, not 'craft', is not 'made out of' pre-existent emotions. (Op. cit., p. 24.)

B] Compare:

> The poet converts human experience into poetry not by first expurgating it, cutting out the intellectual elements and preserving the emotional, and

then expressing this residue; but by fusing thought itself into emotion: thinking in a certain way and then expressing how it feels to think in that way. Thus Dante has fused the Thomistic philosophy into a poem expressing what it feels like to be a Thomist.

Collingwood, Principles of Art, p. 295.

Collingwood, of course, elaborately works out the process whereby 'sensation' plus 'emotion' rises into thought.

CHAPTER V

Style and Feeling: Middleton Murry

How widespread is the Romantic tendency to appeal to feeling as a means of *explanation* in literature is shown by an examination of Middleton Murry's *The Problem of Style*. This little book is almost contemporary with *Tradition and the Individual Talent* and is highly Eliotean both in doctrine and phraseology. Murry has his own doctrine of the 'objective correlative', believes that poets produce not thought but its emotional equivalent, and sets out a theory of style which centres around a particular view of the place of emotion in literature.

Early in the book Murry writes:

> By accepting the view that the source of style is to be found in a strong and decisive original emotion, we can get a closer grasp of the intention that lies under the use of the word as meaning a writer's personal idiosyncrasy. An individual way of feeling and seeing will compel an individual way of using language.[1]

Later Murry draws a contrast between what he considers to be the unhealthy artificiality in the later work of both Meredith and James, and the artificiality of Milton which is "the natural language of an original and unfamiliar mode of feeling". With Meredith and James there is

> (an) artificiality which supervenes when the desire for accomplishment is present without any distinctive mode of feeling, or when the capacity for feeling has withered, leaving what was once a natural and healthy method of expression to run riot in a factitious existence of its own.[2]

One thing that Murry strikingly does not do in *The Problem of Style* is to offer a catalogue of 'styles'. The last thing we can see the book as is a handbook of rhetoric in the traditional sense. This may seem too obvious a point to remark, but I shall show that it is important. What we are offered instead is an account of the *essence* of style, and this is said to be the expression of 'an individual way of

[1] Op. cit., p. 15.　　　　[2] Op. cit., p. 18.

feeling and seeing'. Now Murry's remark that an individual way of feeling and seeing will compel an individual way of using language certainly seems to mark an advance on Eliot, for according to Eliot – as we saw – there is no intrinsic connection between the feeling and the language used to express it. Yet Murry's formulation betrays a fundamental uncertainty, and is brought out with a certain air of paradox. The uncertainty resides in the use of 'compel' – "will compel an individual way of using language". What sort of compulsion is this? If we say that Shakespeare could not have 'expressed' his way of seeing and feeling in the language of Milton, are we saying that his way of seeing and feeling *caused* him to use language in the way he did? It would be a very odd sort of causality since the entity which is supposed to be doing the causing can very often only be described in terms of its effects. For instance the feelings that *The Tempest* expresses can only be described via a description of the play. Here the only account we can give of the way of feeling and seeing is in terms of the play itself. Shakespeare's language is (in some wide sense) a *criterion* – the central criterion – of how he is seeing and feeling, not evidence on the basis of which we can make an inference. Where what is seen and felt is essentially bound up with a mastery of language, the language is the only criterion.[1] Macbeth's capacity to feel as he does when he hears of his wife's death is bound up with his capacity to speak as he does: the feelings 'expressed' by the 'tomorrow and tomorrow and tomorrow' lines are inseparable from a mastery of language. To try to talk about these feelings apart from their expression would be to try to talk about a non-entity. All we can say is that these are the feelings expressed by the words – in which case the feelings (as something separable) "drop out of consideration as irrelevant".[2] To say, then, that an individual way of seeing and feeling will compel an individual way of using language is not to assert a well-established causal law; the connection is not contingent but logical – as is the connection between a man's feeling of pain and his 'pain-behaviour'. (It is possible for some men to smile when they are in pain, but it is not possible for all men characteristically to do so. We should either have to revise our notion of what pain is, or to insist that they were not really smiling but grimacing.)

[1] See Kenny, op. cit., pp. 62–3. Fear of an economic recession would be an example.

[2] See p. 9.

Of course when I say that Shakespeare's language is the *central* criterion of how, in some wide sense, he is feeling and seeing, I am not asserting that any other criterion is logically impossible. There is a continuum from rather simple and primitive feelings which seem capable of being expressed in a number of different ways, to other less simple feelings which can only be expressed verbally, but for which any one of a number of verbal expressions would be suitable, to those complex structures of thought and feeling – such as works of literature – where any substitution would be, for all practical purposes, impossible. We can, then, allow for the notion of a description of what someone else is 'trying to say' – at least at the more 'primitive' levels. A man's actions can, in such cases, help to show (can be important criteria for) what he is trying with only partial success to put into words. Indeed his actions and his words may, as criteria, conflict, and it is the possibility of such conflict of criteria that gives the impression that the feeling or thought which they express is something behind them of which they are symptoms. But even if there is a continuum from the most primitive to the most sophisticated and complex, it is still the case that criteria other than verbal criteria will, at the latter end, play little or no part. In the most complex cases, such as works of literature, the verbal criteria will be patterns of language which are, for all practical purposes, unique. There is a remark of Wittgenstein's which perhaps has bearing on this notion of a continuum, to the effect that pain language *replaces* the natural expression of pain (crying for instance) but does not describe it.[1] I take this to suggest that in some circumstances a man's (non-verbal) behaviour is as central a criterion for his feelings – as fully expresses his feelings – as anything he could *say*. Now as the feeling becomes less and less primitive so the verbal expression of it becomes more and more the *natural* expression, until we come to those emotions which can *only* be expressed verbally; but the highly complex verbal expression does not *describe* anything – any more than the primitive behaviour did. This suggests the way in which we can learn the possibility of new forms of feeling which is at the same time the possibility of new forms of expression. It also suggests the way in which art is, on the one hand, something conventional or artificial – created rather than discovered – but also, on the other hand, something natural, a type of discovery of both formal and emotional possibilities. "For how", as Wittgenstein

[1] *Philosophical Investigations*, 244.

asks, "can I go so far as to try to use language to get between pain and its expression?"[1] And how, we can equally ask, could there be any way of getting between the language of a poem and what it expresses?

Murry's insistence on the intimate connection between style and feeling is a valiant attempt to bridge the gap between the subjective and the objective, a gap which, as we have seen, is such a characteristic feature of Romantic criticism. But unfortunately Murry soon slips back into the very dualism he is trying to avoid: in a later passage he says:

> The test of a true idiosyncrasy of style is that we should feel it to be necessary and inevitable: in it we should be able to catch an immediate reference back to a whole mode of feeling that is consistent with itself. If this reference is perceptible to us, it will be accompanied by a conviction that the peculiarity of style was inevitable, and that the original emotion of which we were made sensible demanded this method of expression and this alone.[2]

The trouble here is that if we could in this way compare the 'original emotion' with the language in which it is expressed we should have no right to say that the emotion 'demanded this method of expression and this alone'. Where there is any genuine comparison we cannot say that. We may, for instance, say that a Reynolds portrait is a very good rendering of the subject (meaning by 'subject' the actual person whose portrait Reynolds painted), but we could hardly say that the subject demanded this rendering and this alone. And when we cannot make such a comparison then we have no way of knowing whether or not the original emotion demanded this method of expression and this alone. Emotions are not inner events which language succeeds in pointing to or naming, or standing in a relation of logical analogy to. We cannot adopt a more or less modified version of the mimetic theory – works of art as imitating emotional states rather than things in the outer world – and expect it to apply to the expression of emotion. It is exactly this sort of theory that is incapable of asserting the intimate connection between the emotion and its expression, an incapacity that cannot be rectified merely by proclaiming the connection with an air of insistence. But if we abandon a quasi-mimetic theory the insistence loses all point, and becomes no longer unjustified but meaningless. If there is a logical connection between emotions and their expression we cannot say that the emotion demanded *this* ex-

---

[1] Op. cit., 245.   [2] Murry, op. cit., p. 16.

pression – as though there were some other expression which we are thereby excluding. To say that the *King Lear* emotions demanded to be expressed only in the form of the play *King Lear* is very like saying that a thing is identical with itself (of which Wittgenstein says that "There is no finer example of a useless proposition"[1]).

We cannot invoke a feeling to 'explain' genuineness or originality of style, since the qualities of style are our only criteria of qualities of feeling. If I am unable to see that a vulgar and sentimental piece of writing *is* vulgar and sentimental, and take it rather as expressing delicate and subtle emotion, my mistake is not in the nature of an incorrect inference. It would be better to say that my attitude is inappropriate, my response unintelligent. If I come to change my mind about the passage, this will not take the form of my deciding that, after all, this fine and delicate writing expresses vulgar and sentimental feelings, but that this is, after all, a vulgar and sentimental piece of writing. I come to 'see' that by comparing this with other pieces of writing, by looking at it more closely, learning to attach less value to certain emotions and more to others.

This is linked with the difficult problem of form and content. When Murry asserts that the test of true idiosyncrasy of style is that the reader becomes convinced that the feeling could only be expressed in the way it *was* expressed, he is attacking the sort of separation of form and content that we find in, for instance, Eliot and (as we shall see) Yvor Winters. But Murry's own view of the connection between the inward state and its outward expression – a view more or less in the main empiricist tradition[2] – most naturally goes with just the sort of separation which he is attacking. To see how deeply Murry's theory of style is imbued with traditional empiricist presuppositions, and how difficult it becomes for him, as a result, to give any coherent account of the place of emotion in literature, let us examine the distinction he attempts to draw between creative and other forms of writing:

> However much [the creative writer] may think, his attitude to life is predominantly emotional; his thoughts partake much more of the nature of individual emotions, which are symbolised in the objects which aroused them, than of discursive reasoning.[3]

[1] *Philosophical Investigations*, 216.
[2] On the traditional empiricist account of the emotions, see Kenny, op. cit. especially Ch. I and II.
[3] *The Problem of Style*, p. 26.

Again:

> The great writer does not really come to conclusions about life; he discerns a quality in it. His emotions, reinforcing one another gradually form in him a habit of emotion; certain kinds of objects and incidents impress him with a peculiar weight and significance. This emotional bias or predisposition is what I have ventured to call the writer's 'mode of experience'; it is by virtue of this mysterious accumulation of past emotions that the writer, in his maturity, is able to accomplish the miracle of giving to the particular the weight and force of the universal.[1]

This account of creative writing certainly seems to remove it from the realm of the rational. It is not allowed that the creative writer may see something which the scientist, for example, does not see (after all the writer has access to no more 'facts' than are available to the scientist). Rather the writer adds an emotion to facts which are common to them both. This is the familiar picture of various emotions being conjoined with neutral facts, the emotions being looked upon as strange inner events or processes which mysteriously 'accumulate'. There is no logical connection between any particular emotion and any particular form of expression – grief could be expressed by hearty laughter – and no logical reason why the same emotion should not find two entirely different forms of expression. The result is a sharp separation of form and content. This all comes from trying to apply what Wittgenstein calls the 'object-designation' model of language to talk about the emotions, or, as Bedford says, from treating emotion words as *names*.[2] This points to the generality of the mistake, which is, as I suggested in Chapter I, to treat naming as the pre-condition of language. If language is simply attached in some neutral way to things (and it is in that way that I have been using 'naming' – naming is supposed to represent *the* relation, the general form of the relation, between word and thing) then there is no reason why two different forms of language should not present, or represent, or 'locate' the same thing. A similarly sharp separation of form and content can arise when we ask whether two different ways of putting something 'say the same thing' – "Does *Oedipus Coloneus* say the same thing as *The Tempest?*" – as when we ask whether they 'express the same feelings'.

One way of trying to deal with the form/content problem is (as the foregoing suggests) to connect it with the problem of identity

---

[1] Op. cit., p. 27.   [2] See pp. 12–13, 27–8.

statements. Examples of identity statements are "The man in the corner is the Professor of Philosophy", "The Morning Star is the Evening Star", "That Carthage, Sir, is Tunis", "A thing is identical with itself" (Wittgenstein's prize case of a useless proposition). Each part of the sentence, we might say, refers to the same entity: 'the man in the corner' and 'the Professor of Philosophy' are being used to refer to the same man. Now in terms of the model of language which – as we saw in Chapter I – Wittgenstein rejects in the *Philosophical Investigations*, it seems easy and natural to make such statements where they cannot be made – as easy and natural as to say that 'the broom-stick and the brush which is fitted on to it' always and in any circumstances designates the same object as 'the broom'. For instance, on the picture theory of language 'The cat is on the mat' and 'The mat is under the cat' would be two different expressions, or projections, or locations of the 'same' fact – a fact that could be neutrally represented by a photograph, or by a perfect photographic or iconic language which simply represented things as in themselves they really are. But along with the rejection of this model of language goes a loss of the ease with which we can say that these different phrases refer to the same objects, or that different poems say the same thing or express the same feelings.

Let us take the example of 'The Morning Star is the Evening Star'. Suppose that there is a tribe who invest the Evening Star with all sorts of divine qualities and magical properties, none of which they attribute to the Morning Star. They perhaps pay no attention to, and even have no name for the Morning Star. Can we say that they are unaware of the fact that the Morning Star and the Evening Star are the same thing, that the Morning Star *is* the Evening Star? Suppose someone tries to prove to them that they are the same thing by plotting the course of the star during the hours of daylight and showing that the mass which causes the light they see had moved in a continuous path from the position occupied by the Morning Star to that occupied by the Evening Star. Would this prove the identity? Surely the tribe might reject this on the grounds that what *they* mean by the Evening Star is "the star which presides over our destiny, makes our crops grow, vanquishes our enemies" etc. – none of which functions do they attribute to the Morning Star. The man who is trying to convince them that they are the same might well describe the Evening Star quite differently – in terms, for instance, of astrophysics. Now it is tempting to say that the astrophysicist and the primitive tribe have different concepts of what a star is, and hence what the Evening Star is. They each mean something different by 'Evening Star' and are both right according to their own usage.[1] But this is both too simple and too drastic a solution; it is not clear that they have different concepts just because they are prepared to offer very different descriptions. It is clear that the Evening Star *qua* possessor of magical powers and so on is not the same as the Morning Star, but *qua* large celestial mass (that is, in modern astronomical terms) it *is* the same thing.

Should the tribe give up their old description and adopt the new one? Let us take the comparable example of the relation between the ordinary, solid, coloured, immobile table and the 'scientific' table consisting of particles in motion separated from each other by vast spaces – 'not solid at all' – and so on. In what sense is the physicist's table the same as the plain man's table? Do the different descriptions refer to the same thing? Could we produce an identity statement of the form 'The plain man's table is the scientific table', or, to give the more interesting version, 'Tables are particles in motion' (elaborating the scientific description as much as is necessary)? To answer this we should, perhaps, stop asking whether the descriptions 'refer to the same thing' and try to decide instead whether we could *replace* one description by the other. We can recall Austin's remark which I have already quoted:[2] "The total speech act in the total speech situation is the only actual phenomenon which, in the last resort, we are engaged in elucidating." We can only discover what 'object' the descriptions refer to by seeing how the descriptions are used: questions about the 'object' are a, perhaps misleading, way of investigating that. Now if the descriptions are being used to the same purpose, have the same function, one can without logical impropriety – although possibly falsely – suppose that one description could be replaced by the other. But when we examine the case of the 'two' tables we find that there is very little opportunity for replacement or translation. The scientific description serves, among other things, to relate the table, in a particular way, to other phenomena, and to bring it under certain general

[1] This is the sort of thing N. Malcolm says in *Dreaming*. Fodor and Chiara discuss his mistake (*American Philosophical Quarterly*, October 1965) and attribute it, astonishingly, to Wittgenstein. It would be truer to say that the tribe have a 'different but related' concept.

[2] See p. 39.

laws. It would not be primarily interested in distinguishing tables from chairs and pictures. If we stop asking what the scientific description refers to – if, in other words, we stop trying to distinguish different 'language-games' by reference to different objects[1] – then the only 'actual phenomenon' which we are trying to elucidate is the way in which the scientific description fits into a whole type of discourse. The ordinary 'plain man's' description fits into a different sort of discourse, has a different purpose and a different function. The nature of each description is determined by the type of language into which each fits. In the case of the two tables we have clearly such a great difference of function that it is impossible to replace one description by the other.

It is not that the identity statement is false in these cases so much as that it is difficult to give any sense to it. To take another example, if sensations are the 'same' as brain-processes ('Sensations are nothing but brain-processes') we can perfectly well ask 'The same *what?*' What force is 'same' supposed to have? If the identity statement means that descriptions in terms of sensations can be replaced by descriptions in terms of brain-processes, then it is false, for the test whether one description can be replaced by another is whether they both have the same point, the same function. If it means that sensation statements *ought* to be replaced by talk of brain-processes, then it amounts to the suggestion that we should all become scientists and talk all the time in scientific language – a suggestion we are likely to ignore. But of course what it really means is that they refer to the same 'thing', although there is no way of saying what this thing is – the old fallacy of invoking an alleged difference of object. The neutral monists, indeed, went so far as to suggest an entity which is under one aspect mental and under another, material.[2]

The question 'The same *what?*' might itself seem to fall into this fallacy. To show why it does not do so I shall draw again on Miss Anscombe's extremely interesting and important article 'The Intentionality of Sensation: A Grammatical Feature'. According to Miss Anscombe an 'intentional' object "is given by a word or phrase which gives a *description under which*".[3] For example, if a man aims at a dark

[1] See Chapter I.
[2] See for instance W. T. Stace, 'Russell's Neutral Monism', *The Philosophy of Bertrand Russell*, ed. Schilpp.
[3] Op. cit., p. 166 (her italics).

patch against the foliage, thinking it to be a stag, when it is actually his father's hat with his father's head in it, then his father is the 'material-object' of his aiming, but not the intentional object.[1] (We see here, incidentally, why Miss Anscombe spells 'intentional' with a t rather than an s – the description of the intentional object of an action describes the action you intended, not any one which may come about.) I think this is connected with Wittgenstein's treatment of the 'duck/rabbit'. When we see this drawing as a duck, the duck is (as I suggested earlier)[2] the intensional object of our seeing; we are able to see it as a duck by fitting it in some sense into an appropriate context – by comparing it, for instance, with unambiguous drawings of ducks. This would also be a way of *justifying* seeing it as a duck – akin to the way in which we would justify seeing *King Lear* as tragic. Now the description under which we view *King Lear* or the 'duck/rabbit' gives us the intensional object. It is not, as Miss Anscombe's article shows, only emotions which take intensional objects; intensionality is of as wide a scope as Wittgenstein's treatment of 'seeing as', and is, indeed, intimately connected with that.

Analogously, then, to say that we can replace the ordinary description of the table with the scientific one is indeed to say that two different objects are the 'same' object; but the object which is 'given' in each case is an intensional object. It then becomes clearer that in saying that the ordinary table is identical with (or reducible to) the scientific one, or that sensations are the same thing as brain-processes, we say that one type of description can be replaced by another, which involves our saying that each description has the same purpose and function and fits into the same sort of discourse as the other. But in several of the cases I have mentioned this would be false. The intensional object, unlike the material-object, is part of the 'total speech situation', part, that is, of the phenomenon which Austin considers himself to be engaged in elucidating.

Let us, at this point, return to the form/content problem, since that was what the discussion of identity statements, and thence intensionality, was meant to illuminate. Murry's incapacity to achieve the sort of connection which his instincts tell him should exist between the expression and the way of seeing or feeling expressed, arises from a confusion of material and intentional objects. Kenny shows how deeply ingrained in the empiricist tradition is this confusion in the

---

[1] Op. cit., p. 167.   [2] See p. 70.

case of theories of the emotions, and Miss Anscombe extends the application to epistemology. Now the emotion expressed by a particular poem is the *intensional* object which the poem as a whole (and as part of a whole literary context) 'gives'. In this sense the 'content' is given by the 'form', and it is in *that* sense that content and form are inseparable. The same applies to a way of 'seeing' which a poem expresses. We cannot talk of the way of feeling or seeing apart from the expression of it, because intensional objects are given by the mode of language in which they are expressed. To suppose that 'content' is not in this way bound up with 'form' is to suppose that it is a *material* object. In other words, to say that one poem expresses the same feelings or says the same thing as another is to say that, without loss or gain, one can replace the other. This is a tame conclusion, but it takes some of the mystery out of the problem of form and content. We have to decide not the general problem of whether any poem can ever express the same feeling as any other, but the question in particular cases of whether this poem can be regarded as a suitable translation of that one. For in adopting what Wittgenstein calls the 'language-game' and what Austin calls the 'speech-act' as the proper object of investigation, rather than some entity to which all propositions must refer (the *Tractatus* 'simples'), we must not therefore decide that every usage of language is so different from every other that no translation is ever possible. We can still distinguish between difference of nuance and difference of meaning. But when we do apply this solution of the problem to literature we soon see that the formalists are more nearly right than their opponents. *Oedipus Coloneus* and *The Tempest*, for instance, have their place in such immensely different contexts that it would be absurd to say that one expresses the same feelings or says the same thing as the other – as absurd as to say that sensations are identical with brain-processes. And this will surely be the case for most poems and plays because of their complexity both internal and in relation to the cultures from which they spring.[1] After all, even such simple sentences as 'The mat is under the cat' and 'Bring me the broomstick and the brush which is attached to it' are rarely likely – and then in rather unusual circumstances – to mean the same as (and hence be

---

[1] This brings out also the sense in which 'language-games' *are* distinguished one from another by different objects. The object is what is 'given' by each form of language. We cannot appeal to the object to explain the different forms since it can itself only be mentioned in terms of them.

replaced by) 'The cat is on the mat' and 'Bring me the broom'. How much more unlikely is it that we could successfully translate Euripides into Swinburnian verse (as Gilbert Murray did – thereby interposing, as Eliot puts it, between Euripides and ourselves "a barrier more impenetrable than the Greek language"), or sense-datum statements into material-object statements, or sensation statements into brain-process statements, or mythological statements about the Evening Star into astronomical remarks about the planet Venus.

The other conclusion that emerges is that, in talking about style it is necessary to be sure whether one is doing philosophy or criticism. If one is doing philosophy one should avoid trying to give, as Murry does, an account of the 'essence' of style. One can no more do this than one can give the 'essence' of propositions (the 'general form' of propositions). One *can* set out in some detail the relations between different 'language-games' (one can elucidate the various types of 'speech-act', to use the Austinian phrase). One cannot appeal to 'feelings' as a means of by-passing this enquiry ('long long ago' feelings, feelings of intention and so on) any more than one can look to different material or metaphysical or mental entities to correspond to the different forms of discourse. But equally, if one is doing criticism, one has to set out in some detail the relation between different plays and poems, or, if a more general approach is preferred, one can write a text-book on Rhetoric, listing 'styles' and cataloguing them. (Philosophers influenced by Wittgenstein and Austin have investigated the various ways in which language is used almost in the spirit of grammarians; but the cataloguing of 'styles' is quite out of fashion among critics – Kenneth Burke being a notable exception.)

Another important conclusion is that Murry's tendency to remove emotions from the realm of rationality is clearly mistaken. He says: ". . . to communicate an emotion means, in fact, to impose an emotion. To do this, I have to find some symbol which will evoke . . . an emotional reaction as nearly as possible identical with the emotion I am feeling."[1] Elsewhere[2] he suggests that the image the writer chooses to objectify his emotion ". . . would exercise a kind of compulsion upon the mind of the reader, so that given an ordinary sensibility, he must share the emotion or the experience that the writer intended him to share." The foregoing discussion has, I hope, shown that there is no

---

[1] *The Problem of Style*, p. 75. See also Note A, p. 118.
[2] Op. cit., p. 96.

such gap as Murry suggests between our understanding the images, style and so on of the writer and our understanding the emotion which he 'intends' to convey. We have seen how the emotion which the author intends is bound up with the language he uses; the quality of his intention is revealed when – as Croce says[1] – he crosses the *pons asinorum* of expression. It would be *prima facie* odd to describe *King Lear* in the conventional way and then to call it a comedy. Its being tragic does not depend upon the majority of the audience having 'an ordinary sensibility' (whatever that might be). An unconventional judgement requires an unconventional description. To take another example: it would be odd for someone to describe at length, and in a conventional way, the training given to doctors and then to say 'Doctors ought to kill people' or 'The purpose of this training is to teach doctors to kill people'.[2] In fact anyone wishing to uphold this position would certainly describe the training differently. He might say: 'Doctors are taught to wake people up too early in the morning in hospitals, obviously with the intention of lowering morale, and, hence, resistance to disease'. Such a description might be satirical, or paranoid, or even – which no one had realized before – true.

Argument about the appropriateness of emotions is bound up with argument about the appropriateness of descriptions. Expressions of attitude, expressions of emotion all have a logic. In a celebrated article[3] Rudolph Carnap asserts that metaphysics is really always the expression of an emotional attitude, and that metaphysical arguments are, therefore, not really arguments:

> The (pseudo) statements of metaphysics do not serve for the *description of states of affairs*, neither existing ones (in that case they would be true statements) nor non-existing ones (in that case they would be at least false statements). They serve for the *expression of the general attitude of a person towards life*.
> ... But the metaphysician supports his statements by arguments, he claims assent to their content, he polemicizes against metaphysicians of divergent persuasion by attempting to refute their assertions in his treatise. Lyrical poets on the other hand do not try to refute in their poem the statement in a poem by some other lyrical poet; for they know

---

[1] *Aesthetic*, p. 18.
[2] This was an illustration used by Miss Anscombe in a paper to the Cambridge 'Theoretical Amoralists'. I may well not be using it to a similar purpose.
[3] Carnap, 'The Elimination of Metaphysics', *Logical Positivism*, ed. Ayer.

I

they are in the domain of art and not in the domain of theory. (Op. cit., pp. 79–80.)

Now even if Carnap were right about the nature of Metaphysics, it would not follow that argument would have to be abandoned. Lyrical poets, according to Carnap, do not criticize the emotions expressed by other lyrical poets. It is true that parody – which is an important form of criticism – is generally out of place in lyrical verse, but when Eliot, for instance, takes Sappho's lines about the coming of evening and uses them as the opening of a passage describing a squalid seduction ("At the violet hour") then he has produced an ironic commentary on the availability for the present age of a certain sort of Romantic poignancy. And we can certainly say that a central aim of 'practical criticism' has been the assessment and criticism of the quality of emotion expressed by poets.

Murry's *The Problem of Style* is, then, something of a *locus classicus*. It brings to the surface and attempts to resolve the central paradoxes of romantic expressionism, and at the same time shows how deeply embedded in romantic expressionism are certain philosophical assumptions which have to be discarded. This, in itself, is no mean achievement.

NOTE TO CHAPTER V

A] Mary Warnock does not avoid this confusion in an article called 'The Justification of Emotions'. She says (p. 54) that in order to *justify* an emotion we often describe the object that arouses it. This is also to *name* 'nameless' emotions.

> By doing this we may hope to show that it was understandable to be moved, and we may even, if we are good at describing, get our audience actually to experience what the feeling was.

If we cannot win sympathy by such a description, there is no more to be done:

> I am enjoying an emotion but I cannot hope to share it, and my defense, such as it was, was more of an attempt to get someone else to feel what I felt than a reasoned justification.
>
> *Supp. Proc. Arist. Soc.*, 1957.

Mrs Warnock is producing a theory which is very close to Eliot's theory of the 'objective correlative', and which suffers from comparable weaknesses. In the first place, it is mistaken to suggest that we describe the object which arouses our emotion in order to "get our audience actually to experience something of the same emotion . . ." We can justify our emotion to someone without his having, in any sense, to 'experience' it. Secondly, even if our audience *did* experience the emotion, *this* would not necessarily show that it was appropriate or justifiable. (*King Lear* is not tragic merely because 'I feel sad when I see it'.) Our description may be – as Mrs Warnock says – 'as far as we can go', but since we are not primarily aiming at getting our audience to 'experience' anything it is quite far enough.

CHAPTER VI

Reason Defended: Yvor Winters and the Nature of Criticism

Yvor Winters – in whom an erratic boldness of critical judgement is strikingly combined with an unembarrassed eagerness to lay bare the theoretical foundations of his work – is a critic to whom it is both tempting and easy to be unfair. Yet this temptation must be resisted, both because Winters is, as a critic, undeniably impressive, and because his *a priori* conception of criticism is interesting in its own right. We can, broadly (and crudely) speaking, elicit from Winters's critical writings two 'theses'. The first is most succinctly expressed in the essay on James, called 'Maule's Well':

> For practical purposes, the New England moral sense was merely an intensification of that of New York; like that of New York it derived ultimately from the pre-American Catholic discipline but unlike that of New York, or at least of English New York, it had experienced a Calvinistic interlude, which intensified it, notwithstanding the fact that such an interlude, rationally considered, ultimately did destroy it, but long afterward, by severing its connection with the one and only source of its nourishment, the Aristotelian ethical tradition, as embodied in the Catholic Church.[1]

This idea of the severance of things which, if they are to make sense – if they are to be 'rational' – should be intimately connected, is central to Winters's thought. Morality is separated from the only tradition which can provide it with discipline and objectivity; emotions have been cut adrift from concepts; ethical choice (in James at any rate) has been detached from manners. These various forms of dissociation produce, or amount to, irrationality, hallucination,[2] and even insanity.[3] Winters intends this historical thesis to have vast explanatory power. It is invoked to explain, for instance, the "margin of obscurity"[4] which Winters finds in nearly all of James's novels.

[1] Yvor Winters, *Defense of Reason*, London 1960, p. 305.
[2] Op. cit., p. 327.   [3] Op. cit., p. 317.   [4] Op. cit., p. 317.

James, we are told, inherits from Hawthorne the New England tendency to allegory[1] and converts this into an extraordinarily fine sense for moral discrimination. But this sense has lost contact with the only sorts of context in which it can fruitfully operate; it has no firm grasp upon either the realities, the pressures, in society which give moral choices meaning, or upon the coherent *Weltanschauung* which gave sense to the Puritan tendency to read enormous significance into the minutiae of everyday experience. James is left with his moral sense operating, as it were, in a void – like some vast mammoth retaining its elaborately protective coat long after the ice age has passed. James's power of suggestion is in excess of his power of understanding – or in excess of his capacity to provide an 'objective correlative' to the mental and emotional states he contrives to create. Winters considers, for instance, that Fleda Vetch's renunciation in *The Spoils of Poynton* is ultimately inexplicable and unmotivated.[2] The decision by Newland Archer and Countess Olenska not to elope in Edith Wharton's *The Age of Innocence* is, by contrast, not at all obscure. The complex values of New York society are so convincingly present that we see how the life they would be forced to live would be, by contrast, squalid and degrading.[3] Similarly, the terror which Isabel Archer and Pansy feel towards Osmond in *Portrait of a Lady* cannot fully be accounted for by what we are *shown* of his character.[4] We can, perhaps, gloss Winters slightly and say that whereas it is perfectly possible for a New England farmer – say, at the time of the Salem Witch Trials – to see the work of the devil in some apparently trivial occurrence (like the disposition of sticks in a plough furrow), it is not equally possible for James to see fathomless evil behind what is, on all accounts – including the only account which James himself can actually give – a perfectly innocent action. Indeed, Winters seems to be suggesting, the sort of evil at which James characteristically hints is really best ascribable to the devil. That is, we are more or less to take *The Turn of the Screw* – minor though it may be – as the paradigm Jamesian novel. The evil there is separated "from all determining or qualifying elements";[5] it exists as a thing in its own right – lurid, obscene, but ultimately mysterious. James can only hint at, suggest the nature of the corruption which, in its various forms, plays so large a part in his novels. He "gives us a sequence of facts without being able to pass judgement on

---

[1] Op. cit., p. 316.   [2] Op. cit., pp. 318–19.   [3] Op. cit., pp. 309–10.
[4] Op. cit., pp. 331–2.   [5] Op. cit., p. 342.

them . . ."[1] Conversely (to take an example which Winters does not use) the goodness ascribed to Milly Theale in *The Wings of the Dove* is vastly in excess of what is actually presented.

Whatever we may think of this analysis, it is obvious that the *historical* part of Winters's thesis has great explanatory power, is of enormous scope and generality. It is intended to explain the main lines of development of American literature, and at the same time to provide a standard by which to judge particular works, the latter being for Winters the end to which the former is the means.

We can pass to what I shall call Winters's second 'thesis' by way of further consideration of these examples. We may prefer to say of *The Spoils of Poynton* that Fleda Vetch's motives for her renunciation are too private to James, that they are the product of a personal obsession. James is unable to bring into the light the rationale of her behaviour – like Eliot's Hamlet. Similarly, we could say that James has deliberately failed to 'present' Milly Theale fully in order that some rather personal, private feelings which he wishes to indulge in towards her may be freed of all qualifying elements; and, according to Cleanth Brooks's definition of sentimentality,[2] this is to indulge a sentimental and unreal attitude. Now this idea of a disparity between an emotional state and the situation with which it is ostensibly connected, is central to Winters's second, *analytical* 'thesis'. Winters sets it forth as follows:

> The theory of literature which I defend in these essays is absolutist. I believe that the work of literature, in so far as it is valuable, approximates a real apprehension and communication of a particular kind of objective truth. . . . The poem is a statement in words about a human experience. Words are primarily conceptual, but through use, and because human experience is not purely conceptual, they have acquired connotations of feeling. The poet makes his statement in such a way as to employ *both concept and connotation as efficiently as possible. The poem is good in so far as it makes a defensible, rational statement about a given human experience . . . and at the same time communicates the emotion which ought to be motivated by that rational understanding of that experience.*[3] [My italics.]

It may, at first, appear that Winters's analysis of the relation between concept and emotion is similar to that which is sketched in the

[1] Op. cit., p. 246.
[2] Cleanth Brooks, *Modern Poetry and the Tradition*, p. 46.
[3] *Defense of Reason*, Foreword, p. 11.

first two chapters. The similarity will, however, soon be seen to be apparent rather than real.

I have suggested that Winters's historical analysis aims at establishing a standard of value; this is also true of his theory of language. For Winters – as for Osborne – the goodness or badness of a poem is to be deduced, more or less directly, from a general definition. What exactly this definition is, is not as clear as it may at first appear to be. It seems, however, that the goodness of a poem follows from the definition of poetry; a good poem is whatever is fully a poem. Now language can be used (according to Winters) first, to express concepts, and secondly, to evoke emotion. Poetry combines both functions to the highest level of efficiency; therefore we can say that poetry (and hence *good* poetry) is merely language being most fully itself. We can, then, move by sheer deduction from a definition of language to a definition of poetry, and thence to a criterion of value. When Mr Winters calls his theory 'absolutist' he seems to mean that it is rigorously deducible from unquestionable first principles.

The definition we have been offered certainly suggests a strikingly fearless readiness on Winters's part to do what is so often demanded of critics – 'state his criteria'. Yet such ostensible boldness also makes us suspicious, for we have become used to being confronted with definitions of great sweep and apparent vulnerability, only to find, upon examination, that little or no evidence which could be brought forward could possibly count against them. It would, after all, be *prima facie* surprising – not to say staggering – if a critic, even a critic of Mr Winters's philosophical interests, were to be able to offer, with scarcely any preliminaries, a theory which should be at once all-inclusive, informative and correct. So we prepare, almost instinctively, to reduce Mr Winters's theory to a 'linguistic recommendation' or to a schema or a tautology.

We do, of course, apart from such an instinct, feel straight away that there is a difference between the definition we have been offered and one which would run, say: "A poem is good in so far as it deals with the coming proletarian revolution". This would be either a highly idiosyncratic (and unacceptable) recommendation ('From now on only value highly poems which . . .' etc.), or, if it is not to be taken as a recommendation, but as a critical remark, clearly false. The difference between this assertion and Winters's is not just that the former is fairly obviously wrong-headed, but that when confronted with it we are likely to find ourselves thinking of exceptions, of contrary instances. We know how to set about showing that as a definition it is inappropriate, and as a critical assertion, false. But when presented with phrases like '. . . defensible rational statement about . . . human experience' and an emotion which 'ought to be motivated by that understanding of experience', we scarcely know where to begin objecting even if we wish. For what could we produce as a counter-instance? And would our counter-example motivate an emotion which ought *not* to be motivated? It would, of course, be impossible to produce a poem which contradicted Winters's criteria, and yet which still used *language* (as language has been defined). Much will depend upon how we are using phrases like 'defensible rational statement'. We could, after all, so interpret the phrase as to rule out the greater part of the poetry which we normally value. We might, for instance, deny that poems containing accounts of events which, historically, did not take place, can be 'defensible' or even 'rational'. One of Plato's objections against poets was that they "tell lies about the gods". In this case we should have to examine Winters's actual critical practice in order to find out what these terms mean.

First, however, we should prepare ourselves for the characteristic manœuvre practised by those who offer definitions of such generality as Winters's and then attempt to draw particular conclusions in accord with them. In Winters's case the move would be as follows: His definition – 'defensible rational statement' – is initially acceptable because it emphasizes a continuity – a continuity between, say, (1) *O, my Luve's like a red, red rose* and (2) *The earth is many years old.* Here the contrast implied is between such utterances and, say, (3) cries like 'Oh! Oh!'[1] In emphasizing the continuity between the first two utterances, and their difference from the third, Winters is not saying anything which is straightforwardly true or false; that is, there *is* this continuity and difference, and Winters may draw attention to it if he thinks it valuable to do so. But there is also a difference between the first and the second expression, and a similarity to which Carnap (and other logical positivists) have drawn attention – between the first and the third. We can complete the picture by pointing out a continuity between the second and the third (as an extreme expressionist might do). When all the continuities have been pointed out we may still wish to go on marking the original differences – in which case we will go

[1] Which Carnap, we remember, assimilates 'on a higher level' to lyrical verses.

on using language in the same way as before. Winters, anyway, begins by emphasizing an undoubted continuity and distinction.

The second part of the manœuvre consists in arriving at a series of particular judgements in accord with a sense of continuities and distinctions quite different from the original one – but without this shift being avowed. That is, having stressed the continuities between poetic and scientific utterances, and concluded that, because of the similarities, both are 'rational' – as opposed, say, to cries of pain – you now point to a new discontinuity between, perhaps, lyrical and didactic verse, assimilating the didactic verse to the scientific type of rationality and denying the name of 'rational' to lyrical verse. So you are showing that poetry 'must' be 'rational' by exhibiting one set of continuities, and then that only some poetry *is* rational by exhibiting another set. Or, to put it another way, you show that all poetry *must* be rational by so using 'rational' to stress the similarities; and you then show that only certain poetry *is* rational by so using 'rational' as to stress the differences. That is, you are having the best of two, contradictory, worlds.

If Winters is perpetrating this manœuvre, then his original distinction feels compelling because we understand it in the first sense; and his particular judgements seem compelling because they appear to proceed from it – only it is now being understood in the second sense. Both senses stress undoubted continuities and differences – which accounts for our feeling puzzled how to object, since we can find fault with neither. But used in conjunction they are contradictory, for they stress different continuities and different differences.

Assuming that Winters is making this move – and there is little doubt that he is – then we may wish to say to him: 'Yes, poetry *is* rational and defensible – but not in the way that science is; if you wish to assert the rational nature of poetry by denying science to be the paradigm of the rational, you cannot then proceed to slip the scientific paradigm in again in order to deny rationality to, say, Pound's *Cantos*.' There is a sense in which there is – compared with the *Divine Comedy* – no rational progression in the *Cantos*; and another sense in which – compared, say, with the babble of a child or the phantasies of a lunatic – there obviously *is*.

Winters certainly means something definite by 'rational and defensible statement about human experience', but this cannot somehow emerge as a criterion of value by means of the definition. Its meaning and validity can only be established by particular judgements. Or rather, particular judgements will bring out more fully the continuities to which he seeks to draw attention.

The status of Winters's definition is further brought out by comparison with some alternative formulation, such as: 'Poetry is incantation', or Eliot's view of poetry as offering 'the emotional equivalent of thought'. Formulations such as these insist on the *difference* between 'The earth is many years old' and 'O, my Luve's like a red, red rose'. They are also liable to be stressing the difference between 'O, my Luve's like a red, red rose' and

> 'A milk-white hind, immortal and unchanged
> Fed on the lawns, and in the forests ranged'

– a difference insisted on by Arnold.

Are we to ask which of these two formulations is 'correct'? The answer would be that neither is correct and neither is an entirely acceptable recommendation. But both may be useful: it is not merely that they are more interesting through being 'paradoxical' (that way of talking, though justifiable, perhaps sounds too facile) but, by exhibiting opposite ends of the spectrum, they relate poetry to other forms of expression, and so help to show what it itself *is*.

In *The Function of Criticism*[1] Winters *defines* a poem as "a statement in words . . . about a human experience". In the Foreword to *In Defence of Reason* he says, as we have seen, that a poem is good in so far as it makes a "defensible rational statement about a given human experience". The poem has, in some sense, to be *true*. Later[2] he says: ". . . truth is not poetry; poetry is truth and something more. It is the completeness of the poetic experience which makes it valuable." Here again, as against Poe, Winters is stressing a sense in which 'truth' is indeed a criterion in the judgement of poetry. But it also has to be pointed out that, say, historical or scientific truth is not always required. Winters is again presenting a general schema, and then giving it a special, limited sense – and hence giving a new schema which does not proceed from the old one, but has to be justified on its own merits. As with 'defensible, rational statement' the procedure is quite clear.

---

[1] pp. 81 and 103.
[2] *Defense of Reason*, p. 241. From 'Edgar Allan Poe, a Crisis in the History of American Obscurantism'.

We may set it out as follows:

In assessing 'Poetry is truth', either

(*a*) You exclude from 'poetry' verses of type X on the grounds of their not being truthful. If this exclusion departs from established usage, it is a recommendation which may be argued for or against; or

(*b*) By 'truth' you mean something so vacuous that nothing is excluded.

Both *a* and *b* can be argued for and against on the grounds of helpfulness, appropriateness and so on (as, for instance, can the question 'Is Sociology a Science?').

(*a*) and (*b*) are obviously distinct and, indeed, contrary methods. (*a*) delimits the concept of truth arbitrarily; (*b*) empties it of content.

To return to the original definition of value:

> . . . a poem is good in so far as it makes a defensible, rational statement about a given human experience . . . and at the same time communicates the emotion which ought to be motivated by that rational understanding of that experience.

This definition will hardly do. For instance it does not exclude the nursery rhyme 'Jack and Jill', which undoubtedly makes a statement about human experience, is perfectly rational, and in some sense defensible – and yet entirely trivial.

Perhaps some later definitions help matters: ". . . poetry is truth and something more. It is the completeness of the poetic experience which makes it valuable."[1] Later Winters suggests that what distinguishes better poems from worse is the perfect arrangement in the former whereby denotation is efficiently supported by connotation. He quotes two lines from Browning's *Serenade at the Villa*:

> So wore the night; the East was gray,
> White the broad-faced hemlock flowers;

and comments:

> . . . I wish to point out . . . the relationship between the words 'wore' and 'gray'. The verb 'wore' means literally that night passed, but it carries with it connotations of exhaustion and attrition which belong to the condition of the protagonist; and grayness is a colour which we associate with such a condition. If we change the phrase to read 'Thus night passed', we shall have the same rational meaning, and a meter quite

[1] *Defense of Reason*, p. 241.

as respectable, but no trace of the power of the line: the connotation of 'wore' will be lost, and the connotation of 'gray' will remain merely in a state of ineffective potentiality.[1]

This is an important passage and is connected with that part of the original definition which mentions 'the emotion which ought to be motivated by the rational understanding of that experience'. Now in the case of so trivial a piece of verse as 'Jack and Jill' what 'emotion' *should* be communicated by the presented situation? Pity? Fear? Contempt? How could we decide? Winters replies:

> The poem is a statement in words about a human experience. Words are primarily conceptual, but through use, and because human experience is not purely conceptual, they have acquired connotations of feeling. The poet makes his statement in such a way as to employ both concept and connotation as efficiently as possible.[2]

Here Winters seems to be offering not only a short and easy way of distinguishing poetry from other forms of expression, but a formula for telling a good poem from a bad one. A poem communicates *emotions* as well as concepts, and a good poem efficiently welds a sufficient charge of emotion to its appropriate concept. The poem presents a situation and evokes the emotions appropriate. Philosophy presents concepts to which no emotions are appropriate, and hence evokes none.

But what *is* the situation presented in, say, the nursery rhyme? The model suggested by Winters's definitions is of some hard 'conceptual' centre to which some sort of emotional response is to be conjoined. This model hides from Winters the force of the question 'What *is* the situation?' He seems to think of the 'situation' as something neutral, purely 'descriptive' – 'This is how things are': that is how he uses the word 'conceptual'. In life there are situations and the behavioural responses they demand; in language there are concepts and the emotive associations they have collected. It is odd that Winters should present such a theory 'in defense of Reason'. Surely we do not decide whether the situation is fearful or pitiable by paying attention to the connotations which the words describing it have (accidentally?) gathered.

Rather we decide what the situation *is*. When in *The Sea-Gull*

[1] From 'The Anatomy of Nonsense', *Defense of Reason*, pp. 365–7.
[2] Op. cit., pp. 365–6.

Konstantin calls for the curtain to be drawn, and later when he uses to Arkadina the words of Hamlet to Gertrude, a context is suddenly established which turns the situation (for the moment) from one of comedy to one of tragic betrayal. Within a few moments we are presented with a *different* situation; or we see the situation 'under a new aspect'.[1] This change has nothing to do with the emotional associations of the words used. In fact the only words are 'Draw the curtain! Draw the curtain!' Nor is it a matter of how the audience feels. It is the situation on the stage, rather than the emotions in the spectators' breasts, which has changed. Certainly the audience will feel differently, but their emotions can only be described with reference to what has taken place on the stage.

In the case of the nursery rhyme we have no real grasp of any particular situation. This is not because of any excess of 'connotation' over 'denotation' or vice versa, but because the situation is only barely sketched.[2] A political or psycho-analytical account of the rhyme might give us something to go on by eliciting a hidden meaning, but in any event the nature of the situation is not determined by the emotional associations of the individual words in the rhyme.

Even if Winters's model were correct,[3] it would by no means follow that the emotion evoked 'ought to be motivated by that rational understanding of that experience'. If words are 'primarily conceptual' and only accidentally 'emotive', there can be no intrinsic connection between the conceptual and emotive aspects of words, and hence no emotional response which is intrinsically appropriate to any given situation or experience. What emotion *is* 'motivated' would be merely a matter of fact – perhaps a well-established causal law. An example of the latter would be '*King Lear* must be tragic because I always feel sad when I see it'.

Like the logical positivists Winters sets up a sharp dichotomy between *concept* and *feeling* and between the scientific and emotive uses of language. Like them he restricts the 'rational' to the scientific, to the concept. In his discussion of the Browning lines, we remember,

---

[1] Wittgenstein, *Philosophical Investigations*, II, xi, p. 206.

[2] It should be mentioned that Winters consistently misuses these technical terms. In Mill the 'denotation' is the referent, the thing mentioned, the 'connotation' the qualities ascribed to it. Winters's 'denotation' and 'connotation' are both strictly part of the 'connotation'.

[3] See Note A, p. 139.

he said: "If we change the lines to read: 'Thus night passed', we shall have the same rational meaning . . ." There is only an 'emotional' difference between 'passed' and 'wore'.[1]

Following Kenny I should like to characterize Winters's mistake as a confusion of 'material' and 'formal' objects. Kenny says:

> Anything which can be ϕd is a material object of ϕing. Beer, for example, can be seen, and so beer is a material object of seeing. . . . The formal object of ϕing is the object under that description which *must* apply to it if it is to be possible to ϕ it.[2]

We can form not only trivial examples of formal objects by modalizing verbs – e.g. only what is tangible can be touched – but we can find non-trivial examples: only what is difficult to obtain can be striven for.[3] To treat the relation between an emotion and its object as merely contingent, rather than as logical, is to treat formal objects as though they were material objects.[4] Kenny's analysis can be related to the discussion in the first chapter of the sort of impossibility there is in feeling pity for stones, or of *taking the attitude to* a corpse that it is in pain.[5] To say that we give *reasons* for finding *King Lear* sad – that we *justify* our response – is to say that the play is the *formal* object of our emotions. To regard the play as the *cause* of our emotions would be to treat it as a *material* object. To justify my finding *King Lear* funny I would (as I suggested earlier) have to describe it in an unorthodox way – or perhaps I would have to describe the world in an unorthodox way. It is in this sense that the relation between an emotion and its formal object is logical not contingent. When we say that a particular type of emotion 'ought' to be motivated by the play, the 'ought' is logical and not, say, moral.

Winters's insistence on the descriptive function of language is a classic case of regarding 'naming' as the basis of linguistic activity. (This is certainly how he uses 'denotation'.) This leads – as I suggested in Chapter I – to the attempt to distinguish different 'language-games' by reference to a private inner state. That is exactly the move Winters makes, and he explicitly connects it with his rigid distinction between 'paraphrasable content' (where language is being used to describe, or rather to name) and 'feeling'. He quotes a sonnet[6] – 'The Subway' –

---

[1] See Note B, p. 139.   [2] *Action, Emotion and Will*, p. 189.   [3] Ibid.
[4] Op. cit., p. 191.   [5] See p. 12.   [6] *In Defense of Reason*, p. 20.

by Allan Tate, and then comments on its 'attitude': "This attitude is defined only by the entire poem, not by the logical content alone; it is a matter not only of logical content but of feeling as well." Winters tries to 'indicate' what the feeling is: "It is a feeling of dignity and self-control in the face of a situation of major difficulty, a difficulty which the poet fully apprehends." Yet Winters goes on to say that the feeling is "particular and unparaphrasable". But if the feeling is 'of dignity', 'of self-control' and so on, what is the mysterious residue which cannot be described (or 'paraphrased')? Clearly it is the 'inner state' which the situation 'motivates'. The inner state has come to mean 'that which the emotion word designates'; and in that case – as Wittgenstein says – it 'drops out of consideration as irrelevant'.[1] If we describe emotions by their objects this is not in default of our being able to describe them 'in themselves'. A state in itself (as Eliot said) is nothing whatever. Here we have a case of the model of language as name/object leading to the idea that emotion words refer to ineffable inner states. It is clear that Winters's analysis of the place of emotion in literature, like Eliot's doctrine of the 'objective correlative', is bound up with the notion of a private language.

There is much significance in Winters's extraordinary remark that there is no 'rational' difference between 'passed' and 'wore' – only a difference of 'feeling'. But of course the two words have a different *meaning*.[2] That there is 'no rational difference' between 'passed' and 'wore' means that they can be substituted for one another in many contexts. Yet there are many other contexts – including the poem – in which they could not be interchanged; and this difference of use is a difference of meaning – one that goes a long way to explain the otherwise mysterious difference of 'feeling'. Similarly, if you describe the plot of *King Lear*, you are not giving the 'paraphrasable content' which then has to be filled out with emotion at a full reading or performance of the play. What is lacking is not a 'particular and unparaphrasable' feeling but a great deal of the detail, a great deal of the *content* of the play. Of course lines, even scenes, can be left out without seriously damaging the 'effect' of the play – but this does not mean that there is a certain minimal number of features which have to be retained in order that the mysterious fusion which 'motivates' the

---

[1] See p. 9.

[2] For a number of the examples in this chapter, as well as the general method, I am indebted to an unpublished paper by Renford Bambrough.

'*King Lear* emotions' can take place. We cannot describe these emotions without describing the play (emotion words are 'intensional'[1] in that they are essentially directed to objects);[2] it is logically impossible that they should be produced by a drug, or by *Macbeth*.

Winters, then, despite his intense desire (to which I have referred earlier) to avoid the severance of emotions from concepts – with the consequent 'irrationality' – has produced just such a severance, and in as extreme a form as Eliot's (whom he criticizes so severely).

Let us now return to the question of whether Winters has gone any way towards establishing a criterion of value. Here we can invoke the distinction between his 'historical' and 'analytical' theses. By means of his historical theory Winters goes a good way towards accounting for the 'margin of obscurity' which he finds in James. When we say that his theory has explanatory power we mean that it enables him to grasp large-scale patterns in American literature, to draw our attention in a peculiarly coherent way to sets of features, and to relationships which we might not otherwise have grasped. But does this add up to providing a standard from which value judgements can be deduced? It is here that we see most clearly the defects in Winters's idea of the nature of criticism. If it is true that "Mr Pound's *Cantos* are decadent in relation to *Paradise Lost*, since their structure is purely qualitative",[3] then is not something implied as to the value of the *Cantos*? Similarly, if it is true (and it is not a part of our argument to assert that it is or that it is not) that

> . . . T. S. Eliot abandoned Laforguian irony not to correct his feelings, but to remain satisfied with them: his career since has been largely a career of what one might call psychic impressionism, a formless curiosity concerning queer feelings which are related to odds and ends of more or less profound thought[4]

then have we not said something about Eliot's value as a poet? Winters, however, is not satisfied with this; unless a judgement of value is entailed by these descriptions, together with his definition of a poem, it would always be possible to come to a different conclusion – and that means that taste is not absolute but only relative. Such a conclusion

---

[1] Kenny's spelling.
[2] See Kenny, op. cit., Ch. ix.
[3] 'Primitivism and Decadence', *In Defense of Reason*, p. 92.
[4] *In Defense of Reason*, p. 10.

would be radically detrimental to the function, indeed to the possibility of criticism:

> The professor of English literature, who believes that taste is relative, yet who endeavours to convince his students that *Hamlet* is more worthy of their attention than some currently popular novel, is in a serious predicament, a predicament which is moral, intellectual, and in the narrowest sense professional, though he commonly has not the wit to realize the fact.[1]

Mr Winters, who *has* the wit, takes a drastic way out. Our descriptions of works of literature, conjoined with unquestionable principles of value, must produce unquestionable evaluative conclusions. The move is familiar enough, but Winters's version of it is unusual. He manages somehow to combine elements of both Hare and Mrs Foot. We shall try to examine how he arrives at this interesting position.

Winters enlarges on the definition of poetry we have already quoted as follows: ". . . a poem, in so far as it is good, represents the comprehension on a moral plane of a given experience."[2] Again:

> Poetry . . . should offer a means of enriching one's awareness of human experience and of so rendering greater the possibility of intelligence in the course of future action. . . . It should, in other words, increase the intelligence and strengthen the moral temper . . .[3]
> Poetry is a refined and enriched technique of moral comprehension.[4]

Winters would presumably claim to have arrived at this position by a strict deduction from his original premises. Poetry is language at its fullest stretch; language is both conceptual and emotional – as is human experience, which language expresses. So poetry must be about human experience. Now morality is merely human experience, conceptual and emotional, rationally understood (or 'judged'); but poetry, because of its essential conceptual content, is merely human experience rationally understood; therefore the qualities of poetry are *moral* qualities. It hardly requires the most penetrating logic to pick holes in this, but we shall not do so here. What is important for present purposes is that Winters, having identified poetry and morality, is in a position to advance his final grand criterion for making moral judgements:

If morality can be considered real, if a theory of morality can be said to

[1] Foreword, op. cit., p. 10.   [2] 'The Morality of Poetry', op. cit., p. 25.
[3] Op. cit., p. 29.   [4] 'Edgar Allan Poe', *Defense of Reason*, p. 243.

K

derive from reality, it is because it guides us towards the greatest happiness which the accidents of life permit: that is, toward the fullest realization of our nature, in the Aristotelian or Thomistic sense.[1]

We can arrive at an idea of our highest realization by considering clear examples of maladjustment, such as insanity or neurosis. This leads us to conceive of better adjustment, and, hence, perfect adjustment. Works of art are ultimately to be judged good in so far as they contribute, cognitively and emotionally, to the 'fullest realization of our nature'. Poetry "trains our power of judgement"[2] and, hence, indirectly affects our behaviour.[3]

In the *Nicomachean Ethics* Aristotle defines happiness as "an expression of the soul in considered actions",[4] that is, an activity in accordance with reason. Since Reason is the distinguishing and defining characteristic of man, it is the function[5] and perfection of man to be rational. For an Aristotelian, presumably, if one ascribes to a man the virtues of courage, liberality, magnificence, magnanimity, proper ambition, good temper, etc., then it makes no sense to assert that he is a *bad* man. A man with all the virtues is fully human, and a good man is whoever is fully human. The question 'Why be human?' can hardly arise. If one asserts that one's ideal of a man is someone who is mentally defective, lame, blind, and syphilitic, then one's ideal is not of a *man* but of something else. We can decide what man's 'function', his proper excellence *is* purely in virtue of our *concept* of a man; there is no gap between the fact or description and the value we attach to it. So if Winters can show that a particular poem does not contribute to the highest realization of man – is not, that is, fully 'rational' – then he has shown that it is a bad poem, or, rather, that it does not succeed in fully being a poem, and is, therefore, not a *good* one.

Clearly the Aristotelian account of goodness is akin to the analysis of the connection between fact and value which we find in Mrs Foot. Winters, however, also bears comparison with Hare in that he characteristically thinks of an argument as proceeding to the more general until it reaches a point where it can go no further. All of Winters's judgements are related, as it were, vertically to the standard of Reason.

---

[1] 'The Anatomy of Nonsense', op. cit., p. 370.
[2] Op. cit., p. 372.
[3] Ibid.
[4] Book I, Ch. 8.
[5] Op. cit., Book I, Ch. 7, p. 38.

To assert that a particular poem is 'irrational' is to say that it is bad. I have already tried to show that there are enormous ambiguities in phrases like 'defensible rational statement', and important fallacies in the theory of language – its division into 'conceptual' and 'emotional' – which is intended to explain them. Of course we could interpret Winters as saying that the idea we have of a poem's being valuable inevitably involves the idea of its being rational. This will certainly be true if we build the concept of rationality into the definition of poetry – as Winters tries to do, and still more so if we build it into our definition of *language*. In that case, however, our idea of what is rational will be determined by and constituted of what we think is good poetry, appropriate language and so on. We have still not arrived at an absolute and unquestioned standard from which all these judgements can be derived. Similarly, if we can have an idea of varying perfections – insanity less perfect than sanity and so on – and if our alleged knowledge of absolute perfection is based upon this apprehension of these relative ones, then we are not judging the relative by reference to the absolute. In *The Function of Criticism*, there is a passage relevant to this. Winters is discussing R. S. Crane – one of the 'Chicago Aristotelians' – who recommends detailed study of the different literary 'forms'. Winters insists that the literary forms should be 'arranged hierarchically':

> Yet ... [this] would be impossible unless we had a clear idea of what the final cause of literature should be, so that we could evaluate the different forms in relation to this cause; nor ... would we have, in fact, ... [any] ... basis for saying that a given work was an admirable example of its kind unless we could see the kind as a related division of the whole.[1]

Here again we have the idea that judgements of value are not possible unless they are ultimately to be deduced from 'norms' at the highest level of generality. Yet if we cannot apprehend the particular instances, how can we apprehend the more general formulation, which collects and draws attention to the particular instances?

What then is left of Winters's theory? Certainly we have, at any rate, a schema of considerable explanatory power. The concept of 'reason', in the concrete sense which Winters gives it, does enable us to organize our experience of literature, or at any rate, of a great deal of American literature, to a high level of coherence. It therefore helps

[1] 'The Function of Criticism', *Problems for the Modern Critic of Literature*, p. 20.

us to judge it. We have, then, a concept at least comparable with 'significant form'. The sorts of continuities upon which such schemata rely have also been sketched. Yet to talk of 'schemata' is to be too vague; we have still to decide what is the status of such a schema as is represented by the phrase 'defensible rational statement'. We must not obscure the fact that questions of truth and falsity still apply, and to re-emphasize this we should talk of Winters's *theory*. Now it is clear that we can only understand what Winters means by his general formulations by paying attention to his particular judgements. Yet we find that some of Winters's particular judgements – especially his admiration for writers such as Elizabeth Daryush and Adelaide Crapsey – are only explicable in terms of his general criteria understood in a special sense. How would we refute either his particular judgements or his general theory?

In the first place we would exhibit the ambiguities upon which the general statements rely; this would, in Winters's case, remove much of the force of the theory, and much of our feeling of puzzlement how to object. Secondly we would examine his particular judgements in the light of what we can unambiguously understand of the general theory. If we combine the two we undoubtedly have a theory of what makes literature good. It is also a theory of why certain literature is good. That is to say, we *can* elicit a general principle from our particular judgements, but this general principle is always open to correction by further particular judgements. Particular judgements are universalizable in the sense that two situations which are not significantly dissimilar must be given similar descriptions. Yet this is trivial – it is merely the principle of rationality itself. Particular judgements are not deduced from these general standards, and true in virtue of their being so deduced, for the general standards are corrigible by particular judgements. Hare at one point compares moral reasoning with scientific method as analysed by Popper.

> What has happened is that a provisional or suggested moral principle has been rejected because one of its particular consequences proved unacceptable. But an important difference between the two kinds of reasoning must also be noted; it is what we should expect, given that the data of scientific observation are recorded in descriptive statements, whereas we are here dealing with prescriptions.[1]

Now this difference may be what Hare would expect, but in literary

[1] R. M. Hare, *Freedom and Reason*, p. 91.

criticism, indeed in aesthetics generally, our disagreement with a general principle may well be on the grounds of its misdescribing the artistic (or the ethical) facts. Scientific theories – as I have already suggested – may be valuable in virtue of the enormous number of phenomena they connect, even if not much is added, in the way of predictive power, to the current theories. If we drop Hare's grand 'prescriptivity' distinction between ethical and 'descriptive' language, we have a very close parallel between scientific reasoning and some forms of ethical reasoning. We can accept Hare's adoption of the principle of falsifiability as a method of testing ethical and aesthetic principles. We can then ask whether this particular critic adequately, or appropriately or helpfully, describes the facts with which he deals. Yet what is this but to ask whether he is a good critic? I have argued that we cannot agree with a critic's description and yet 'deny the conclusions of value' which the description involves (to make the point deliberately tautologous). So Winters's theory – when we have finally located it – is 'falsifiable'; it seeks to describe facts and is falsified when it is shown to misdescribe them.

At this point a qualification is called for. A critic need not suggest general principles – he may rather go on describing works in their particularity. This would not prevent our falsifying his particular judgements, and, hence, his 'theory'. Universalizability will still apply. If work A is to be described as 'sentimental' then so is work B, unless significant differences can be pointed out.

It is no part of this account of Winters to assess – at least in the most blatant sense – his value as a critic. Nevertheless, what I have already said amounts to some sort of valuation. It cannot be denied that Winters arrives at some grotesque positions, both practically and theoretically – for instance he believes that his theory of criticism entails the existence of God.[1] It equally cannot be denied that he suggests a new and powerful 'literary map', and a new and suggestive 'value map'. What becomes obvious is that valuing is a much more complicated process than Winters imagines it to be. His attempt to derive his judgements from such an ambiguous formula as 'defensible rational statement' is symptomatic of his over-simple idea of what evaluation is. When he accuses Hart Crane and Yeats of attempting to escape from the complexity of experience rather than to 'master and understand it', and claims that the result is that ". . . one's feelings are certain

[1] Op. cit., p. 14.

to be confused, and one's imagery . . . is bound to be largely formulary and devoid of meaning",[1] we want to say that this is not, at any rate, the end of the matter. For Winters it *is* the end of the matter; Crane and Yeats are irrational, and it is absurd, not to say contradictory to allow that a poem is irrational and yet to claim that it is good – or even that it is a poem at all. Winters is too fond of phrases like 'devoid of meaning', too fond of bringing discussion to a halt with a formula. We do *not* instantly know what to think of escapes from complexity, or deliberate obscurity, unless we have a map, a sense of how things stand, where different experiences come, which gives us a very good sense of our bearings. We cannot expect the critic to provide us with such a sense, if it is lacking in the society or culture in which we live – just as we cannot take over, for example, Jane Austen's exquisite, and balanced, sense of values. Johnson, who wrote within a fairly clear critical and ethical framework, had so much the greater right to bring discussion to an end with a formula. Winters is trying to provide himself with as sure a framework by the erection of the criterion of 'reason'; but this cannot have the function Winters intends for it unless the reader already has a sufficiently sound conception of literature, and indeed of 'life', to know how to use it. Of *course* insane gibbering (and insanity is, for Winters, the ultimate end of obscurity) is inferior to Shakespeare; but to say that is not to go very far. If all we are told about Pound's *Cantos* is that they produce a "blur of revery"[2] and that that is "irrational", then we are perfectly entitled to ask "Well, in that case, what is wrong with irrationality?" The trouble is that Winters, instead of pointing out more and more features of 'irrational' works – and no formula can lay down in advance where this process must stop – might well reply with an argument in favour of rationality!

I have not questioned Winters's belief in Objectivism, or what he calls 'Absolutism', but I have tried to show that the sorts of standards that he thinks such an absolutism implies neither can exist, nor can have the function he intends them to have. The idea that particular judgements, if they are to be objective, have to be deduced from general principles, or entailed by general descriptions, is the fundamental fallacy. To defend a judgement of a poem one has to go on describing it, relating it to other poems and so on, until the person one is trying to convince is satisfied. There are no general laws which will take the place of this, or which will unquestionably 'bring the

[1] *Defense of Reason*, p. 27.   [2] Op. cit., p. 59.

discussion to an end' (a favourite phrase among writers on ethics and aesthetics).

Finally, would all those unfortunate American obscurantists, from Poe and Henry Adams to James, Pound, Eliot and Hart Crane, really have written better, more enduring, more *rational* works of literature, if only they had read their *Nicomachean Ethics?*

NOTES TO CHAPTER VI

A] For another attack on Winters's 'dualism of intellect and emotion', see Cleanth Brooks's *The Well Wrought Urn*, p. 217.

B] Cleanth Brooks discusses Winters's treatment of the Browning lines under the heading of 'The Heresy of Paraphrase', *The Well Wrought Urn*, p. 184.

For Brooks, of course, poetry is not 'statement' but rather "a pattern of resolutions and balances and harmonizations, developed through a temporal scheme" (op. cit., p. 186). Brooks associates his own position with Burke's – poetry as 'a mode of action' – and with R. P. Blackmur's – poetic language as gesture, 'the outward and dramatic ploy of inward and imaged meaning'.

This leads Brooks – plausibly enough – to a preference for poetry of wit, irony and complexity. Sentimental verse would not be expected to exhibit 'a pattern of resolutions and balances and harmonizations'. Conversely, Winters's assertion that poetry is 'statement' consorts easily with an admiration for Bridges.

CHAPTER VII

A 'Science' of Criticism: Northrop Frye

The hay, ye ken, is cut down by scythes in meadows; meadows lie by water sides; the teeth of the hippopotamus is as big as scythes; and he slumbers and sleeps in the rivers of Afrikaw; so the snuff, smelling like hay, brings a' thae things to mind; and therefore it is like a hippopotamus – for surely there is a likeness somewhere in everything that brings another thing to mind –.

John Galt, *The Entail.*

Northrop Frye's proclaimed aim is to place criticism upon what he at times calls a 'systematic' and at times a 'scientific' basis. The fact that these two terms tend to be interchangeable in Frye's writings is an indication of a fundamental difficulty and, perhaps, confusion, in his whole theory of criticism (and literature): it is a difficulty or confusion upon which M. H. Abrams seizes in a masterly review of *The Anatomy of Criticism*[1] – a review upon which much of this chapter is a commentary. Vastness of scope is, perhaps, Frye's most striking quality, as well as his chief ambition, and any attempt at summary must here be avoided.[2] I shall merely try to deal with what I take to be the central problem – Frye's attempt to establish criticism as a 'science'.

The present study of literature is, according to Frye,[3] in a state of 'naive induction', and on its present basis incapable of becoming truly systematic. Although critics may expend considerable labour in assessing works of literature, relating them to each other, constructing genres, and so on, all their efforts are vitiated by a chronic and radical defect: they treat each work as a *datum*. The ultimate items out of which the larger patterns – the critical traditions and so on – are to be constituted are whole works of literature. The rejection of this 'naive' method is the central move in Frye's attempt to reform and systematize the critical pursuit.

[1] *University of Toronto Quarterly*, 1958–9.
[2] For such a summary see the essay in F. Kermode's *Puzzles and Epiphanies* and also Abrams's review.
[3] *The Anatomy of Criticism*, p. 15.

Frye begins with an account of the conceptual innovations which were necessary for the inauguration of modern science. Physics becomes a true science when the concepts 'hot', 'cold', 'moist' and 'dry', are abandoned as the ultimate data out of which the science is to be constructed and an investigation is begun into the constitutive principle of these data themselves. As the science develops, the principles behind the phenomena are simplified more and more, so that the essential structure behind the complex and confusing manifold is gradually revealed. A similar conceptual revolution inaugurates the systematic study of history in place of the naive writing of 'chronicles'. The chronicler becomes an 'historian' in the modern sense when he ceases merely to catalogue events, employing no principle other than that of chronology, and begins to bring them under wider explanatory categories. He learns to discern the principles behind the events, and in the light of these his arrangement – and, indeed, understanding and description – of the events changes. In a sense he looks at the same event and sees something different from what the chronicler sees, but in another sense he is looking at something different. The historian does not accept his material at its face value; he is able to perceive the essential similarity between two dissimilar events, and the real dissimilarity between two apparently similar ones.

The scientist and the scientific historian make an "assumption of total coherence".[1] They see events as "a complication of a relatively restricted and simple group of formulas".[2] The study of literature, too, can become systematic when critics learn to make assumptions similar to those involved in all truly scientific studies.

> It is clear that criticism cannot be a systematic study unless there is a quality in literature which enables it to be so. We have to adopt the hypothesis, then, that just as there is an order of nature behind the natural sciences, so literature is not a piled aggregate of 'works' but an order of 'words'.[3]

It is natural to compare what Frye says about 'naive inductivism' with Popper's attack on naive empiricism in science. In *The Logic of Scientific Discovery* Popper argues that the scientist does not merely assemble data, but forms very general explanatory hypotheses which are then tested deductively by rigorous experimentation. But we soon

---

[1] *The Anatomy of Criticism*, p. 16.   [2] Op. cit., p. 17.
[3] Op. cit., p. 17.

realize that such testing plays little or no part in Frye's scheme. His very formulation suggests how unPopperian is his idea of a 'scientific' method. He talks of the assumption 'that there is an order of nature' behind the natural sciences. But this assumption is very unlike a Popperian scientific hypothesis. It is easy to see how such an assumption could be continually confirmed, but less easy to envisage conditions under which it could be considered to have been decisively refuted. It is, in fact, very much the sort of theory which J. W. N. Watkins, following Popper, would class as 'metaphysical' – "easy to confirm but practically or logically impossible to test".[1]

So although a part of Frye's proposal for the establishing of criticism as a science accords with the Popperian analysis of scientific procedure, another part ignores the equally important requirement of Falsifiability. Abrams makes the same point when he insists that the relation of Frye's general principles or archetypes to his particular interpretations is not that of general scientific hypotheses to particular experiments – like the Theory of Relativity to the bending of light waves – but more like the relation of the One to the Many in a metaphysical system.[2] I will consider the justice of this reduction later.

Frye's theory is certainly misleading in another way. He suggests that the ancient chronicler accepts events in some sense at their face value, as basic data. He lacks principles for ordering them, or if he has principles they are as primitive as the critic's distinction between 'prose' and 'poetry', or his division of literature into 'novel', 'play' and 'epic'. But this is certainly fallacious. The ancient chronicler certainly does see and describe his material in the light of particular categories. At the lowest level, the sorts of fact he thinks worthy of mention, or irrelevant, and, at a more sophisticated level, those events he stresses and those upon which he places less weight, are all evidence of and constitute his conceptual scheme. It is, we might say, the conceptual scheme out of which he constructs *his* facts. The sorts of fact we single out already depend upon our principles of selection. The distinction we make between 'chronicler' and 'historian' is not between one who has and one who has not a conceptual scheme, or even a relatively elaborate one, but between one of whose scheme we

---

[1] 'Between Analytic and Empirical', *Philosophy*, 1957, p. 127. See also 'When Are Statements Empirical?', *B.J.P.S.*, 1960, and 'Confirmable and Influential Metaphysics', *Mind*, 1958. See also Note A, p. 152.

[2] Op. cit., p. 195.

approve – say, as 'scientific' – and one whose notions of explanation we might think ill-founded or 'superstitious'. The distinction is not between the naive and the systematic, with the latter being a synonym for 'scientific', but between those forms of enquiry which are scientific, say in that they yield hypotheses which are falsifiable to an approved degree, and those systematic forms of enquiry which are *not* also scientific: "... a realistic dividing line between scientific and un-scientific statements cannot coincide with a realistic dividing line between meaningful and meaningless sentences. . . ." We need ". . . a criterion which distinguishes empirical from non-empirical statements *within* the class of meaningful statements".[1] There is also, of course, the question of distinguishing between the more and the less valuable non-empirical (here meaning *non-scientific*) systems.

It is clear that, in one sense, it is not of central importance whether or not Frye is 'scientific' according to the Popperian formula. After all, his work could be 'unscientific' but, nevertheless, of great value. Popper and Watkins leave room for 'metaphysical' theories which, although not scientific, are none the less rational and systematic. We may, however, find a connection or coincidence between the question whether Frye is scientific, and the question whether he is useful as a critic; between 'Is this science?' and 'Is this criticism?'

Let us take, for instance, Frye's assertion that if we 'stand back' from *Tom Sawyer* we see ". . . a youth with no father or mother emerging with a maiden from a labyrinthine cave, leaving a bat-eating demon imprisoned behind him".[2] Could even an initiate, asks Abrams, have predicted in advance that Frye would discover this pattern in Tom Sawyer? Abrams concedes that the pattern *may* be 'there' – but only in the way that triangles or quincunxes are 'there' – not in the way that four-leafed clovers are. In the end we can only accept as 'real' patterns which would be recognized by independent, neutral ob-servers.[3] "One may doubt whether many archetypal statements are even, in the strict sense, significant empirical propositions".[4] This last remark of Abrams suggests that he is using 'empirical' to mean 'mean-ingful' – a confusion upon which Popper mounts his main attack.

What are we to say about the connection Newton saw between the fall of apples and the movement of stars? Was it 'there' to be seen in

---

[1] J. W. N Watkins, 'When Are Statements Empirical?', p. 291.
[2] *Anatomy of Criticism*, p. 190.
[3] See Note B, p. 152.   [4] Op. cit., p. 194.

the way that a four-leafed clover is, or as a quincunx is?[1] It is not sufficient to say that the question is settled by an appeal to independent
observers. After all, a quincunx can be recognized by an independent
observer when he has been taught what it is. It is true that we do not,
in the same way, have to be taught to recognize four-leafed clovers;
but we *do* have to be taught to see the connection between apples
falling and stars moving. Now it is true that the law of gravity is testable. The discovery of the planet Uranus helped to confirm it, and one
can conceive of events which would tend to refute it. To say that the
law of gravity is a scientific hypothesis, and that a belief in the ubi-
quitous presence of quincunxes is not, is perhaps to say something
about comparative testability. Now are we saying something of the
same order when we ask whether the pattern which Frye discovers in
Tom Sawyer is critically relevant? We must remember that Frye does
not posit any causal connection between the archetypal formulae and
their particular instances; nor does he appeal to a 'collective unconscious'. He merely says that the patterns are there 'however they
came there'. Yet this seems to make Frye's interpretations less, not
more, plausible. If a particular view of *King Lear* is suggested by a
critic, we may see the play in a new light. But equally we may ask:
'Could Shakespeare have *meant* that?' This might be an entirely relevant question. In asking it we would not be seeking to infer an entirely
hidden intention, which could only be revealed to us by Shakespeare
himself. Rather we would be asking about the plausibility of the
interpretation in the light of what we take to be the pattern of the play.
We can compare this with the way in which we could seek to show,
by a description of medical training, that a doctor's proper function
is to cure, rather than kill people.[2]

Now if we say that a pattern is there 'unconsciously' – that there is
an 'unconscious Oedipal situation' in *Hamlet* for instance – are we not
suggesting that in some way the writer 'meant' or that the work
means – perhaps 'really means' – that? If Freud, while analysing a
dream, suggests that a house stands for the patient's mother, this
interpretation is tested by being found to fit into the patient's history
and to throw light on his situation. Similarly we can try to justify an
assertion that a particular man intended to murder his wife in the light
of what we know about his background, his character and so on.

Can the archetypes which Frye claims to discover as the organizing

<hr />

[1] See Chapter I, pp. 17–18.   [2] See p. 117.

principles of literature be 'tested' in the same way? Can we, for instance, show that *Tom Sawyer* is *not* an example of the Minotaur
archetype?

Perhaps this can be put in another way. Even if we see a particular
work in terms of a larger archetype, does this explain anything? What
are we to make of the bat-eating demon in the cave? The archetypes
stand just as much in need of explanation as the particular works. And
we understand the archetypes in so far as we see them as constituted
of particular works. The significance of an archetype is constituted of
the significance of the particular works which make it up.

Here we are in a position somewhat analogous to that in which we
land when we seek to justify ethical or aesthetic judgements of value
in terms of certain very general criteria. The giving of some formula –
such as Winters's 'Reason' – is often an attempt at a short cut, a substitute for the particular 'placings' which make up a value scheme.
Similarly with Frye's archetypes; these have to justify themselves by
reference to particulars – as has any general formula of *value*. One has,
as it were, to put as much into the archetypes as one wishes to get out
of them. Would Abrams compare the relation of Winters's particular
judgements to his general formula of Reason, or Leavis's particular
'placings' to concepts like 'Life' or 'Maturity', to 'the relation of the
Many to the One'?

To find whether an archetype is validly, genuinely present in a work
is certainly to 'test' it. Without this testing we are entitled to ask 'So
what?' when the various archetypes are triumphantly produced out of
the hat. This is a request for justification – perhaps in the form of
further description – analogous to one we may make when someone
describes a poem as 'immature'.

Here, then, we have what may be a way of distinguishing within
the class of quincunx (as distinct, that is, from four-leafed clover) patterns. There is a sense in which all of these patterns are really there:
but, nevertheless, only some are 'really' there. For the pattern to be
genuinely there, the poet or the poem will, in some sense, have to
'mean' it. The test will be very like that for an interpretation of a
dream – a relation to undeniable intentions, meanings and so on. But
this means that to understand whether the bat and cave archetypes are
present in *Tom Sawyer*, and in what way they are present, and what
it *is* for them to be present, we must already understand *Tom Sawyer*.
Hence the archetype cannot enable us to understand the novel, and

archetypes cannot be the constitutive, explanatory principles of literature.

This may become clearer with another comparison. In the commentary on the *Song of Songs* in the Douay version of the Bible 'I am black but beautiful' is interpreted as "The Church of Christ founded in humility appearing outwardly afflicted, and as it were black and contemptible; but inwardly, that is, in its doctrine and morality, fair and beautiful". Here we see why Frye's refusal to posit a 'collective unconscious' – or some other such explanation of the archetypes – makes his theory (on one level at least) less, not more plausible. The traditional theological defence of the 'mystical' interpretation of the *Song of Songs* from the charge that it is ludicrously far-fetched and arbitrary, is the appeal to a polysemous reading. The *Song of Songs* has both a natural and a theological meaning. Now for Christians who believe in God who reveals himself through scripture this is not altogether implausible. The second level of meaning is God's – who stands in place of the 'collective unconscious'. Or, we can say that the writer of the *Song* intends a secular love poem, but God through him intends a revelation of the mystical bridal relationship between Christ and the Church. We can see how, with reference to what he believes himself to know of God's nature and purposes more straightforwardly, as it were, a Christian could build up a fairly coherent system of two-level interpretations embracing both prophecy and typology. In this way would be provided a method of justifying some otherwise rather implausible interpretations.

It is perfectly testable whether or not the theological reading of the *Song of Songs* is valid. The appeal is to what the song *means* – and, of course, theologians have special reasons for believing that it means two things at once. And we can find out what the song means by the usual literary and historical methods.

Similarly Northrop Frye's archetypes can be tested. We can distinguish between those patterns which we might want to call arbitrary or far-fetched, and those which are genuine and relevant. The comparison with the Freudian theory of symbolism is again helpful. Abrams says:

> Freud's system permits him to apply alternatively, according to circumstances, the canon of literal meaning (A is A), displacement or substitution (A is B), condensation (A is A+B+C+D ...) and inversion or transvaluation (A is the contrary of A). .... The cardinal modes of proof,

however, in Freud's theory as in all theories of natural symbolism, is analogical. The implicit canon here is that analogy justifies identification; if A is in some respects like B, then A is identifiable as B. This appears to be the standard formula of archetypal reasoning.[1]

But surely Abrams is ignoring what is *in practice* the cardinal mode of proof in Freud. Freud interprets a patient's dream by means of free association and connection with his waking life. An argument is gradually constructed, a context built up, which convinces the patient that he must see a particular dream image as a symbol of a wish or situation in his waking life. It is true that Freud's total theory of dreams – that they are all, in some way, wish-fulfilling – leaves ample room for logical manœuvre: dreams are either straightforward wishes, or disguised wishes (often inverted in the dream), or masochistic wishes. There are also dreams dictated by the wish of refuting the analyst's theory! But the room for manœuvre is not total. We can argue about the propriety of this extension of the notion of 'wishing'. Whether all human actions are governed by appetency and aversion, or by appetency alone, is arguable – although it is not a matter that can be settled in the psychological laboratory. It is 'a question of words', but questions of words are no more *mere* questions of words than taste is a matter of taste. And within the theory a strict weighing of evidence is possible.

It is important that the analyst does not believe that a dream can be interpreted without detailed knowledge of the patient's life, or apart from the context of an analysis. The patient must co-operate in 'free-association', remembering and so on. Similarly, when Frye claims to find in *As You Like It* a green forest world in which an old, corrupt world is metamorphosed and reborn, and finds the same pattern[2] in *The Two Gentlemen of Verona*, *A Midsummer Night's Dream*, *The Merry Wives of Windsor* and *The Winter's Tale* – we can test what he says quite easily. Has the forest this function? Has it this importance? These are perfectly settleable *critical* issues, and are decided like all critical issues – finally with reference to the work. When Frye goes on to say that "In *The Merchant of Venice* the second (i.e. 'green') world takes the form of Portia's mysterious house in Belmont, with its magic caskets and the wonderful cosmological harmonies that proceed from it in the final act."[3] we can settle this also. Similarly we can

[1] Op. cit., p. 194.   [2] *The Anatomy of Criticism*, p. 182.
[3] Ibid., p. 194.

argue with the critic who claims that Ross is the real villain in *Macbeth*,[1] or with the man who believes that the world is controlled by Jews.
Abrams says:

> Even if we grant . . . that these heroines are all Proserpine figures who act out a ritual death . . . our task as practical critics has not even begun. For few works differ more radically from each other in consitution, characterisation, qualitative feel and emotional effect than do *The Winter's Tale*, *Bleak House*, *Pamela*, and *The Rape of the Lock*, and the job of the practical critic is to account for each work in its minute particularity.

Of course Abrams is right; but we may well consider this a misleading way of expressing the point. For if the emotional and structural qualities of these works are as different as Abrams says, both from each other and from the original archetype, then this is a reason *against* granting that 'the heroines are all Proserpine figures . . .' The figure of Proserpine, the Proserpine myth, *involves* particular emotions, a particular 'qualitative feel'. These emotions, this 'feel' are not mere extraneous, additional elements. It is by remembering this that we see how the very presence of the archetype can be tested in the particular works. All the archetypes are highly complex pieces of mythology; both Christ and Proserpine die ritual deaths, but they are dissimilar figures and easy to distinguish. There is, as it were, a point about the myth of Proserpine; it has meaning. The point, the meaning is embodied in the form. Similarly *King Lear* has a point, or meaning; and one of the reasons why *King Lear* is not to be seen as an instantiation of the Proserpine archetype is that it has a different point, a different meaning. This difference in meaning is bound up with and involves a difference in 'constitution, characterization, qualitative feel and emotional effect . . .' For all of these reasons we can safely deny that King Lear 'is' Proserpine or any other mythological figure. Should Frye insist on such an identification then he would be practising what Abrams[2] calls 'wit criticism' – the seeing of similarity in dissimilars.

It would be useful at this point to take note of what Professor J. A. Passmore calls two different 'models' of intention, the 'coherence' model which seeks only to pick out a purposive pattern in behaviour, and the 'planning' model which "assimilates intending to deliberately

---

[1] See Arden edition of *Macbeth*, xlix.
[2] Op. cit., p. 195.

planning a course of action".[1] Now it is clear that when a critic says
that a writer 'means' or 'intends' something by a work of literature,
he is talking more in terms of the first – the 'coherence' – model. In
psycho-analysis this model makes possible the attribution of an 'unconscious' intention to the patient, such that although the patient's
agreement with the attribution may be a criterion that it is correct,
his refusal to agree might not be evidence that it is false. In the same
way, in arguing that a test of whether an alleged pattern in a work is
really 'there' is that the writer must, in some sense, 'intend' it, I am
not proposing a test so rigorous that it allows a work to mean only
what a writer *thinks* it means. This would be far too easy and crude
a way of refuting Frye. The writer's opinion about his intentions is a
far less important criterion than it would be on the 'planning' model,
so that we might even say that the writer is in no better position to
interpret his work than the informed reader. At any rate, if he is in a
better position, this is because he is liable to know his own work
better than most readers – but as a matter of fact, not of logic. This is,
I think, what underlies the attack on the 'Intentional Fallacy' by
Wimsatt and Beardsley. On the other hand it also helps to show where
they exaggerate. For instance, in their discussion of whether the line

> I have heard the mermaids singing each to each

in *Prufrock* is an allusion to Donne's

> Teach me to heare Mermaides singing

they suggest that the only 'true and objective' method of criticism
would be to enquire 'whether it makes any sense if Eliot-Prufrock *is*
thinking about Donne'.[2] This is certainly right, but an important
test of whether such a supposition makes sense is whether the poem
'means' that, or whether the poet can be said to 'intend' that (in the
'coherence' sense of 'intend'). In other words, the 'true and objective'
method in criticism involves the picking out of patterns of intention.

We see, then, that the testability of Frye's archetypes is connected
with their critical usefulness. To say something valid about the presence
of an archetype is to say something relevant about the 'constitution,
characterization, qualitative feel and emotional effect . . .' of the work.

---

[1] 'Intentions', *Arist. Soc. Supp.*, 1955. There is a discussion of this by MacIntyre,
op. cit., Chapter IV.
[2] 'The Intentional Fallacy', *The Verbal Icon*, p. 18.

L

To 'interpret' *The Rape of the Lock* as a Proserpine myth is so to describe it that the interpretation is correct. This description will include an analysis of the emotional tone, qualitative feel and so on. This returns us to the familiar point that interpretation is not merely conjoined with description.

The rather tame conclusion we come to is that Frye's archetypes are valid in so far as they are appropriate and useful descriptions of the works to which they are supposed to provide the key. The validity and appropriateness is a matter of the fidelity to what Abrams calls the 'minute particularity' of the literature which is being 'interpreted'. Whether Frye's scheme *is* valid and useful is not my immediate concern. I have merely sought to set out some of the conditions under which it could be valid and under which the interpretations could be tested.

We might notice here a connection with the discussion in Chapter V of statements of identity. I there suggested that in saying that the ordinary table is identical with the scientific one, or that sensations are the same thing as brain-processes, we say that one type of description can, in some circumstances, usefully be replaced by another, which involves our saying that each description may have enough similarity of purpose and function as to fit into the same discourse as the other. Analogously, only if there is some such similarity or equivalence of function can one expression be a 'translation' of another. This also applies to other sorts of translation. If a Freudian analyst suggests that the house of which the patient dreams 'is' the patient's mother, he can only 'prove' this through fitting the image into the general pattern of the patient's preoccupations and anxieties. In showing that it does fit he is showing that such a translation is possible. A criterion of the correctness of the interpretation is that the patient come to see the house *as* his mother – not that he decide to accept the hypothesis that the house stands for his mother, a hypothesis backed up by the supposed general law discovered by Freud that in dreams houses represent mothers. The arrow points only in the application that a living being makes of it – and an image can only be a symbol if we can take it as such. Another way of putting it is that the patient has to 'accept' that the house symbolizes his mother – has to accept that he in some sense 'means' his mother by the house. Now when such a body of insights is treated simply as though it were a body of scientific laws the result is a failure to convince. If, for instance, it is suggested that the Dragon in *Siegfried* 'is' The Terrible Mother[1] and if the proof offered for this assertion is a resemblance to an appropriate archetype, we are at a loss. No connections have been established which enable us to see Fafner *as* The Terrible Mother, or, indeed, to see The Terrible Mother as terrible or in any way significant. The archetype is pretending to function as an 'explanation' in a way far too naively imitative of scientific explanation. When these connections have not been established it is simply impossible to see the *meaning* in the statement that Fafner 'is' The Terrible Mother; just as it is initially very difficult to see what is meant by the assertion that sensations are brain-processes or that tables are particles in motion. It is notable that Freud very frequently presents his findings in the form of case-histories – a method which emphasizes the relevance of the patient's history to the interpretation of the symbols. Something of the distinction between criticism and science comes out here; the difficulty of establishing a fixed body of symbolic meanings of the model of scientific laws is akin to the difficulty of writing literary history on the model of political or economic history.

All this means that the resort to archetypes cannot replace the insights of criticism. The relation of the archetypes to the particular work is more like the relation of a general category of dream in Freud to a particular dream than like the relation of a scientific law to its instances. Reverting to the distinction of Chapter I we may say that neither archetypes nor Freudian categories 'explain' in the sense in which scientific theories explain – although the distinction is not an absolute one. Like Mrs Langer, Frye attempts to give a 'profound' explanation of literature, more profound than any that can be given by mere criticism. It is not that criticism cannot be useful at a high level of generality, but that general schemes can never escape from dependence on particular insights. And this means that in the end the only relevant question about Frye is the one I have not discussed – how good a critic he is.

[1] See Robert Donington's *Wagner's* Ring *and its Symbols*, p. 193.

NOTES TO CHAPTER VII

A]

> ... the dogmatic attitude is clearly related to the tendency to *verify* our laws and schemata by seeking to apply them and to confirm them, even to the point of neglecting refutations, whereas the critical attitude is one of readiness to change them; to refute them; to *falsify* them if possible. This suggests that we may identify the critical attitude with the scientific attitude, and the dogmatic attitude with the one which we have described as pseudo-scientific.
>
> Popper, 'Conjectures', from *Conjectures and Refutations*, p. 50.

B]   Abrams is over-simplifying: we cannot lay down a *formula* for the separation of real from arbitrary patterns. Hepburn discusses the impossibility of legislating in advance "where the boundary between the plausible and the strained will fall . . ." in the case of alleged 'typographical patterns' in the Bible.

See 'Poetry and Religious Belief', from *Metaphysical Beliefs*, ed. MacIntyre, p. 94.

CHAPTER VIII

Object, Feeling and Judgement:
F. R. Leavis

I. THE PARTICULARITY OF CRITICISM

... in all decisions of taste or external beauty, all the relations are before-hand obvious to the eye; and we thence proceed to feel a sentiment of complacency or disgust, according to the nature of the object and the disposition of our organs.

Hume, *Enquiry Concerning the Principles of Morals*, Appendix 1.

The critic's aim is, first, to realize as sensitively as possible this or that which claims his attention; and a certain valuing is implicit in the realizing.

F. R. Leavis, 'Criticism and Philosophy', *The Common Pursuit*, p. 213.

In this chapter I shall try to bring together certain themes which I have discussed in other parts of the book. I shall, in particular, try to show how problems about the place of emotion in literature and criticism are closely connected with problems about the objectivity of value judge-ments. Some of these connections have, I hope, already emerged. We have seen, for instance, how Murry's expressionism leads to, and goes with, a dichotomy between thought and emotion which, in its turn, goes with a radical subjectivism. In the chapter on Eliot I argued to-wards a very similar conclusion which had bearing on the relations be-tween 'art' and 'life'. In examining Winters I traced the connections between the view of the relation between emotion and concept which he holds in common with the others, and his attempt to set up an external, *a priori* standard – 'Reason' – as a means of avoiding the subjectivism which his own premises involve. In Leavis we have a critic who becomes aware of the paradoxes inherent in romantic expressionism, and whose solution is a remarkably interesting syn-thesis of expressionist and mimetic theories. In his criticism we have the most thoroughgoing attempt to retain, on the one hand, the emphasis on the emotional importance of literature, and yet to provide,

153

on the other, objective criteria for judging the quality of emotion a
poem presents.[1]

The attempt to establish these connections will, however, be sub-
sidiary to a larger analysis: an examination of the means by which
Leavis attempts to justify his critical judgements, and the consequences
for the theory of value.

The first thing to be noticed is that Leavis's critical arguments do
not characteristically proceed from the particular to the general. We
find ourselves producing an account which is quite the opposite of
R. M. Hare's.[2] To assert this at the outset may seem merely dogmatic.
It is, after all, very easy to point to some extremely general terms in
Leavis's vocabulary – 'life', 'maturity' and so on – which seem to be
paradigms or central criteria, the ultimate premises of a critical 'system'.
If we deny the premises we are entitled to deny the conclusion. Hence
arises the demand[3] that Leavis 'state his premises' in order that we may
first understand his particular judgements and secondly that we may
be in the position either to accept or reject them. Sympathizers with
Leavis's position sometimes suggest that the real motive behind this
demand is an objection to Leavis's actual judgements.[4] However, as
may already be clear from my discussion of Hare and Mrs Foot, it is
a perfectly natural demand, and one which can be explained in terms
of a particular view of the nature of evaluative argument, and indeed
of the nature of argument itself. It is a view with wide philosophical
support – and one which is in fact held by both parties to the dispute
(although not by Leavis himself). In the course of this discussion I
shall try to indicate further why I think it is mistaken.

When Leavis describes de la Mare's poetry[5] as predominantly
'glamorous' and 'dream-like' one is tempted, particularly if one ad-
mires de la Mare, to retort, 'But what is wrong with the poetry of
day-dream?' However, we soon notice that his attitude to 'dream'
poetry is more complex than that; he contrasts with de la Mare and
the Victorians, Yeats and the Romantics.

[1] This is meant to suggest a logical centre and not, of course, the centre of
Leavis's *critical* interests.
[2] In *The Language of Morals*.
[3] See René Wellek, *Scrutiny*, Vol. V, No. 4, and George Watson, *The Literary
Critics*, pp. 213–14.
[4] I cannot give documentary evidence for this, but it is common.
[5] *New Bearings in English Poetry*, pp. 50–6.

It was possible for the poets of the Romantic period to believe that the interests animating their poetry were the forces moving the world, or that might move it. But Victorian poetry admits implicitly that the actual world is alien, recalcitrant and unpoetical, and that no protest is worth making except the protest of withdrawal.[1]

> For Mr Yeats's Irishness is more than a matter of using Irish themes and an Irish atmosphere. It means that his dream world is something more than private, personal and literary; that it has, as it were, an external validation.[2]

Here we see that Leavis is suggesting that if we are to take de la Mare's 'dream' poetry seriously we have in some way to blot out or diminish our normal everyday awareness of how the world really is.

Now in isolation this is highly questionable. To read *The Divine Comedy*, *Paradise Lost* and even *King Lear* properly we have to suspend some of our criteria of 'reality'. This is why some critics wish to insist that all literature is, in some sense, 'dream'.[3] But, as the quotations suggest, Leavis is himself trying to distinguish between 'dream' and 'day-dream'. A day-dream is a 'yielding', a shutting off of intelligence.

> The switching-off of intelligence that is necessary if the sentiments of the third stanza (of Shelley's *When the Lamp is Shattered*) are to be accepted has now to be invoked in explanation of a graver matter – Shelley's ability to accept the grosser, the truly corrupt, gratifications that have just been indicated. The antipathy of his sensibility to any play of the critical mind, the uncongeniality of intelligence to inspiration, these clearly go in Shelley, not merely with a capacity for momentary self-deceptions and insincerities, but with a radical lack of self-knowledge.[4]

In discussing de la Mare's late poem *The Veil* Leavis says:

> ... The poignancy turns into a duller, heavier desolation; the dream takes on a nightmare quality; and the unwholesomeness of the fantasy habit is, implicitly and explicitly, admitted. It is as if the disastrous consequences of drug addiction were being recognised. Life seems now not tragic but flat and empty.[5]

Already we can see that the distinction (to label it crudely) between dream and day-dream is supported and given meaning by a fairly thick

---

[1] Op. cit., p. 15. [2] Op. cit., p. 34.
[3] For instance, Northrop Frye, "In the anagogic phase literature imitates the total dream of man", *Anatomy of Criticism*, pp. 117–19.
[4] *Revaluation*, p. 221. [5] *New Bearings*, p. 54.

context. The correlation of 'failure of intelligence' with a tendency to 'yield' to various forms of subjectivity, or 'self-indulgence' or 'self-absorption' or 'unreality' is further brought out in the chapter on George Eliot in *The Great Tradition*. Leavis is criticizing what he takes to be the conventional view (it is, for instance, James's) of George Eliot as a writer whose strength lies in her 'capacity to feel' and her weakness in her care for 'the reason of things'.[1]

> ... the emotional 'fulness' represented by Dorothea depends for its exalting potency on an abeyance of intelligence and self-knowledge, and the situations offered by way of 'objective correlative' have the day-dream relation to experience; they are generated by a need to soar above the indocile facts and conditions of the real world.[2]

Again:

> There is nothing against George Eliot's presenting [Maggie Tulliver's] immaturity with tender sympathy; but we ask, and ought to ask of a great novelist, something more. 'Sympathy and understanding' is the common formula of praise, but understanding, in any strict sense, is just what she doesn't show. To understand immaturity would be to 'place' it, with however subtle an implication, by relating it to mature experience. But when George Eliot touches on these given intensities of Maggie's inner life the vibration comes directly and simply from the novelist, precluding the presence of a maturer intelligence than Maggie's own.[3]
>
> Maggie Tulliver, in fact, represents an immaturity that George Eliot never leaves safely behind her ... where it prevails her intelligence and mature judgment are out of action.[4]

It is easy to see how the groupings are developing; intelligence, self-knowledge, maturity, reality stand together against immaturity, self-dramatization, sentimentality, day-dream, self-indulgence. It is obvious that there is a large set of terms in Leavis's criticism which are closely interrelated, and sometimes even equated. We quickly see what the paradigmatic terms are. (A rough appendix of the terms associated, in *Revaluation*, with 'life' is included as an illustration.[5]) Leavis's 'key' terms are so thickly interrelated that it is at any rate misleading to talk about his 'premises' – as though 'life', 'maturity', etc. existed in isolation and *a priori*, to be accepted or rejected entirely in their own right. On the other hand there *is* a sense – a point to which we shall

---

[1] Henry James, *Daniel Deronda: A Conversation*.
[2] *The Great Tradition*, p. 93.
[3] Op. cit., p. 54.   [4] Op. cit., p. 55.   [5] See p. 177.

return – in which they can be described as premises. This description of the relation between Leavis's critical terms will have important bearing on the discussion of the nature of evaluative arguments.

Leavis's attitude to expressionism is characterized by a similar tendency to connect apparently distinct concepts. Much of Leavis's critical terminology can be seen in terms of a tension between expressionism and its opposite. Overwhelmingly his language is the sort which normally characterizes an 'expressionist' rather than a 'mimetic' theory of literature. A word like 'sincerity', for instance, obviously has more affinities with the lamp than with the mirror.[1] Early in *New Bearings* we find the following:

> [The poet] is unusually sensitive, unusually aware, more sincere and more himself than the ordinary man can be. He knows what he feels, and what he is interested in. . . . poetry can communicate the actual quality of experience with a subtlety and precision unapproachable by other means.[2]

Again: "But the only technique that matters is that which compels words to express an intensely personal way of feeling."[3] This is the orthodox language of expressionism. It is a language which, concentrating as it does on the state of mind and emotion of the author, is obviously liable to pass into *moral* discriminations. I have, however, left out an important part of the first passage: ". . . [the poet's] power of making words express what he feels is indistinguishable from his awareness of what he feels; . . . he is a poet because his interest in his experience is not separable from his interest in words . . ."[4] Here we see that Leavis, although finding it natural to use expressionist language, tries to avoid the usual expressionist difficulties, by denying the expressionist distinction between the thing expressed and the expression of it. We may schematize the procedure as follows: the expressionist asserts that 'behind' the words on the page is an emotion or idea which the words express, or for the expression of which the words are a 'medium'. (For a relevant comment see Leavis's 'Tragedy and the Medium'.) This, however, leads to the difficulties I have diagnosed in the earlier chapters. Broadly speaking, there is no way of inferring the 'thing expressed' from the passage which 'expresses' it. One response to the dilemma is to insist that nothing about the author can be inferred

---

[1] See M. H. Abrams, *The Mirror and the Lamp.*
[2] *New Bearings*, p. 13.   [3] Op. cit., p. 25.   [4] Op. cit., p. 13.

from his work. (This is a loose formulation, but I wish to suggest what are in practice the positions taken up in criticism.) Words like 'sincerity' are to be avoided, as are all phrases that have moral overtones. Biographical criticism is impermissible; we recall Proust's attack on Sainte-Beuve for daring to think that there can be any connection between a writer's life and his art (the latter being an expression of his 'soul'); 'the greater the artist, the greater will be the separation between the man who suffers and the mind which creates'.

Another solution is to reduce the 'thing expressed' to the 'expression' of it, and this is something like the position Leavis adopts. It is a position which can easily lead to an extreme formalism, and formalism hardly goes with an emphasis on moral criteria in criticism. However, as we shall see, the reputation which both Leavis and Matthew Arnold have of being moralists is rather paradoxical.

We can best begin to illustrate by examining Leavis's attacks upon Milton.

> . . . Milton is using only a small part of the resources of the English language. The remoteness of his poetic idiom from his own speech is to be considered here. . . . *a man's most vivid emotional and sensuous experience is inevitably bound up with the language that he actually speaks.* [My italics.]

Leavis wishes to characterize Milton's defects as failures of intelligence, of awareness.

> He has 'character', moral grandeur, moral force; but he is, for the purposes of his undertaking disastrously single-minded and simple-minded. He reveals everywhere a dominating sense of righteousness and a complete incapacity to question or explore its significance and conditions. *This defect of intelligence is a defect of imagination . . . It involves too a great poverty of interest.*[1] [My italics here and throughout, except where otherwise stated.]

C. S. Lewis suggests that he and Dr Leavis 'see the same things' in *Paradise Lost* but "He sees and hates the very same that I see and love".[2] This is a remark to which we shall have occasion to return. Here it suffices to notice that Leavis is strenuously attempting to make it impossible to see the same things in Milton but value them differently. He does this in two ways, one of which concerns us now. (We shall

[1] *Revaluation*, p. 54.
[2] *A Preface to Paradise Lost*, p. 130. (I am indebted to an unpublished paper of Renford Bambrough for this example.)

come to the other when we examine his exchange with Wellek on the nature of Criticism.) That is, he is trying to 'build in' to his description of Milton's verse terms which, from the very beginning, would be accepted by almost everybody as in some sense 'evaluative'. However – a central point – this *could* be denied; Leavis *usually* insists on what might be called a 'strong criteriological', rather than a deductive relationship between terms. At some points, though, this does amount to a 'reductionist' *equation* of terms. He doesn't say that lack of 'concreteness' in the verse 'tends to go with' a relative lack of interest in what is supposed to be going on in the poem, which, in turn, tends to go with a general lack of awareness, which, in its turn, is usually to be associated with a failure of intelligence. If he were to say this it would be possible to give a similar or even identical description (leaving out the 'overtly evaluative' words) while insisting on a different judgement of value without any appearance of strain. This is not just to say that a critic opposed to Leavis's opinions about Milton could invoke 'the fact/value distinction'. (That would be the second of the two ways; we are here considering the first.) Rather he could say something like this: 'I grant Leavis's (or Eliot's or Pound's or Murry's) description of Milton's verse, but I insist that the verse can have all these qualities and still be the vehicle of intelligence, awareness and so on.' He might add that in Milton there is a 'different sort' of intelligence from what we find in Shakespeare which is, nevertheless, intelligence. Then – as we shall see – a great deal will depend on what he means by 'different sort'. This could be an 'intuitionist' move (i.e. 'This passage leads me at any rate to infer intelligence'). It could, on the other hand, be a preparation for a detailed counter-attack. That – as will be argued when we come to the general question of how Leavis's judgements could be refuted – is the only genuinely *critical* move, even though it is not the only logically possible move. It could also be a merely sceptical move; the critic would refuse to make any inference about the mentality of the author. This refusal might well be connected with a reluctance to use terminology which would suggest moral judgements about the author. 'Bad men can write good verse', etc.

Leavis's rejoinder is, as I have suggested, to equate the terms. A lack of concrete grasp *is* a failure of imagination, which *is* a failure of intelligence.

> But it is in the 'versification' everywhere that the essential inaptitude [for justifying 'the ways of God to men'] appears: "*the man who uses words in*

this way has (as Mr Eliot virtually says) no 'grasp of ideas' and, whatever he may suppose, *is not really interested in the achievement of precise thought of any kind* . . .[1]

We can relate this to what he says about Pound:[2]

> In 'Mauberly' we feel a pressure of experience, an impulsion from deep within. The verse is extraordinarily subtle, *and its subtlety is the subtlety of the sensibility it expresses. No one would think here of distinguishing the way of saying from the thing said.*

Despite the obviously expressionist language ('impulsion from deep within') which is most pronounced in *New Bearings* and *D. H. Lawrence, Novelist,* there is the clear intention of avoiding the pitfalls. In fact *New Bearings in English Poetry* is something of a *locus classicus* for illustrating (in connection, that is, with the central preoccupations of this book) the growth of a critical language and the development of a characteristic sort of critical position. The general formulations in the book are couched – to almost an extravagant extent – in the language of romantic, as opposed to mimetic, theory. "Poetry matters because of the kind of poet who is more alive than other people, more alive in his own age. He is, as it were, at the most conscious point of the race in his time. . . . He is unusually sensitive, unusually aware . . ." Clearly such an emphasis in one's received critical terminology on consciousness, sensibility, capacity for experience and so forth must lead – if one becomes aware of the dangers – to a rather violent reaction. And that is what we have in "his power of making words express what he feels is indistinguishable from his awareness of what he feels".

Leavis sets out his position more clearly and explicitly in a *Scrutiny* essay entitled ' "Thought" and Emotional Quality'.[3] In comparing Cory's 'Heraclitus' with Scott's 'Proud Maisie' he distinguishes between what he considers to be the insistent emotionalism of the first and the "emotional disinterestedness" – for which "we can substitute 'impersonality' " – of the second. He explains the distinction in terms of the presence or absence of the proper object of emotion. ". . . in reading 'Proud Maisie' we never seem to be offered emotions as such; the emotion develops and defines itself as we grasp the dramatic

---

[1] *The Common Pursuit,* p. 23.   [2] *New Bearings,* p. 138.
[3] *Scrutiny,* Vol. XII, No. 1, p. 53.

elements the poem does offer . . ."[1] Let us, for a moment, compare this with some remarks about George Eliot:[2]

> [At her 'highest level' her] sensibility is directed outward, and she responds from deep within. At this level, 'emotion' is a disinterested response defined by its object, and hardly distinguishable from the play of intelligence and self-knowledge that give it impersonality. But the emotional 'fulness' represented by Dorothea depends for its exalting potency on an abeyance of intelligence and self-knowledge, and the situations offered by way of 'objective correlative' have the day-dream relation to experience. . . . They don't, indeed, strike us as real in any sense; they have no objectivity, no vigour of illusion.

The reference to the 'objective correlative'[3] reminds us of some of T. S. Eliot's other remarks: "The poet does not aim to excite – that is not even a test of his success – but to set something down; the state of the reader is merely that reader's particular mode of perceiving what the poet has caught in words."[4] Again: "The sentimental person in whom a work of art arouses all sorts of emotions which have nothing to do with that work of art whatever, but are accidents of personal association, is an incomplete artist."[5] Unlike Eliot, Leavis tries to work out consistently this equation of 'the emotions aroused by' the object with 'the contemplation of' the object.

To return to ' "Thought" and Emotional Quality': Leavis goes on to examine Lawrence's poem 'Piano'. He notes that the imagery in 'Piano' is more particular, more concrete than any in 'Tears, Idle Tears', which he uses as a foil, and goes on:

> The main immediate point . . . is that in all this particularity we have something quite other than banal romantic generality: this is not the common currency of sentimental evocation or anything of the kind. *The actuality of the remembered situation is unbeglamouring* . . .[6]

Perhaps we can concentrate, for the moment, on the last sentence, and particularly upon the word 'unbeglamouring'. In discussing Ernest Jones's psycho-analytical account of *Hamlet*, and relating this to Eliot's essay on *Hamlet*, and to his theory of the 'objective correlative', I said: ". . . to say that Shakespeare has failed to transmute a personal experience into a work of art . . . is to say that we, the audience, are

---

[1] Ibid.   [2] *The Great Tradition*, p. 93.
[3] See the discussion of this in Chapter IV.
[4] See p. 89.   [5] Ibid.   [6] ' "Thought" and Emotional Quality', p. 57.

unable to locate precisely the peculiarly insidious glamour that we may find in *Hamlet*. It is not that there has been no transmutation of the original experience into the symbol, but that the connections between the symbol and the original situation – that is, the *context* of the symbol (the symbol is *part of* the situation; it does *not stand for* it) . . . have remained unconscious." This is not to say that unconscious models are necessarily 'glamorous' or even 'insidious'; whether they are is an empirical question. But the quotation may help to draw attention to a recurrent theme of this book; for the "aspect" to change, the context has to change. This is a banal enough remark, but it has, I hope, been given its relevance in earlier chapters. Now Leavis is equating what he calls sentimentality with a particular form of incompleteness of context. To illustrate this let us suppose that Lawrence's poem were much more similar to 'Tears, Idle Tears'; in other words, granting for the argument the justice of Leavis's account of the Tennyson, vague and sentimental. We could say to Lawrence: "But your mother's piano was a very bad one and all she played were those dreadful pietistic hymns." The tone of noble nostalgia which in Leavis's view characterizes 'Tears, Idle Tears' would be vulnerable to such attack. Or, if Lawrence's poem had ended on the straightforwardly nostalgic note – without, that is, any of the qualifications of attitude that Leavis and Harding[1] find in it, we might say to Lawrence, "But after all, you can't go back and anyway, do you *really* (i.e. with the whole of your personality, now that you are a man of . . . years of age, too big for one thing to sit under the piano any more . . .) want to?" If this had no effect we might even say "But really you *hated* your Mother, didn't you?" – which, whatever its psycho-analytical validity, would be an even more radical challenge.

For Leavis a 'sentimental' attitude is false in a peculiarly radical way, for an attitude just *is* a grasp of a particular set of objects.

> [In 'Piano'] something is, we see, held and presented in this poem and the presenting involves an *attitude towards* [Leavis's italics] an element of disinterested valuation. For all the swell of emotion the critical mind has its part in the whole; *the constatation is at the same time in some measure a placing.* That is, sensibility in the poem doesn't work in complete divorce from intelligence; *feeling is not divorced from thinking.*[2]

[1] 'A Note on Nostalgia', *Scrutiny*. Republished in *Determinations*, ed. Leavis, p. 70.
[2] ' "Thought" and Emotional Quality', p. 57.

This passage will have bearing when we come to consider Leavis's views about the nature of evaluation.

To revert to the attack on Milton, it is easy to see how Leavis is so constructing his critical concepts that his initial description of Milton's lack of local concreteness and precision will *immediately* involve further descriptions, the pejorative quality of which would be universally recognized. If one accepts the initial description one seems compelled, ultimately, to accept the final judgement, except at the price of extreme scepticism, that is, at the price of refusing to go on taking part in the critical activity. This bears certain similarities to 'reductionist' moves. In fact these are *not* the only alternatives – as I shall suggest later. The connection between 'thought' and 'local organization' is further brought out in the chapter on Keats in *Revaluation*. He is attacking the view that Keats, unlike Shelley whose poems have 'an intellectual structure', is merely a master of sensuous detail.

> Now, if intellectual structure is what Shelley characteristically exhibits, the 'Ode to a Nightingale' may freely be allowed to lack it. But the super-iority of the Ode over 'To a Skylark', which beside it appears a nullity, is not merely a superiority of details . . . The rich local concreteness is the local manifestation of an inclusive sureness of grasp in the whole. What the detail exhibits is not merely an extraordinary intensity of realization, but also an extraordinary rightness and delicacy of touch; a sureness of touch that is the working of a fine organization.[1]

As an insistence that 'intellectual structure' is not necessarily something standing *behind* 'surface' details this is a useful corrective to the expressionist position. Now sentimentality, and the wrong sort of emotionalism, are, according to Leavis, a matter of the divorce of thought and feeling. But this itself is further explained in terms of concreteness, precision and so on. In fact the conventional distinction between thought and feeling is denied. Emotional attitude *is* a matter of the situation grasped. Sentimentality is in some sense 'interested'; opposed, that is, to the 'disinterestedness' which grasps the whole of the situation. For instance, the Tennyson poem "moves simply for-ward with a sweetly plangent flow, without check, cross tension, or any qualifying element. To give it the reading it asks for is to flow with it, acquiescing in a complete and simple immersion."[2] If the poem were more concrete the situation would have to be qualified. The more

[1] *Revaluation*, p. 245.   [2] ' "Thought" and Emotional Quality', p. 59.

reality enters, the less sentimental a poem can be. And for Leavis, to say this is to say nothing different from 'The more *intelligence* enters the less can a poem be sentimental' (We could apply a similar analysis to 'sincerity'.) To this end he quotes a remark of Yeats:

> I tried after the publication of 'The Wanderings of Oisin' to write of nothing but emotion, and in the simplest language, and now I have had to go through it all, cutting out or altering passages that are sentimental for lack of thought.[1]

Enough has now been said to show first how Leavis's 'key' terms are related to each other, and, in connection with this, secondly how the central questions of expressionism are dealt with. We may take, as a final example of this second point, the question of 'sincerity'. To call a poem insincere is not to make an inference to the state of mind of the author, nor is it to say something of the effect on the audience. For instance, an insincere poem may betray a lack of any real interest in the subject it is supposed to be presenting: to show this we may point to the language which may all be on the level of the vaguely emotional cliché with no precision of expression. Such a use of language *cannot* be the sincere expression of genuine feeling, no matter what facts we may discover about the poet's life, his spiritual struggles and so on. The way the poet uses language is the central criterion of how he feels, and the condition of his having certain feelings is his capacity to use language in a certain way. It is difficult to argue that a poet may experience profound feelings that he is unable to express, or that a humble and inarticulate peasant may be a "mute, inglorious Milton" (in the sense that he may experience profound feelings but never learn to 'express' them) without falling into the over-sharp form/content distinction that I have already discussed.[2] There just are many feelings which are intrinsically verbal and cannot be translated into any other form, or into any other form of words. But similarly, where the poem is sincere in expression, no facts about the poet can of themselves make it insincere. To use an example of Eliot's, if we discovered that Dante wrote the *De Rerum Natura* as well as the *Divina Commedia*, and that he left notebooks scoffing at religion and ridiculing St Thomas, then we would not know what to say. This would be especially true if none of this new information enabled us to *see* elements of insincerity in the *Divina Commedia* which before we had been blind to. Such facts

---

[1] *Early Poems and Stories*, p. v.   [2] See Chapter V.

about Dante would indeed be puzzling, but we cannot predict what our reaction to them would be. We might even decide that the *Divina Commedia* is so obviously sincere that the notebooks must be forged. If the evidence for the notebooks were overwhelming we would just be at a loss. If there were just no connection between these and the poem – if we remained unable to locate insincerity in the poem – then there would be nothing we could do. But the very difficulty of even imagining with any concreteness such a situation points to what we mean when we say that the sincerity of a poem does not depend upon facts about its author.

I suggested at the beginning of this chapter that the main terms in Leavis's criticism find much of their meaning, and support each other, through being thickly interrelated and even capable of being equated. The validity of the attempt to *equate* different concepts as a means of forcing one to *connect* them, and thus making one unable to avoid (except at the price of scepticism, which would mean the abandonment of the critical pursuit) the judgements of value that obviously ensue, will be examined later. An attempt will now be made to establish the connection of the foregoing with the question of the nature of critical judgement.

2. DESCRIPTION AND EVALUATION

Thus, if pressed to justify a decision completely, we have to give a complete specification of the way of life of which it is a part. This complete specification it is in practice impossible to give; the nearest attempts are those given by the great religions, especially those which can point to historical persons who carried out the way of life in practice.

R. M. Hare, *The Language of Morals*, p. 69.

...I would ask you ... to defend this position more abstractly and to become conscious that large ethical, philosophical and, of course, ultimately, also aesthetic *choices* are involved.

René Wellek apropos of *Revaluation*,
Scrutiny, Vol. V, No. 4, March 1937, p. 376.

In comparing Beatrice's speech from the *Cenci*

> ... O
> My God! Can it be possible I have
> To die so suddenly? So young to go
> Under the obscure, cold, rotting, wormy ground!
> To be nailed down into a narrow place;
> To see no more sweet sunshine; ...

M

with Claudio's in *Measure for Measure*

> Ay, but to die, and go we know not where;
> To lie in cold obstruction and to rot;
> This sensible warm motion to become
> A kneaded clod; and the delighted spirit
> To bathe in fiery floods, or to reside
> In thrilling region of thick-ribbed ice . . .

Leavis says:

> The juxtaposition is enough to expose the vague generalizing externality
> of Shelley's rendering. Claudio's 'Ay, but to die . . .' is not insistently and
> voluminously emotional like Beatrice's ('wildly')
>
> > '. . . O
> > My God! Can it be possible . . .'
>
> but it is incomparably more intense.[1]

Now, according to Hare, if someone were to ask 'But what is
wrong with generalizing externality and voluminous emotionalism?'
Leavis can only reply 'Well, they are unintelligent'. To the further
question 'Why be intelligent?' he can only attempt the desperate
reply: 'To be intelligent is to be human.' The rejoinder is obvious;
'Why be human?' 'Il faut choisir' must be the reply, for Hare's analysis
is, at this point, identical with Sartre's.[2] At this point, we *choose* which
way of life to adopt; we commit ourselves. For Hare, evaluative argument proceeds from the particular to the more and more general; it
has to stop when we can think of no more general formulation. The
sole function of the general judgement is that it entails the particular.
According to Hare's doctrine of the practical syllogism[3] an evaluative
proposition can only be derived from premises one of which is evaluative. Since this is the case, our particular judgements have finally to
be deducible from an Original Imperative.

But as I suggested in Chapter II, we frequently do not argue like
this in Ethics, and still less so in Aesthetics. It is true that we can
proceed to the more general; but we may well not do so. Instead we
may cite facts on the same level. 'Voluminous emotionalism is usually
bad because it is a form of insincerity.' Then, 'Why is insincerity bad?'
'Well, look at this speech by N' (a notably insincere politician). Our
opponent can, of course, reply 'Well, what is wrong with it?' He can

---

[1] *Revaluation* p. 226.   [2] *L'Existentialisme est un Humanisme.*
[3] See also Aristotle, *Nicomachean Ethics* (Penguin), pp. 200–1.

go on doing so whatever examples of insincerity we bring forward. We may then show more fully what we mean by insincerity – may show how it is connected with, and made up of many qualities – let us call them *a . . . n*. If, by the time we have reached *n*, he is still unwilling to concede any sense in which insincerity might be bad, we may well be at a loss what to say; for nothing we have shown entails the judgement of value that we wish to elicit. Hare concludes from this that either value judgements are irrational, or that they must be deducible from original decisions at a very high level of generality. That – as the quotation at the beginning of this section suggests – seems also to be Wellek's position.[1]

In the light of this, let us examine the exchange between Leavis and Wellek. Wellek writes:

> Allow me to sketch your ideal of poetry, your 'norm' with which you measure every poet: your poetry must be in serious relation to actuality, it must have a firm grasp of the actual, of the object, it must be in relation to life, it must not be cut off from direct vulgar living, it should be normally human . . .[2]

In his reply Leavis maintains that to approach literature 'with one eye on the standard' is the negation of criticism.

> By the critic of poetry I understand the complete reader: . . . Philosophy, we say, is 'abstract' . . . and poetry 'concrete'. Words in poetry invite us not to 'think about' and judge but to 'feel into' or 'become' – to realise a complex experience that is given in the words. They demand, not merely a fuller-bodied response but a completer responsiveness – a kind of responsiveness that is incompatible with the judicial, one-eye-on-the-standard approach . . . The critic – the reader of poetry – is indeed concerned with evaluation, but to figure him as measuring with a norm which he brings up to the object and applies from the outside is to misrepresent the process. The critic's aim is, first, to realize as sensitively and completely as possible this or that which claims his attention; *and a certain valuing is implicit in the realizing.* As he matures in experience of the new thing he asks, explicitly and implicitly, 'Where does this come? How does it stand in relation to . . .? How relatively important does it seem?' And the organisation of similarly 'placed' things, things that have found their bearings with regard to one another, and not a theoretical system or a system determined by abstract considerations.[3]

[1] It is fair to add that Wellek denies this.
[2] *Scrutiny*, Vol. V, No. 4, p. 376.
[3] *Scrutiny*. Reprinted, *Common Pursuit*, p. 213.

The key words of this passage are 'and a certain valuing is implicit in the realizing'. That is, by becoming aware of more and more of the features of different works of literature, and of different experiences, we are able to compare them one with another, to relate them to each other. This map of relations *is* our value scheme. 'Placing' is a complicated matter; and to place *is* to value. Here we see a connection with Leavis's attitude to expressionism. As a descriptive, objective account is to be given of 'intelligence', 'sincerity' and so on, so the account of evaluation is not in terms of *description plus an evaluative 'element'*. As the 'thought' or 'emotion' 'expressed' by or in a passage is not something to be inferred as standing behind the words on the page, but is to be described in terms of the language itself, so evaluation is not a matter of description plus some other element or event. Hare, wedded to a particular model of reasoning, sees that description cannot entail evaluation, concludes that evaluation must be an extra element added to description, decides that this element is the 'imperative' element or 'commendation', and seeks to produce an entailment of this 'imperative' in particular cases by positing an Original Imperative at the highest level of generality. ('I ought to behave like St Francis, therefore . . .'; 'I ought to behave like Hitler, therefore . . .') For Leavis valuing is a complex of activities (or a family of activities), 'finding that this wears well', 'coming back again to that' and so on. All this adds up to evaluating; there is no gap to be bridged between it and evaluating.

> . . . we find our description merging into criticism . . . in the examination of [Shelley's] poetry the literary critic finds himself passing, *by inevitable transitions*, from describing characteristics to making adverse judgements about emotional quality; and from these to judgements that are pretty directly moral; and so to a kind of discussion in which, by its proper methods and in pursuit of its proper ends, literary criticism becomes the diagnosis of what, looking for an inclusive term, we can only call spiritual malady.[1]

To ascribe certain characteristics to a poem (or a man) is, in certain circumstances, to evaluate. Leavis's account, as we should expect from a practising critic, does not seek to provide a formula for what these circumstances are. It is not that there is a formulable end in view, such as 'guiding choice' or 'inducing an attitude' – although choices and attitudes will be important criteria for whatever the value scheme is. Similarly, those features of a poem which count towards its being a

---

[1] ' "Thought" and Emotional Quality', p. 60.

good one are criteria – not elements of a definition of value. No enumeration of features will entail a judgement of value, and if someone accepts the description of the features, and agrees that they 'count towards' the conclusion of value, and yet persistently denies the conclusion of value, he cannot be convicted of a formal contradiction.

This is the case in literary criticism. Someone may accept the analysis of a poem as, say, weak in realization, and, by the same token, sentimental, and by the same token unintelligent, but still refuse to accept that it is 'bad'. If he goes through this process of evaluation with us, and yet refuses to admit that what he has agreed to adds up to saying that the poem is a bad one, he is still not contradicting himself. We might, however, wonder what he is saying; we might wonder if he has the concept of evaluation. Similarly, he may refuse any one of the steps in the evaluative process. He may agree that 'Tears, Idle Tears' admits only such aspects of the situation that will permit of an 'easy, plangent flow', but deny that it is sentimental. If, however many sentimental-making features we point out, he persists in his denial (without giving cogent reasons) we cannot convict him of contradiction, although we may be permitted to wonder what, if anything, he *is* saying, and whether he *has* the concept of sentimentality. I distinguished earlier, in discussing the interrelation of Leavis's terminology (pp. 158–9), between two ways in which Leavis seeks to compel critical agreement. The first was to connect – practically to equate – the initial description with further descriptions which almost anyone would admit carried pejorative implications of value. The second, which I have just been considering, is to equate certain descriptions with certain evaluations: 'and a certain valuing is implicit in the realizing'. But we are now in a position to see that there is really no distinction between these two procedures. For the same scepticism that would permit someone to refuse to call a certain family of activities in which he has just taken part 'evaluating unfavourably' would equally permit him to accept certain descriptions of a poem and yet refuse to call it 'sentimental' or 'morbid' or 'unintelligent'. And the two replies to these moves are, in fact, the same reply. That is, respectively: 'But this just *is* evaluating', and 'But maturity *involves* intelligence'. This is the only way of convicting the denier of contradiction. I have suggested that this may be a move which Leavis makes; it is certainly a move towards which he is tempted when he is trying hardest to convince. In some of his writings about D. H. Lawrence, for instance, the equation of concepts reminds one of the language of theologians on the divine attributes – 'God is His Knowledge', 'God's Knowledge is His Will', etc. "Lawrence's genius manifested itself in sympathetic insight and an accompanying diagnostic intelligence, and cruelty was not in him."[1] That is, if one admits Lawrence's 'genius' – as everyone does – it is, by this very admission, impossible to ascribe cruelty to him – although some people who *think* that they recognize his genius do so. Perhaps the most extraordinary example is:

> And this genius here we see as a penetrating human intelligence, something indistinguishable from a complete and irresistibly impersonal disinterestedness that, without condescension, overbearingness, self-blinding or indulgence on his part, enables him to be on sympathetic terms of person to person, or human life to human life, with the other.[2]

It is not that one could not make sense of this passage (except for the 'irresistibly' – who might offer the resistance?) but that one objects to the irresistibly interested equation of terms. 'This' genius may or may not deserve Leavis's description, but whether it does so is a matter of fact not of logic. 'Genius', on any normal understanding of the word, may well go without several of the intellectual qualities ascribed to Lawrence, and such intellectual qualities may well go without some or most of the moral qualities. Whether they do is a matter of fact which has to be shown – it does not all follow from the definition of 'genius'. The passage commits a typical philosophical confusion, in that it both suggests that it follows as a matter of principle ('genius ... indistinguishable from ...') and at the same time guarantees that it *shall* follow by establishing it as a matter of fact ('*This* genius ...'). If Lawrence's genius involves all these qualities, that is because it is *Lawrence's* genius, not because it is Lawrence's *Genius*. Of course this does follow from Leavis's usage of the terms 'genius', 'intelligence' and so on (one could say 'from his redefinition'), but it is just this usage, or redefinition, that one might wish to quarrel with.

Leavis seems here to be reverting to the traditional model which he usually, and explicitly, avoids. He seems to be insisting that his equation of genius and objectivity in Lawrence is either a matter of definition, or else must simply be *seen*. He is here arguing intensively, asserting

[1] *Sewanee Review*, Vol. LXXI, No. 1 (Winter, 1963), pp. 30–1.
[2] Op. cit., p. 33.

the connection by insisting on the terms in which it is made, whereas the critical alternative would be to argue extensively – to point out in detail, by comparison with other passages and other writers, how Lawrence's genius and his objectivity are connected. In doing this he might persuade us to take a different view – as no terminological stipulation could – of what had appeared to be defects in Lawrence. I said earlier that Leavis's two 'procedures' for supporting his judgements of value were not in the end distinct, and I suggested that the objection to either procedure would be a form of scepticism. Now the mistake Leavis seems to be making here is a typical reaction to such scepticism, and is essentially the same as Mrs Foot's. That is, he is treating qualities which are criteriologically related as though they were deductively related, or, in other words (as I suggested earlier), he is *equating* terms in order to force us to *connect* them.

But even here we must be careful not to react too far in the opposite direction. Leavis's equation of terms is not merely arbitrary. It is no use saying 'On *my* definition of genius, intelligence etc. a man may have genius as a novelist and yet be immensely imperceptive in his private life'. This dispute may be about words, but it does not follow that the positions taken up are arbitrary. Nor, on the other hand, can we say, if we have shown that Leavis is using these words in an unconventional sense, that he is simply 'wrong'. If Leavis has been successful as a critic, he has, perhaps, shown that there is a much closer connection between, say, intelligence and maturity than had been previously recognized. If, in his analysis of George Eliot, in *The Great Tradition*, he has shown a connection between a sentimental treatment of Dorothea and Ladislaw and a failure of grasp, of reality, and if this connection was not already made in our conventional concepts of reality and sentimentality (although in this case the connection probably already was there), then he has extended the concepts, and his extension has justified itself.

Now this returns us to the point mentioned at the beginning of this chapter. I there denied that Leavis starts from 'premises' in the sense, at any rate, that Winters's 'Reason' is a premise. Rather, I suggested, his terminology justifies itself in terms of a context which is gradually built up. But we see that we are still left with the possibility that the whole terminology may be, in the end, unjustified. That is, although the 'system' may be complete in itself we can question the 'premises' if by 'premises' we mean the application given to the terms. Whether this would amount to a 'falsification' of the system is a point I shall come to later.

We have, then, an account of description and evaluation which denies the sort of gulf between them which many moral philosophers since Hume have posited. In an article called *Critical Communication* Arnold Isenberg says:

> And if communication is a process by which a mental content is transmitted by symbols from one person to another, then we can say that it is a function of criticism to bring about communication at the level of the senses; that is, to induce a sameness of vision, of experienced content. If this is accomplished, it may or may not be followed by agreement, or what is called 'communion' – a community of feeling which expresses itself in identical value judgments.[1]

According to Leavis's account, a sameness of vision does not 'issue' in identical value judgements, but rather it *is* identical value judgements. '. . . the presenting involves an *attitude towards*, an element of disinterested valuation'[2] (Leavis's italics). Leavis correctly sees that 'community of feeling' and 'identical value judgements' are *criteria* of sameness of vision. There can be no severing of the 'vision' and the emotion or value judgement in which it 'issues'. The description under which the work of art is given, our way of seeing it, are what determine and constitute our attitude to it. The connection is not, as Isenberg seems to think, a matter of chance, but of logic.

Leavis's attack on the notion that evaluation consists in adding an attitude to 'neutral facts' is elaborated in an exchange with F. W. Bateson over the nature and role of literary history.[3]

> Mr Bateson can suppose his position reasonable only because he invokes an absurdly simple notion of criticism: the critic, he suggests, says, pointing to this or that work which lies there for him, the historian and all of us as a common fact, 'this is good' or 'bad'. Actually Mr Bateson as a literary historian can have access to the works he proposes to deal with – to his most essential facts – only if he is sufficiently a critic; only by an appropriate and discriminating response; a response, that is, involving the kind of activity that produces value judgements. And these judgements are not, in so far as they are real, expressions of opinions on facts that can be possessed and handled neutrally (so to speak).

[1] *Aesthetics and Language*, ed. Elton, p. 137.
[2] ' "Thought" and Emotional Quality', p. 57.
[3] *Scrutiny*, Vol. IV, No. 2, pp. 186-7.

This is surely true. We might even say that the greater part of the critical effort of the past has gone not into writing criticism but in preserving and re-reading those works of literature which are now central 'facts' in the literary histories. Value judgements do not take the form merely of inducing an attitude to the facts, or persuading people to 'choose' in a particular way (a way of talking which reduces the cognitive element in evaluation), but also in persuading them to 'see' the facts in a particular way. Bateson, like Hare, is relying upon the notion of a purely 'descriptive' use of language.

But Leavis seems to be in danger of denying that there can be *any* distinction between describing and evaluating. His description of evaluation is very close to Mrs Foot's and, like her, he seems to be suggesting that descriptions entail judgements of value. But whether 'This clock tells the time correct to nth of a minute' is a value judgement depends upon the use to which the sentence is being put, not merely upon its being a description.

3. FALSIFICATION OF A CRITICAL THEORY

In the exchange with Wellek, Leavis suggests that the typical critical move is 'This is so, isn't it?' and the reply is 'Yes, but . . .' Of course the initial reply can be 'No'; we may refuse to accept the description of a work of literature as in any way accurate. Or the 'Yes, but . . .' may suggest further, qualifying descriptions. Now would it be possible to *falsify* Leavis's particular critical judgements?

There is first of all the test of consistency. If the treatment of Dorothea in *Middlemarch* manifests an indulgence, a lack of control, how can one not use such terms of *St Mawr*? If ". . . a breathing, blooming girl, whose form, not shamed by the Ariadne, was clad in Quakerish grey draper . . ." is sentimental, why are we not to describe the account of St Mawr kicking a young man in the face and "spoiling his beauty" as sadistic? If Leavis were to deny the comparison we might argue that he is in some obvious way abusing or stretching his terms. Of course, someone may go on denying that two similar cases *are* similar without ever contradicting himself – he can do this in science as well as in aesthetics or ethics.

The most obvious method of falsifying a critical system would be to present a counter-instance. If, then, Leavis's critical 'placings' seem to imply that one whose characteristic attitude to experience is disgust and rejection cannot be a great writer, we may ask 'But what about Swift?' Now, either Leavis's criteria

1 do not exclude Swift, or
2 they exclude Swift as we have described him, but we have mis-described him; or
3 they do exclude him, or
4 they can be made to include him.

These four categories are only meant to be a very rough sketch of the possibilities; I wish to concentrate on 3 and 4.

If Swift is excluded, what can we do? We may suggest that Swift is a great writer because he has qualities A, B, C, D. If our opponent grants that Swift has these qualities, but denies that they make for greatness in a writer, do we merely assert that in our system, at any rate, Swift is great? Can we not, after all, argue about rival critical systems?

Rival critical systems at a high level of generality are comparable to Hare's "characterizations of a whole way of life";[1] and again the remedy is recourse to the particular. Different value systems involve, in the end, different descriptions of the facts. In this case we have to argue that one description is more appropriate than another. Where we are confronted with a new way of seeing the world (either by a painter such as Giotto, a composer such as Beethoven, or a philosopher such as Plato), then such argument becomes extremely difficult, or, for practical purposes, impossible.

If a man insists on describing something as being like *this*, despite all the evidence we bring that it is like *that*, there may be little we can do – but this would be the position in science as well as in aesthetics.

The inclusion of Swift when, as it were, he ought to be excluded presents a more interesting case. Swift does not show "a kind of reverent openness towards life" as do (according to Leavis) the great English novelists. Yet the chapter on Swift in *The Common Pursuit* begins:[2] "Swift is a great English writer". According to Leavis the case of Swift calls for paradoxical descriptions[3] – but we might well consider that paradox is only the result of the usual criteria being under strain. Swift expresses 'negative emotions' but the negative in some sense involves a positive: "The positive appears only negatively – a kind of skeletal presence, rigid enough, but without life or body; a necessary

---

[1] See Chapter II.   [2] Op. cit., p. 73.   [3] Op. cit., p. 79.

precondition, as it were, of directed negation." Later he writes: "In his use of negative materials – negative emotions and attitudes – there is something that it is difficult not to call creative, though the aim is always destructive." Again, ". . . the only thing in the nature of a positive that most readers will find convincingly present is self-assertion-*superbia*. Swift's way of demonstrating his superiority is to destroy – but he takes a positive delight in his power." The conclusion finally reached is that Swift, though a great writer, lacks "moral grandeur or human centrality; our sense of (his greatness) is merely a sense of great force. And this force, as we feel it, is conditioned by frustration and constriction; the channels of life have been blocked and perverted." Finally:

> He was, in various ways, curiously unaware – the reverse of clairvoyant. He is distinguished by the intensity of his feelings, not by his insight into them, and he certainly does not impress us as a mind in possession of its experience. We shall not find Swift remarkable for intelligence if we think of Blake.

Presented with this piece of criticism, we might wish to insist upon the strain, the paradox. The most obvious feature is, perhaps, ingenuity. Does this mean that Leavis is refusing to allow his value scheme to be 'falsified' by an apparent counter instance? This question could only be answered by a detailed *critical* analysis of a sort that is not being attempted here. The question in fact is 'Taking into account both Swift and Lawrence, is this the most appropriate way to describe the literary facts as they are?' If Leavis is extending the word 'life' to cover writers who should be excluded if it has any real meaning, this is what we can argue about – whether the extension is justified. And this is ultimately a question about how good a critic Leavis is – does his theory give the best account of the facts, including the best evaluation of the facts. And, as with a scientific or moral[1] theory, an important way of testing this is to bring counter instances. And if the usage of terms seems to exclude counter instances then we can argue about the usage (are philosophical or legal disputes 'matters of words'?) by, again, bringing counter instances; i.e. 'If you call this x mustn't you call that non-x?' And there is no radical difference between this sort of bringing of counter instances and the sort where one cites Swift's disgust or the bending of light-waves. There is, in other words,

---

[1] For a similar analysis in Ethics see R. M. Hare, *Freedom and Reason*, pp. 87–92.

no radical difference between this sort of fact and 'hard' or 'existential' facts. (Yet it is upon a belief in such a radical distinction that Popper bases his theory of Falsifiability as a principle of demarcation between science on the one hand and metaphysics, ethics, aesthetics, psycho-analysis, Marxism, etc. on the other.)

A good example of an over-simple application of this view to aesthetics is to be found in an article by Beryl Lake, in *Aesthetics and Language*.[1] Miss Lake's argument is simple – that Clive Bell's theory that 'Art is Significant Form' and Croce's that 'Art is expression' are both merely the product of a *decision* to use words in a particular way, and are irrefutable by any appeal to empirical facts. A dispute between them would be interminable, neither being able to convince the other.

> This does not happen in empirical disputes. For example, a dispute about whether or not the word 'art' is, as a matter of fact, used only for paintings would be terminated by consulting a dictionary. A dispute about whether more people went to plays in England than in France would be terminated by making a survey and getting statistics. In the case of an argument between Croce and Bell, it seems to me that no appeal to facts, linguistic or about experiences, canvases, paintings or anything else, would settle it to the satisfaction of both sides.

One indeed longs for a world in which there are only *genuine* aesthetic disputes – those solved by 'making a survey and getting statistics'. But what if someone says 'I don't call *that* a painting' or 'I don't call *that* a play' or even 'I don't call *that* collecting statistics' – what statistics would solve that? What Miss Lake calls hard, empirical facts are those which, in *fact*, are hardly ever questioned. This, of course, rules out most of the questions that we are interested in arguing about. Indeed, it rules out all innovation. And this is a general point about 'merely a linguistic recommendation' theories in philosophy.

A more sympathetic view is put by W. E. Kennick:[2]

> Although the formulae of the aestheticians are useless for the role usually assigned to them, we must not ignore the live purpose they frequently serve as slogans in the effort to change taste and as instruments for opening up new avenues of appreciation.

When Clive Bell says that 'Art is Significant Form' he has not, as he thinks, discovered the 'essence' of art, but he may help us to appreciate

---

[1] 'The Irrefutability of Two Aesthetic Theories'.
[2] 'Does Traditional Aesthetic Rest on a Mistake?', *Mind*, 1958, p. 334.

Cézanne if, up to then, we had concentrated our attention upon (probably sentimental) *subjects*. This would be a means of freeing our taste from, say, Victorian anecdotal pictures.

But Mr Kennick does not make it sufficiently clear that, if such slogans are helpful, it is not by accident. And we can argue about whether they are the most appropriate descriptions, whether they illuminate or distort, without reference (in this sense) to their pragmatic value. Indeed, their pragmatic value will very often depend on their appropriateness. It is an empty victory for aesthetics to leave the impression that it is always the other way round.

It is clear that all this has bearing upon the question of the objectivity of value judgements. What emerges is that arguments towards a radical (and subjectivist) distinction between description and evaluation, and between 'falsifiable' science and only 'confirmable' metaphysics,[1] rest, in the end, upon a general scepticism.

4. CONCLUSION

The sense in which Leavis has produced a synthesis of mimeticism and expressionism should now be clear. Inner states are essentially expressed and judged in terms of objective qualities; there is no room for essentially private emotions, subjective responses. And in the same way valuing is not the arbitrary addition of an 'attitude' to neutral facts, but is involved in the way we see and know the facts. All this amounts to a rejection of certain presuppositions about 'facts' and 'emotions' which are very deeply ingrained in the empiricist tradition and which have generally dominated critical theory since Wordsworth. For a critic to have arrived at such a theoretical position is a very remarkable achievement. In the next chapter, however, I shall explore what I take to be some of the limitations.

APPENDIX TO CHAPTER VIII

Words associated with 'life' in *Revaluation*.

intelligence   single-mindedness
consciousness   lack of self-knowledge

[1] J. W. N. Watkins, op. cit.

complex	simple; (single-minded)
organic complexity (Lawrence)	willed contrivance (Joyce)
sensitive	insensitive; coarse; heavy; vulgar; mechanical
whole	
spontaneous	willed
spontaneity; alertness; actuality; variety	ritual; routine; hieratic; distanced; solemn; mechanical; stylized
ambiguity; richness	neat; formal (stylized)
dramatic; poetic; pressure of speech	eloquence; rhetoric
strength	energy
enacting; realizing	stating; saying
from within (whole; spontaneous)	external; (willed); imposed
rooted Englishness; fullness of experience; firm grasp of the actual; adult response; poise; precision; consciousness	ritual; (distanced); hypnotic; dream; day-dream; indulgence
(Chaucer, Shakespeare, Donne, Pope, Hopkins, Eliot)	(Spenser, Milton, Shelley)

CHAPTER IX

Art and Morality

His first defect is that to which may be imputed most of the evil in books or in men. He sacrifices virtue to convenience, and is so much more careful to please than to instruct, that he seems to write without any moral purpose.

Johnson, *Preface to Shakespeare*

The superior character of truth and seriousness in the matter and substance of the best poetry, is inseparable from the superiority of diction and movement marking its style and manner. The two superiorities are closely related and are in steadfast proportion one to the other. So far as high poetic truth and seriousness are wanting to a poet's matter and substance, so far also, we may be sure, will a high poetic stamp of diction and movement be wanting to his style and manner. In proportion as this high stamp of diction and movement, again, is absent from a poet's style and manner, we shall find, also, that high poetic truth and seriousness are absent from his substance and matter.

Matthew Arnold, *The Study of Poetry*

It has never been clear whether Arnold was a moralist or an aesthete. That he was a moralist in criticism does seem to be a fairly widely held view. For instance, in his book *Poetry and Morality* Vincent Buckley says: "He is quite as much a moralist as Johnson was; but his view is more complex and sophisticated than Johnson's."[1] The opposite view has, however, found support. Eliot, for instance, speaks of ". . . the degradation of philosophy and religion, skilfully initiated by Arnold [and] competently continued by Pater".[2] Eliot also suggests that 'Art for Art's sake' is the offspring of Arnold's 'Culture': ". . . and we can hardly venture to say that it is a perversion of Arnold's doctrine, considering how very vague and ambiguous that doctrine is."[3] There is a more penetrating analysis by Wimsatt apropos Arnold's insistence that mankind will find it ever more necessary to turn to

---

[1] Op. cit., p. 86. [2] 'Arnold and Pater', *Selected Essays*, p. 437.
[3] Eliot, op. cit., p. 439.

poetry "to interpret life for us, to console us, to sustain us". Wimsatt remarks:

> It is easy to see that a morality of this sort, determined by poetry, is not really a morality in the sense of a code, but a relative morality of almost infinite diversity and flexibility – for such is poetry – and that hence what theorists of this school mean in the end is that they do not subscribe to a code. For these we may say that in the large sense the problem . . . does not exist since there is no distinction between, and hence no need of explaining the relation between, poetry and morals.[1]

I shall return later to Wimsatt's criticism. For the present I shall merely remark that even Wimsatt concentrates too little on what Arnold says about the relation between the form or style of a poem and its moral content, and too much on the larger and much more vulnerable assertions about the function of poetry in the modern world. Yet the passage of Arnold which I have quoted is of great importance, not only in the light it sheds on the perennial problem of literature and morality, but also in the questions it raises as to the nature of moral judgement itself.

It is not, indeed, clear whether Arnold is introducing moral criteria into the criticism of literature, or aesthetic criteria into morality. The guarantee of the 'truth and seriousness' of a poem is its 'style and manner', but the excellence of its 'style and manner' is a matter of the 'truth and seriousness' of its *content* ('substance and matter'). It is this sort of language which has earned Arnold a reputation for intellectual looseness. But far from being loose, this is one of the subtlest statements of the relation between form and content ever made by a critic. Arnold is avoiding, on the one hand, the aestheticism which is involved in trying to assess poetry purely in terms of its 'formal' qualities and, on the other, the moralism or didacticism which seeks to judge the moral or emotional or intellectual 'content' of a poem separately from its 'form'.

The question most obviously prompted is: 'But cannot a poem be well written but morally bad?' There certainly seems to be no room for this in Arnold's system. Now I have already suggested (particularly in the chapters on Middleton Murry and Leavis) why that is plausible. Sentimentality in a poem will betray itself in the language used, and in so far as 'sentimental' is a moral term we can say that here we have

[1] Wimsatt, *The Verbal Icon*, p. 88.

a case where the moral 'content' of a poem is inseparable from its 'form'. Leavis makes some remarks to the same effect:

> But [Jane Austen's] interest in 'composition' is not something to be put over against her interest in life; nor does she offer an 'aesthetic' value which is separable from moral significance. The principle of organisation and the principle of development, in her work is an intense moral interest of her own in life that is in the first place a preoccupation with certain problems that life compels on her as personal ones.[1]

Again:

> As a matter of fact, when we examine the formal perfection of *Emma*, we find that it can be appreciated only in terms of the moral preoccupations that characterise the novelist's peculiar interest in life. Those who suppose it to be an 'aesthetic matter', a beauty of 'composition' that is combined, miraculously, with 'truth to life', can give no adequate reason for the view that *Emma* is a great novel, and no intelligent account of its perfection of form.[2]

It is important to notice what Leavis does *not* say. He does not say that Jane Austen arrives at the right moral *conclusions* about life; indeed a criticism he makes of Johnson's complaint against Shakespeare is that "Johnson cannot understand that works of art *enact* their moral valuations".[3] Nor does he suggest that the moral code which emerges in Jane Austen's novels is one which, if we admire her as a writer, we should in some sense be prepared to adopt, or at least to approve. Indeed the question arises whether the word 'moral' is being used with anything like the force it traditionally has. Jane Austen's work is not said to be 'moral' in a sense in which it could alternatively be described as 'immoral', but rather as opposed to 'amoral'. And this of course is very close to Arnold's proclamation that "A poetry of revolt against moral ideas is a poetry of revolt against life". Jane Austen is said to have "an intense moral interest . . . in life", and this in turn is characterized as "a preoccupation with certain problems that life compels on her as personal ones". The moral significance of her work, then, lies in its dealing seriously, or intensely, or maturely with experience. The opposite of this would be triviality, or sentimentality, or self-deception. Neither Arnold nor Leavis is committing himself to the proposition that no serious work of literature is ever morally

---

[1] *The Great Tradition*, p. 15.   [2] Op. cit., p. 17.
[3] *Johnson and Augustanism – The Common Pursuit*, p. 110.

bad; but this is because the notion of the 'morally bad' in any traditional sense hardly seems to exist in their systems at all. To insist that
a serious concern with certain problems of life is a 'moral' concern
is not the same thing as to say that it is a morally *good* concern; it
is rather to say that it is the sort of concern which is in the province
of morality, or which is the material of moral judgements. Jane Austen
takes a moral *interest* in life, which is to say that she takes a *serious*
interest, and the criterion of that is that she has produced serious
works of art.

To see what sort of moral judgement this allows, let us examine
Leavis's treatment of Shelley. The moral corruption which he infers
in Shelley is a function of "a radical lack of self-knowledge" which in
its turn goes with "the antipathy of his sensibility to any play of the
critical mind". In the end Shelley's emotional corruption is a matter
of failure of intelligence – a "switching-off of intelligence".[1] The
moral judgement here is a diagnosis of certain intellectual and emotional failings. Indeed (to recall a passage I quoted in the last chapter)[2]
Leavis suggests that there is a direct passage from 'judgements about
emotional quality' to 'judgements that are pretty directly moral', and
thence, eventually, to diagnosis of 'spiritual malady'. But what happens when no such diagnosis of spiritual malady is plausible? Can there
not be a poem which is mature, intelligent, poised and yet, at the same
time, wicked? And if we claim that any poem which is mature and
intelligent is thereby morally admirable, are we not leaving out something important in the notion of morality? Wimsatt presents the case
of an acknowledged masterpiece – *Antony and Cleopatra* – in which
"The poetic values are strictly dependent – if not upon the immorality
as such – yet upon the immoral acts."[3] He goes on to argue that the
'immorality' of the play is not a matter of triviality, immaturity or
unintelligence:

> Even though, or rather because, the play pleads for certain evil choices,
> it presents these choices in all their mature interest and capacity to arouse
> human sympathy. The motives are wrong, *but they are not base, silly or
> degenerate.* They are not lacking in the positive being of deep and com-
> plex human desire. *It is not possible to despise Antony and Cleopatra.* If
> one will employ the classic concept of 'imitation', the play imitates or
> presents the reasons for sin, a mature and richly human state of sin.[4]
> [My italics.]

[1] See p. 155.   [2] See p. 168.   [3] *The Verbal Icon*, p. 17.   [4] Ibid.

In the light of this it is interesting to see how a critic who expects a moral valuation to emerge from a 'close reading' deals with *Antony and Cleopatra*. Let us take Derek Traversi's treatment in *Shakespeare: The Roman Plays*. How does Mr Traversi deal with the 'mature and richly human' state of sin? In fact he does not deal with it at all because he sees no such thing in the play. Antony, for instance, is throughout presented as self-deceived. His gesture in thrusting aside the intrusion of a messenger from Rome to turn back to Cleopatra "indicates rather petulant self-indulgence than the noble generosity to which he lays claim".[1] Antony's "efforts at moral realism" are rare, since he is habitually afflicted with "surrender to the feeling of the moment".[2] Antony's weakness is a "giving way to his emotions whilst waiting for the arrival of the external stimulus which he craves, which alone can give him the illusion of self-respect".[3] An "essential aspect" of the tragedy is Antony's decline into "self-regarding pity"[4] which is accompanied by "the element of sadistic resentment which is a principal sign of his collapsing integrity".[5] In defeat it is typical of Antony "that only in hysteria can he bring himself to look upon his situation in its true light".[6] Finally, Antony's passion for Cleopatra is, "seen from one viewpoint", no more than "the instrument of (his) self-deception".[7]

I am not concerned with whether this is a critically acceptable description of Antony. What is important is that Traversi does not allow that the play presents evil choices "in all their mature interest and capacity to arouse human sympathy". The Antony he gives us is subjected to a sort of technique of degradation; it is certainly possible to despise him (although not *simply* to despise him) and his motives are in effect characterized as base, silly *and* degenerate. Such a reading avoids altogether the problem Wimsatt raises. The play is made to 'enact' the right sort of moral judgement, so that we never have to reject what the play presents in the light of a moral code to which we adhere (or to modify the moral code to which we adhere in the light of what the play presents).

This is the point which Wimsatt rightly takes to be central: we are not here faced with a moral code which can be transgressed or complied with. Indeed a central part of the aim of modern criticism

[1] Traversi, op. cit., p. 82.   [2] Op. cit., p. 88.   [3] Op. cit., p. 140.
[4] Op. cit., p. 142.   [5] Op. cit., p. 148.   [6] Op. cit., p. 149.
[7] Op. cit., p. 154.

is to avoid coming up against any such code. The interest is, as it were, not in the content of the moral valuation, but in its form – and the latter guarantees the former. The key words are 'serious', 'sincere' (Arnold speaks of a "high seriousness born of absolute sincerity"), 'mature' and so on – terms which refer to the emotional or mental state expressed by the poem or play; and both Arnold and Leavis have attempted to correlate the emotional or mental state with the language by which it is expressed. There is no *faith* that a serious, mature, intelligent and sincere work of art will never be wicked as well, because such a faith is unnecessary: to call a work with these qualities 'wicked' would just have no sense. All we can do is to show that it is not really serious and sincere. And all this is, I think, a logical culmination of romantic expressionism. A poem is to embody an individual response to the world; what is important is the emotion with which the poet invests what is before him. But then the task of criticism must be, in some sense, to diagnose the quality of the emotion, and the only way a critic can do this is by examining the 'manner and movement' of the expression, in order to decide whether the emotion is 'serious' or 'sincere'. Hence is evolved a technique of close reading – 'practical criticism' as Richards called it – whereby a diagnosis can be made in terms of minute particularity. (Oddly enough Richards seems not to have realized the logical implications of his method. He loftily dismisses the remark of one of his anonymous contributors that "An insincere emotion betrays itself by slovenly expression if one watches it closely I think", with the comment: "The last remark is more a pious hope than a sound opinion".[1]) The refusal to separate form and content which is characteristic of both Arnold and Leavis is certainly right for this sort of criticism, because the quality of emotion is indeed bound up with the language in which it is expressed, in exactly the way they say it is. In this sense the form does guarantee the content.

But the assessment of the quality of emotional or mental states is not the whole of morality. We do, after all, also judge a man's actions, and we often judge them in terms of their consequences. In condemning an action we do not necessarily commit ourselves to saying that the motives which prompted it were unserious or despicable. We may rather say that it is simply the sort of action which leads to consequences, or even to the sort of world, of which we disapprove. Now in judging *motives* alone we do not necessarily refer to consequences

[1] *Practical Criticism*, p. 114.

at all (although the sorts of motive, the sorts of inward state we tend to admire will not in the end be disconnected from the consequences such states tend to have) and it is here – as I suggested in Chapter II[1] – that moral judgements are most like aesthetic ones, most like judgements of 'ends'.[2] When I condemn a sentimental emotional response I do not justify my condemnation primarily by pointing to the consequences of sentimentality, but by building up a picture of what sentimentality *is*, of what it involves. If, after doing this, I am still unable to convince someone that sentimentality is to be condemned, it is no use my appealing to the consequences of sentimentality, since I will only be able to show that the consequences are bad in the same way that I am trying to show that sentimentality is bad. In judging emotional states, as in judging pictures or poems, we are doing something in the nature of analysis rather than of prediction. Expressionism is entirely geared to this sort of judgement. It is not geared – as mimetic critical theory is – to questions of right and wrong, or truth and falsity.

Arnold's remark that "A poetry of revolt against moral ideas is a poetry of revolt against life" repays attention because in it is much of the ideology of modern criticism. It is a classic case of taking away with one hand what is being given by the other. Arnold does, at first sight, appear to be insisting that moral considerations must come into our judgement of works of literature. But he has so extended the notion of 'morality' as to make it almost unrecognizable – it would, for instance, have been unrecognizable to Johnson, despite his assertion that "He that thinks reasonably must think morally". Arnold indeed says: "A large sense is of course to be given to the term *moral.*" The sense is certainly large: "Whatever bears upon the question, 'how to live', comes under it."[3] When Keats consoles "the forward-bending lover on the Grecian Urn" with the line,

> For ever wilt thou love, and she be fair

he 'utters a moral idea', as does Shakespeare when he has Prospero say (or, as Arnold puts it, when *he* says)

> We are such stuff
> As dreams are made on, and our little life
> Is rounded with a sleep.

[1] See pp. 52–5
[2] I am indebted for this suggestion to a discussion with Renford Bambrough.
[3] 'Wordsworth', *Critical Essays*, 2nd series.

Now Arnold dismisses as worthless the lines from Byron's *Cain*:

> Souls that dare look the Omnipotent tyrant in
> His everlasting face, and tell him that
> His evil is not good;

The dismissal is not on grounds that they are wicked or false, but that they are unserious: "One has only to repeat to oneself a line from *Paradise Lost* to feel the difference."[1] The difference is between a serious and mature vision and one which is callow and bombastic. To revolt against moral ideas is to be not wicked, but trivial (indeed in a footnote in *The Great Tradition* Leavis actually *says* that "out of triviality comes evil"[2]). 'Moral ideas' means something like 'the serious concerns of life', and what is important is that the writer be seriously concerned with life's serious concerns. And this comes close to saying that he ought to be a serious person, or at any rate to be capable of serious responses to experience.

We have seen that Leavis and Arnold insist on a very similar connection of form and content. Leavis argues, quite rightly, that only in the light of such a connection can the conjunction of 'beauty of form' with 'truth to life' be other than 'miraculous'. But one reason why Leavis avoids miraculousness is that the sort of 'truth to life' he demands is highly qualified. He does not, for instance, expect literature to represent events exactly as they are, or as they could ideally be, or as they ought to be (to mention some of the variations of mimetic theory). It is this sort of demand that leads to Johnson's strictures on Shakespeare's morality: "He makes no just distribution of good or evil". For Shakespeare to make no just distribution of good or evil is to misrepresent at any rate the ideal reality which our reason allows us to infer. To act rightly may not, in this or that case, benefit us, but morality is in the long run based upon reality, and it is truer to represent it as beneficial than as harmful. Hence, Cordelia should not have been hanged. This is the sort of moral demand Johnson makes upon literature, and it is connected with the way in which he expects literature to be *true*. But in Arnold both morality and truth tend to dissolve into 'high seriousness', and in Leavis 'reality' and 'sincerity', as we have seen, come close to being equated. As Wimsatt says:

> There is no religion or philosophy that will embrace Homer's heroes and gods, the fatalism of Greek tragedy, the atomism of Lucretius, the

---

[1] 'Byron', op. cit., p. 104.   [2] Op. cit., p. 23.

Heaven, Purgatory and Hell of Dante, the Senecan Stoicism of Shake-speare, the occultism – what has seemed to many the diabolism – of Milton, the world soul of Wordsworth, the flowers of evil of Baudelaire.[1]

Arnold's explanation of the sense in which literature must be moral shows an awareness of this difficulty: "Morals are often treated in a narrow and false fashion; they are bound up with systems of thought and belief which have had their day."[2] Little could be more endearing than the openness with which Arnold exposes his motives. In the past morality has been bound up with theories about what the world is like, or what the next life will be like, or with particular social patterns, or with the needs of a particular race. Now there is no agreement about such things; societies have altered, races have disappeared. Morality must be founded on a new basis, not on beliefs or social preferences, but upon a capacity to decide whether this or that is or is not a serious response to experience, or a 'powerful and beautiful application of ideas to life'. Not only did Arnold wish to have morals without religion, but he wished to have them without beliefs of any kind, and certainly without a moral *code*. The question is how close this comes to morals wthout morality.

It is clear that it would be possible to condemn Antony not on the grounds that he is hysterical, or sadistic, or self-deceived, but simply on the grounds that the course of action he embarks on must lead to disastrous results. In the light of a moral scheme in which public duty comes before private fulfilment (not that this, in itself, would be a very subtle moral scheme) then Antony behaves wrongly in reversing these priorities. On similar grounds we might even object to the play *Antony and Cleopatra* itself. We might say that the moral valuation it 'enacts' is mistaken. In the light of a moral code according to which surrender to sexual passion was the highest good, *Antony and Cleopatra* might be immoral just because it seems to suggest that political obliga-tions have an at least equal claim. An important alternative is that the play might *challenge* such a code. If we were to treat *Antony and Cleopatra* simply as an historical or political document there is little doubt that it would be found wanting as a piece of history and naive in its political concepts.

This would be, of course, to approach the play in an excessively literal spirit. One of the great problems of criticism and critical theory

[1] *The Verbal Icon*, p. 89.
[2] 'Wordsworth', *Critical Essays*, 2nd series.

has been to avoid that sort of literalness while at the same time trying to preserve some sense in which truth and moral goodness could be ascribed to literature. A theory of art as imitation allows ample room for manœuvre. Art can represent reality literally, or ideally or 'in a more general way than history' (and indeed Aristotle's answer to Plato of itself shows how many are the possible moves within an essentially mimetic theory). 'Expressionist' theories start from different premises. Art is the expression of, or symbol for, an inner emotional state. Poetry is fundamentally emotional; perhaps – as Eliot has it – it expresses only the 'emotional equivalent' of thought. Now terms like 'serious', 'sincere', 'sensitive', 'spontaneous' and so on come most naturally in the assessment of emotional states. They go also with an emphasis on 'form' rather than on 'content' – if by an interest in form we mean something like an interest in the way the poem is organized, the relationship its parts have to each other rather than directly to the world, and if by an emphasis on content we mean a concentration upon the relation between the poem and the world as it seems to us, a concentration upon what the poem 'says' or recommends.

Now in explaining what he means by 'moral' Arnold quite decisively shifts the emphasis towards formal qualities. A response to experience is moral if it displays a sufficient degree of complexity, if it is highly organized – not a simple and callow response of the sort suggested by the lines from Byron – if it is sincere and 'powerful'. Leavis, as I have shown, works out in some detail what sort of properties a poem is to have if it is to be 'sincere': one can almost say that he works out a series of formal requirements – intelligence, 'reality', 'consciousness' – qualities which a poem must possess if it is to count as a serious, and hence moral, response to experience. There is a possible analogy with the 'formal' requirements sometimes made of scientific theories – 'richness', 'explanatory power', 'economy' and so on. But whereas in the case of a scientific theory these requirements – as the description of them as 'formal' implies – are a *sine qua non*, they guarantee nothing.[1] The theory can still be false. But for Arnold and, I think, for Leavis there is no requirement beyond the formal. A work which satisfies these 'formal' demands *cannot* nevertheless be 'false' – say in

---

[1] Compare Stravinsky: "Sincerity is a *sine qua non* that at the same time guarantees nothing." As usual Stravinsky expresses in an aphorism what others, including the present writer, labour to articulate.

that it rests upon a set of beliefs about what the world is like which are simply untrue (and nearly all literature in this sense 'tells lies about the Gods') – or 'wicked' – in that it holds up as admirable courses of action which we know have a tendency to lead to disaster (as distinct from states of mind which we now no longer admire).

This is not, of course, to deny that the connection, almost amounting to an identification, of form and content on which Arnold and Leavis insist is of the highest importance. They are also right to insist on formal requirements in moral judgements. It is certainly the case that when a man habitually expresses his feelings at the level of the banal and sentimental cliché there are important categories of emotional seriousness that we cannot attribute to him. He lacks the capacity to have certain feelings just in so far as he lacks the mastery of certain forms of verbal expression. There is no question of separating the thing said from the manner of saying it. (Nor does this apply only to verbal form and content: Salvador Dali could not have meant something serious and deeply felt by his vulgar and sensational crucifixion paintings. Christians who use reproductions of these paintings as devotional objects cannot be experiencing anything profound and serious by means of them – even though they may think that the experiences they have are profound and serious.) This is not only true of emotions. Two poems, novels, mythologies or even scientific theories can only 'say the same thing' about the world in so far as they are formally similar. The 'thing' that they say is not a neutral object to which the words point, or which is their *content*.[1] A ten-line paraphrase of *King Lear* cannot say the same thing as the original because its form gives it no chance of doing so.

But the fact remains that the *truth* of a description of a state of affairs is not simply a formal property of the description. A description could be complex, internally consistent, elegant and false. To say that a description is true is not equivalent to saying that it is serious and complex. To say that an action is good is not simply to say that it proceeds from serious and mature motives. It may be to say that it has good consequences. But to say that a man's motives are good, or that his emotions are admirable, or that he has a noble character *is* to say something about his seriousness, his sincerity, his intelligence, and so on. It *is* to talk about ends without immediate reference to consequences. We stress the relations the qualities have to each other and,

[1] See the discussion in Chapter V on 'intentional' and 'material' objects.

in this sense, what they are like, and this can at the same time be a valuing of the qualities. In judging a man's motives we emphasize formal qualities – richness, seriousness, complexity – of the sort we find important in judging works of art. As we would not decide that a work of art was bad because we were told that it had inspired a madman to assassinate the king, so we would not consider a man's motives bad on the grounds that, in the particular circumstances then prevailing, they led to disastrous results. To use Hume's phrase, we are talking of qualities immediately agreeable or disagreeable to ourselves. Hume distinguishes such judgements from judgements in terms of Utility thus:

> As a certain proof that the whole merit of benevolence is not derived from its usefulness, we may observe that in a kind of way of blame we say that a person is *too good* when he exceeds his part in society and carries his attention for others beyond the proper bounds. In like manner we say a man is *too high-spirited, too intrepid, too indifferent about fortune* – reproaches which really, at bottom, imply more esteem than many panegyrics. Being accustomed to rate the merit and demerit of characters chiefly by their useful or pernicious tendencies, we cannot forbear applying the epithet of blame when we discover a sentiment which rises to a degree that is hurtful; but it may happen, at the same time, that its noble elevation or its engaging tenderness so seizes the heart as rather to increase our friendship and concern for the person.
>
> *Enquiry Concerning the Principles of Morals*, Section VII.

But this does not mean that where, because of important changes in the structure of society, certain qualities – martial valour for instance – which had always been 'immediately agreeable' to ourselves are now seen to have a constant tendency to produce disastrous effects (martial valour is not, for instance, a valuable commodity in officers in command of nuclear missile sites) we will not gradually come to find these qualities 'immediately disagreeable'. It is indeed the case that many people now find the military virtues immediately disagreeable. And something comparable *could* happen in the case of works of art. To return to a case I discussed in Chapter II: if in examining Hitler's admiration for Wagner we come to see that there is a more than accidental connection – if we come to see that Wagner glorifies the 'Nazi mentality'[1] – then, if we disapprove of the results to which the Nazi

[1] Since this view of Wagner actually finds favour in certain quarters – see for instance Sir Victor Gollancz's *Journey Towards Music* – perhaps I should mention that I consider it entirely false.

mentality is likely to lead (apart from any disapproval of the Nazi mentality as such) we might cease to admire Wagner. But here the consequences *reveal* something about the work of art which we might otherwise not have noticed. (Whereas the fact that the madman is 'inspired' by, say, a Cézanne landscape to assassinate the king does not necessarily reveal anything about Cézanne.)

This does not mean that in the end consequences are decisive since, as I have said, we still have to decide what we think of the consequences. If we stress consequences as the ultimate factor in evaluation we are often tempted to resort to a different sort of criterion in order to evaluate *them* – to resort, for instance, to biological or psychological hypotheses.[1] But in referring to consequences in the case of Hitler's admiration for Wagner we are not resorting to criteria of a different order from those involved in a judgement of his works in themselves – as 'ends'; for the resort to consequences may be a way of adding to our picture of what Wagner is like (which marks a distinction – if one of 'degree' – from the case of the madman and Cézanne). Pointing to consequences here could still be something in the nature of analysis rather than prediction. Even when the pointing takes the form actually of predicting consequences the point of the prediction might well be to bring out something of the nature of the works of art.

In saying that judgement of consequences is like aesthetic judgement, judgement of ends, I am not trying to provide an explanation or justification of value judgements comparable with the justification in terms of biological or psychological facts to which Hare and Nowell-Smith resort.[2] To say that in the end we have to assess consequences themselves 'aesthetically' is simply to say that aesthetic judgements are a very good paradigm of judgements of ends. *This* is what judgement of ends is like. And this returns us to the discussion of evaluation at the beginning of the book. A moral philosopher who assumes that the 'ultimate consequences' can just be *seen* to be biologically or psychologically intolerable is taking as direct a reductionist step as that taken by Richards when he seeks to provide an ultimate criterion of aesthetic value in terms of 'balance of impulses'.

Of course, when we change our attitude to certain virtues it is not simply a case of our 'changing our evaluation' while describing the virtue as before. Here we see even more clearly that a rigid distinction

[1] See the discussion in Chapter II.   [2] See pp. 52-5.

between judgements of ends and judgements with reference to consequences cannot plausibly be maintained. When we ascribe a virtue
to someone – say, courage – there is, I think, an implication that the
actions and consequences to which it gives rise will be ones of which
we can approve. Where a man's courage leads him constantly into
foolhardy and dangerous actions we might insist that this was rash-
ness, not courage. The same goes for martial valour. We would,
perhaps, deny that the commander of a nuclear missile base showed
courage in being ready to fire the rockets when given the order to do
so, regardless of the consequences to himself. We might even say that
the only true courage in such circumstances would be in refusing to
obey the order. Or take the case of thrift. Because of changes in
economic theory what would have counted as thrift in the nineteenth
century would, in many cases, be considered useless now. We might
say that it no longer counts as thrift – it is a false notion of thrift. If
we take the second course we would be emphasizing the extent to
which the concept of thrift involves the expectation that the objects
aimed at will have a good chance of being achieved. An assessment
of foreseeable consequences is involved in the description we give of
the virtue. In a simpler case this has always been one of the ways in
which a distinction is drawn between true thrift and a mindless cheese-
paring. The latter description involves the notion of short-sightedness,
confusing means and ends, lack of an intelligent sense of priorities and
so on; there is no very rational expectation that it will achieve the ends
it aims at – as there is in the case of thrift. Talk about the consequences
in these cases is a way of saying something further about the virtue
itself. We have here a connection with the distinction I tried to draw
between the case in which Hitler is 'inspired' by Wagner to behave in
a particular way, and that in which a madman is 'inspired' by a Cézanne
landscape to assassinate the king. The distinction has bearing upon
why it is absurd to try to judge works of art directly, or primarily in
terms of their social or political consequences, to see them as means
rather than as ends. To say that Shostakovitch is a good composer
because he intensifies the revolutionary fervour of the proletariat
would be to appeal to consequences irrelevant to the assessment of
his musical value – as irrelevant as the fact that the king was assassinated would be to Cézanne's goodness as a painter. The consequences
in neither case would be illuminating. They would tell us nothing
about music or painting. And in the Wagner case the defence of

Wagner would be along the lines that Hitler's use of Wagner was of this sort, that it was an accidental or irrelevant consequence, not one which brings out something of the nature of Wagner's art. Wagner's music was the *occasion* of Hitler's response to it, but Hitler's reaction was 'irresponsible'.[1] We cannot provide a formula for distinguishing between relevant and irrelevant consequences any more than we can give one which will distinguish between responsible and irresponsible reactions to works of art or to rules.[2]

This, then, is the sort of distinction that there is between judging a man's motives, character, emotions as ends, and judging his actions by reference to consequences, as 'means'. (We could, of course, judge a man's character purely as a means – 'A man who can be relied on to do X'; and we can judge his actions as ends – 'aesthetically' – as when we describe a dancer's movements as beautiful.) We could call it a distinction of degree in order to emphasize that it is not rigid. But it is a distinction. When I judge ends I concentrate upon the pattern of qualities as they are in relation to each other. One way of putting it is to say that I concentrate on 'formal' qualities, or to say that I make an 'aesthetic' judgement. At any rate aesthetic reasoning is a good model for reasoning about ends. When I judge in terms of consequences – as 'means' – I concentrate more on what is being said about the world, or recommended as a course of action. Although – in the sense in which I have suggested – implications as to consequences frequently do enter into judgements of motive, they do not enter so as to exclude the possibility of someone's being 'a good man but a bad thing'.

But if a person can be a good man but a bad thing, then so can a poem. At any rate, a poem can exhibit beauty of motive, and, indeed, intelligence, poise and maturity, but still tell lies about the gods and, implicitly or explicitly, recommend courses of action or attitudes which are unwise, superstitious or even wicked. Although a poem cannot be aesthetically good if it is morally bad when by 'morally bad' we mean having unserious, or insincere or unintelligent motives, it can be aesthetically good but morally bad if by 'morally bad' we mean recommending or approving courses of action which we now believe to lead to bad consequences. A poem's capacity to embody serious motives or emotions will depend upon its having a serious form; so will its capacity to say something serious about the world in

---

[1] See pp. 29–30.   [2] Ibid.

a more literal sense. But whereas a poem (as Arnold and Leavis insist) will not count as having a serious form unless the motives it expresses are serious, so that in ascribing seriousness of form we will at the same time be ascribing seriousness of motive or emotion, and to that extent *moral* seriousness (which means that the concept of poetic form is less 'pure' than the concept of, for instance, musical form), yet it can count as having seriousness of form – and, hence, moral seriousness – even though what it says about the world be substantially false or superstitious, and even though the courses of action, or the type of society it implicitly or explicitly recommends, or holds up for admiration, are wrong or bad.

One conclusion to emerge is that 'formalism' is much nearer the truth where the judgement of motives, character or emotions is concerned. Here it is indeed difficult to maintain any coherent distinction between excellence of form and excellence of content. It is least near the truth when we see literature in a more literal sense as making statements about the world or, in a broad sense, commending courses of action or types of society. I do not for a moment suggest that a sharp and unambiguous distinction can be established between the two, but the distinction as I have outlined it does seem to throw light upon certain aspects of the development of contemporary criticism. Expressionism has been the characteristically Romantic critical doctrine, and it has tended to see creative literature as the representation, or symbolization, of emotional states. It is to be expected that a critic such as Arnold who is essentially Romantic in his presuppositions – despite yearnings for the classical ideal – should produce a theory of poetry that comes as close to pure formalism as any. The difficulty of reconciling one's 'aesthetic' interest in a poem with one's possible moral disapproval of it has been solved in a very radical way – but at a cost. The cost is, I think, that poetry is too decisively cut off from forms of expression which make true or false claims about the world, and from anything like a moral code. The sort of 'truth to life' which Leavis ascribes to Jane Austen is so essentially a matter of richness and seriousness, and so little a matter of truth in any more literal sense, that there is no problem in ascribing an equal or greater truth to Lawrence. Now if we read Hobbes in such a way that what is important is his completeness, his rigour, his comprehensiveness to experience, then we are concentrating on his 'formal' properties, taking an 'aesthetic' interest in his system. Our emphasis would not be on what he claims to be true about the world in any literal sense. There would be no very great clash between Hobbes and Spinoza, who has a comparable formal excellence. It would similarly be possible to read Newton largely for his formal properties. But to read Hobbes or Newton in this way would certainly be to leave out something important – to leave out, indeed, what they would have considered *most* important. But if we read literature for its 'formal' properties – even when this is understood in the large sense in which Arnold and Leavis understand it – do we lose nothing? In one sense we put litera-ture in a privileged position. It does not have to compete with the sciences in providing information. Indeed Kenneth Burke puts the demand that literature provide information among the 'fallacies'.[1] Since expressionist criticism concentrates on the analysis of motives it will tend to cut literature off from questions of truth and falsity, or from assessment of consequences in just the way in which the judge-ment of a man's character can be independent of such things. One of the results is that it becomes virtually impossible to raise as a critical issue the falsity of a writer's beliefs (which makes criticism of Blake and Yeats, for instance, a matter of great tact). Similarly, with the notable exceptions of Yvor Winters and the Marxists, critics are not very ready to condemn a writer in the light of an ethical code which they hold to be superior. The corollary is that literature does not really challenge one's beliefs. A further consequence is that there is a temptation to present what are really objections to actions in the light of a code as though they are objections to motives. So Mr Traversi has to insist that Antony convict himself out of his own mouth. Yet we *can* condemn a man for his actions without 'diagnos-ing' his motives as despicable. Perhaps the best example I can give of how distorting in such cases can be an emphasis on motives is by drawing a contrast with Dante's treatment of Brunetto Latini who is in Hell for 'violence against nature'. Dante joins an entirely dis-passionate condemnation of Brunetto's actions with an entirely re-spectful, and indeed, reverent, attitude towards him personally. The final picture of Brunetto Latini is of "one of those who run for the green cloth at Verona through the open field; and of them he seemed he who gains, not he who loses".

> ... e parve di costoro
> quegli che vince e non colui che perde.

[1] See p. 86.

We are left with a certain paradox. Both Arnold and Leavis insist that the criticism of literature is inescapably moral, but they both see moral judgement as essentially the diagnosis of emotions, motives, character – an area where it is most like aesthetic judgement. The conclusion is, surely, unavoidable that their notion of the moral, in its extreme formalism, is fundamentally aesthetic. But even in its one-sidedness their achievement is very great, for this is an aspect of morality which *is* central and which has been greatly understressed by moral philosophers.

CONCLUSION

I have been throughout concerned with what can loosely be called expressionist criticism. Expressionism, with its emphasis on emotion, has always had a strong tendency to subjectivism, and my arguments in favour of the objectivity of critical argument have been partly motivated by this fact. To a large extent the development of the technique of close verbal analysis has restored to criticism an objectivity of which remarks such as Wordsworth's – "the feeling . . . gives importance to the action and situation, and not the action and situation to the feeling" – had deprived it. But in this chapter I have tried to explore the limitations of this approach. There can be no doubt that Johnson's notion of how literature can be 'true', or how it can have 'moral purpose', suffers from being excessively didactic and literal. Johnson so emphasizes content, that formal or aesthetic qualities can be no more than ornamental. This means that he, like Leavis's aesthete, must find the coming together of beauty of form with truth to life – or, as he would say, of delight with instruction – little short of miraculous. Against this I have tried to show that if *truth* and *morality* were being used with their full traditional force (and that they are used with such insistence suggests that they trade on an association with their traditional force) then the fact that all literature which happened to be serious, poised, complex and mature was also morally good and true (true to fact rather than to 'life') would indeed be miraculous. But since this is not the case – since most important literature tells lies about the gods and upholds, either explicitly or implicitly, social, political, ethical and religious systems which no one would think of supporting now – no miracle is required. Poetry may be more philosophical than history, but any attempt to cut it neatly off from history, from a particular set of beliefs or from any moral code *must* end in aestheticism. Literature can only remain in a privileged position by refusing to compete. This means that when a work of literature is bound up with a system of thought or belief which, as Arnold engagingly puts it, "has had its day", then it too ceases to remain fully alive. This is, surely, true to our experience. The amount of knowledge and imaginative sympathy required to understand an ancient work of literature is at least as great as, and hardly separable from, the knowledge and sympathy needed to understand an ancient society. Of course Arnold's desire to erect poetry into a kind of super-history (the more plausible since it concentrated on motives; our judgement of motives *is* relatively less subject to change just in that it is less involved in *particular* states of affairs) went with a certain intolerance towards actual history. An alternative view might be that literary criticism must be, at least in part, historical. Indeed the limitations of a 'formal' view of literature are one and the same as the limitations of a 'non-historical' view of criticism. Criticism without history is empty, just as history without criticism is blind.

o

BIBLIOGRAPHY

This list is of books and articles referred to or quoted in the text. Dates refer to editions used. Where there is only a brief reference and no quotation the date refers to the first edition, or the first edition in English.

Abrams, M. H., *The Mirror and the Lamp*, New York 1958
    Review of *The Anatomy of Criticism*, *Univ. Toronto Quarterly*, 1958–9
Anscombe, G. E. M., 'The Intentionality of Sensations: a Grammatical Feature', *Analytical Philosophy* II, ed. Butler, Oxford 1965
Aristotle, *Nichomachean Ethics*, Harmondsworth 1958
Arnold, Matthew, *Essays in Criticism*, 2nd series, London 1938
Austin, J. L., *How to do things with Words*, Oxford 1962
    Sense and Sensibilia, Oxford 1962
Ayer, A. J., *The Problem of Knowledge*, Harmondsworth 1956
Ayer, Rhees, 'Can there be a Private Language?', symposium, *Proc. Arist. Soc. Supp.*, 1954
Bambrough, Renford, 'Universals and Family Resemblances', *Proc. Arist. Soc.*, 1960–1
    'Principia Metaphysica', *Philosophy*, April 1964
Bedford, Errol, 'Emotions', *Proc. Arist. Soc. Supp.*, 1956–7
Bell, Clive, *Art*, London 1914
Bennett, Jonathan, *Rationality*, London 1964
Brooks, Cleanth, *Modern Poetry and the Tradition*, London 1948
    The Well Wrought Urn, London 1960
Buckley, Vincent, *Poetry and Morality*, London 1959
Burke, Kenneth, *Counterstatement*, California 1953
    The Philosophy of Literary Form, California 1957
Carnap, Rudolph, *The Logical Syntax of Language*, London 1937
Carney, J. D., 'Private Languages; the Logic of Wittgenstein's Argument', *Mind*, 1960
Cassirer, E., *The Philosophy of Symbolic Forms*, Yale 1961
Coleridge, *Biographia Literaria*, ed. George Watson, London 1956
Collingwood, R. G., *The Principles of Art*, Oxford 1938
Croce, Benedetto, *Aesthetic*, London 1909
Crow Ransom, John, 'Criticism as Pure Speculation', *The Intent of the Critic*, ed. Stauffer, Gloucester, Mass.
Daitz, E., 'The Picture Theory of Meaning', *Essays in Conceptual Analysis*, ed. Flew, London 1963

Donington, Robert, *Wagner's* Ring *and its Symbols*, London 1963

Edwards, Paul, *The Logic of Moral Discourse*, Illinois 1955

Eliot, T. S., *Homage to John Dryden*, London 1927
  The Sacred Wood, 2nd edition, London 1928
  The Use of Poetry and the Use of Criticism, London 1933
  Selected Essays, London 1963

Foot, Philippa, 'Moral Arguments', *Mind*, 1958
  'Moral Beliefs', *Proc. Arist. Soc.*, 1958-9
  'Goodness and Choice', *Proc. Arist. Soc. Supp.*, 1961

Forster, E. M., *A Passage to India*, Harmondsworth 1959

Freud, *The Interpretation of Dreams*, Complete Works vols. IV and V, London 1955

Frye, Northrop, *The Anatomy of Criticism*, Princeton 1957

Gollancz, Victor, *Journey towards Music*, London 1965

Haezrahi, Pepita, 'Propositions in Aesthetics', *Proc. Arist. Soc.*, 1956-7

Hampshire, Stuart, 'Logic and Appreciation', *Essays in Aesthetics and Language*, ed. Elton, Oxford 1954

Hanson, N. R., *Patterns of Discovery*, Cambridge 1958

Harding, D. W., 'A Note on Nostalgia', *Determinations*, ed. Leavis, London 1934

Hare, R. M., *The Language of Morals*, Oxford 1958
  Freedom and Reason, Oxford 1963

Hepburn, R., 'Poetry and Religious Belief', *Metaphysical Beliefs*, ed. MacIntyre

Hobbes, *Leviathan*, Oxford 1957

Hospers, John, 'The Concept of Artistic Expression', *Proc. Arist. Soc.*, 1954-5
  'Explanation', *Essays in Conceptual Analysis*, ed. Flew, London 1963

Hume, *A Treatise of Human Nature*, Oxford 1960
  An Enquiry Concerning the Principles of Morals, Hafner Classics, New York 1958

Isenberg, Arnold, 'Critical Communication', *Aesthetics and Language*, ed. Elton, Oxford 1954

Johnson, Samuel, *A Preface to Shakespeare*

Jones, Ernest, *Hamlet and Oedipus*, Essays in Applied Psycho-analysis, London 1954

Kant, *Critique of Pure Reason*, London 1963

Kennick, W. E., 'Does Traditional Aesthetics Rest on a Mistake?', *Mind*, 1958

Kenny, Anthony, *Action, Emotion and Will*, London 1964

Kermode, Frank, *Puzzles and Epiphanies*, London 1962

Knox, R., *Difficulties*, London 1932

Lake, Beryl, 'The Irrefutability of Two Aesthetic Theories', *Aesthetics and Language*, ed. Elton, Oxford 1954

Langer, Susanne, *Philosophy in a New Key*, Oxford 1951
Problems of Art, London 1957
Feeling and Form, London 1959

Leavis, F. R., *New Bearings in English Poetry*, London 1932
Revaluation, London 1936
D. H. Lawrence, Novelist, London 1955
The Common Pursuit, Harmondsworth 1962
The Great Tradition, Harmondsworth 1962
' "Thought" and Emotional Quality', *Scrutiny* Vol. XII, No. 1
'Mr Bateson and Literary History', *Scrutiny* Vol. IV, No. 2
'Lawrence's Letters', *Sewanee Review* Vol. LXXI, No. 1

Lewis, C. S., *A Preface to Paradise Lost*, Oxford 1942

Macdonald, Margaret, Review of *Feeling and Form*, *Mind*, 1955

MacIntyre, A. C., *The Unconscious*, London 1962

Malcolm, Norman, *Dreaming*, London 1959
Review of *Philosophical Investigations*, *Philosophical Review*, 1954, reprinted in *The Philosophy of Mind*, ed. V. C. Chappell, New Jersey 1962

Maslow, Alexander, *A Study in Wittgenstein's Tractatus*, California 1961

Mayo, Bernard, *Ethics and the Moral Life*, London 1958

Melden, A. I., *Free Action*, London 1961

Mill, John Stuart, *Utilitarianism*, Bantam Books, New York 1961

Moore, G. E., 'Wittgenstein's Lectures 1930–33', *Philosophical Papers*, London 1959
Principia Ethica, Cambridge 1962

Murry, J. Middleton, *The Problem of Style*, Oxford 1922

Nowell-Smith, P. H., *Ethics*, Harmondsworth 1956

Oras, Ants, 'The Critical Ideas of T. S. Eliot', *Acta Univ. Tart. Hum.* XXVII, 1932

Osborne, Harold, *Theory of Beauty*, London 1952
Aesthetics and Criticism, London 1955

Passmore, J. A., 'Intentions', *Proc. Arist. Soc. Supp.*, 1955

Pears, D. F., 'Universals', *Logic and Language*, 2nd series, ed. Flew, Oxford 1953

Peters, Richard, *Hobbes*, Harmondsworth 1956

Pole, David, *The Conditions of Rational Enquiry*, London 1961

Popper, K. R., *The Logic of Scientific Discovery*, London 1959
Conjectures and Refutations, London 1963

Richards, I. A., *Practical Criticism*, London 1954

Russell, Bertrand, 'The Philosophy of Logical Atomism', *Logic and Knowledge*, ed. Marsh, London 1956

Ryle, Gilbert, *The Concept of Mind*, London 1962

Sartre, J.-P., *Existentialism and Humanism*, London 1952

Stace, W. T., 'Russell's Neutral Monism', *The Philosophy of Bertrand Russell*, ed. Schilpp

Strawson, P. F., *Introduction to Logical Theory*, London 1952

Review of *Philosophical Investigations*, *Mind*, 1954

'On Referring', *Mind*, 1950, reprinted in *Essays in Conceptual Analysis*, ed. Flew, London 1963

Traversi, Derek, *Shakespeare, The Roman Plays*, London 1964

Urmson, J. O., 'On Grading', *Logic and Language*, 2nd series, ed. Flew, Oxford 1953

Waismann, F., 'Verifiability', *Logic and Language*, 2nd series, ed. Flew, Oxford 1953

Warnock, Mary, 'The Justification of Emotions', *Proc. Arist. Soc. Supp.*, 1957

Watkins, J. W. N., 'Between Analytic and Empirical', *Philosophy*, 1957

'Confirmable and Influential Metaphysics', *Mind*, 1958

'When are Statements Empirical?', *B.J.P.S.*, 1960

Watson, George, *The Literary Critics*, Harmondsworth 1962

Wellek, René, 'The Criticism of T. S. Eliot', *Sewanee Review*, 1956

'Criticism and Philosophy', *Scrutiny* Vol. V, No. 4

Williams, Bernard, Review of *Aesthetics and Criticism*, *Mind*, 1958

Wimsatt, W. K., and Beardsley, Monroe C., *The Verbal Icon*, Kentucky 1954

Winters, Yvor, *The Function of Criticism*, Denver 1957

In Defence of Reason, London 1960

Wisdom, John, *Philosophy and Psycho-Analysis*, Oxford 1957

Wittgenstein, Ludwig, *The Blue and Brown Books*, Oxford 1958

Philosophical Investigations, Oxford 1958

Tractatus Logico-Philosophicus, tr. Pears and McGuiness, London 1963

Remarks on the Foundations of Mathematics, Oxford 1964

Wordsworth, Preface to *Lyrical Ballads*

INDEX OF NAMES